CHRONOLOGY OF WORLD WAR TWO

CHRONOLOGY
OF
WORLD WAR TWO

**EDWARD DAVIDSON AND
DALE MANNING**

CASSELL&CO

Cassell & Co.
Wellington House, 125 Strand, London WC2R 0BB

First published 1999
This edition 2000

British Library Cataloguing-in-Publication Data:
a catalogue record for this book is available from the British
Library

ISBN 0-304-35672-7

Distributed in the USA by Sterling Publishing Co. Inc.
387 Park Avenue South, New York, NY 10016-8810.

Designed and edited by DAG Publications Ltd.
Designed by David Gibbons; layout by Anthony A. Evans;
edited by Michael Boxall

Printed and bound in Great Britain by
MPG Books Ltd, Bodmin, Cornwall

CONTENTS

INTRODUCTION

When the Germans invaded Poland on 1 September 1939 the world went to war for the second time in twenty-seven years. One country, albeit overtly expansionist in its aims, had simply invaded another, but the omens were not good. Unbelievably, so soon after 'the war that will end war', nations and their leaders had allowed another conflict to threaten the planet. The scope of this new war was not yet apparent, the truth dawning gradually; this one would last six years, involve more than two hundred countries and influence the lives of the majority of the world's inhabitants to some degree.

Within months of the German move into Poland much of Europe had been occupied by the rampaging Blitzkrieg techniques of the Third Reich's military forces and everyone, even residents of far distant nations, was 'at war', their resources in men and *matériel* committed to the cause, on one side or the other. The Battle of Britain was at its height, Hitler's plans to invade England were close to being given the 'green light', and an awful dread filled many a heart.

Now, fifty years on from the end of that wretched war, only a few remain who can accurately recall the way the war developed on a day-by-day basis, in what order alliances were formed, when summit meetings were held, invasions mounted and repelled, set-piece battles won or lost, how personalities met with success or failure, and the actual reasons why national moods ebbed and flowed. And yet, World War Two is destined to be studied as a momentous historical event for generations to come, by students of all ages, backgrounds and levels of knowledge. The 1939–45 war is history, pure history, and a topic we should all understand and be able to discuss.

PRELUDE TO WAR

The seeds of the antagonism and division which will evolve to become World War Two are sown by the Treaties of Versailles and St-Germain which conclude the 1914–18 conflict. These see Germany disarmed and precluded from fresh military investment, new states born into instant dislike and rivalry, and Japan given control of some Pacific islands. Discontent and right-wing attitudes are prevalent in Germany and that country's leader in the next war enters public life in the early 1920s when he renames a workers' organisation The National Socialist German Workers' Party and campaigns for his doctrine of élite nationalism. Soon, Mussolini leads his Fascist Party to power in Italy and follows similarly dictatorial policies.

Treaties of Versailles and St-Germain

Mussolini leads his Fascist Party to power in Italy

Despite concern about the political unrest surfacing in Germany, the nations which claimed victory in 1914–18 commence a policy of military cuts fuelled by financial problems and the remaining bill of reparation. Adolf Hitler's ill-timed and inadequate attempt to seize power at the end of 1923 fails and sees him imprisoned; while incarcerated he writes *Mein Kampf* (*My Struggle*), the Third Reich's doctrinal guide book.

The powder keg which is Germany is kept quiet enough for that country to join the League of Nations in September 1926, and the Kellogg-Briand agreement of 1928 sees the USA, Great Britain, Germany, Italy, France and Japan forego future wars of aggression, but the decade ends with reparation payments still outstanding and Hitler joining those opposed to the settling of the debt. This stance increases his profile and gives the infant Nazi Party credibility; at the 1930 election it becomes the second party of Germany.

In the east, differences between China and Japan lead to the former appealing to the League of Nations for backing in the dispute, involving that body in such a matter for the first time. Early in 1932 Japan declares the former Manchuria independent and imposes a puppet government

By summer 1932 the political thuggery of the Nazi Party has seen it grow to become the largest group, boasting 230 of the 608 seats in the Reichstag and within six months Hitler is elected Chancellor, exploiting the weaknesses and bickering among his political rivals. The Reichstag fire of 27 February 1933 enables the new regime to assume greater powers, but poor election results in March prompt the Nazis to use force to quell opposition.

Hitler elected Chancellor of Germany

Six months after Japan leaves the League of Nations because of that body's criticism of its moves in Manchuria, Hitler pulls Germany out of the organisation. These moves fuel nationalist thought and action, and encourage public support for more arms expenditure to protect their countries from the perceived threat of those trying to impose their will.

Japan leaves League of Nations and moves against Manchuria

In a purge on 30 June 1934, Hitler eliminates much of the political and military opposition within Germany; more than 1,000 people are assassinated and others are removed from positions of influence. On the death of President Hindenburg in August, Hitler declares himself Führer as well as Chancellor and demands the loyalty of the armed forces and civilians. The Nazi salute and cries of '*Heil Hitler!*', already compulsory between Party members since 1926, now become the norm in German life.

Assassinations of King of Yugoslavia and the French foreign minister

The precarious condition of central European states and their alliances is further harmed by the assassinations of the King of Yugoslavia and the foreign minister of France and, when the people of the Saar region vote for union with Germany, the Nazis benefit from the erosion of such cohesion that remains. Great Britain cannot bring herself to view the Soviet Union as a likely ally against Germany despite the signing by other nations, including France, of co-operation pacts with Moscow. In fact, she looks the other way, an Anglo–German Naval Agreement in June 1935 effectively annulling the Treaty of Versailles by allowing the Kriegsmarine to be built up to 35 per cent of the strength of the British Fleet.

Anglo-German Naval Agreement

Italy invades Abyssinia

When, in October, Italy moves against Abyssinia, international criticism is modest, leading Hitler to believe that such shows of aggression are likely to be allowed to pass unheeded. By the following spring he is ready to move into the supposedly demilitarised Rhineland and this success destroys any doubts of his army chiefs and, in his eyes, further validates the use of force.

Outbreak of Spanish Civil War

The summer of 1936 sees the outbreak of the Spanish Civil War where the new factions within Europe become more deeply etched. For Hitler it offers the chance to play a leading role in a substantial conflict and provides him with a testbed for military strategy and machinery, especially for his Luftwaffe.

By the end of the year the desire to weaken the Soviet Union drives Japan and Germany and, later, Italy, to enter into a pact which aims to pressurise the Communists from the East and West. The Japanese believe that concern about German expansionism will distract the British from imperial matters in Asia.

Hitler rejects Treaty of Versailles

With the confidence of a solid home platform and a proven record of international strength, Hitler uses a speech in January 1937 to reject the restrictions of the Treaty of Versailles on a nation of Germany's importance. These words unequivocally state the Führer's intention of dominance for his country; they destroy the rulings of the victors in the 1914–18 war. By the end of the year he has announced to a conference that he will surely have to use force to impose the changes that he believes are necessary in eastern Europe and that he may have to move against Austria and Czechoslovakia. The British and French leaders agree that they will not react to an invasion of Austria, but existing pacts between France and Czechoslovakia mean that the latter must be assisted; initially the Czechs are urged to make acceptable concessions to German demands.

At about this time the deteriorating situation in the Far East sees Japan offer terms to the Chinese leader, Chiang Kai-shek, against whom incursions and skirmishes have escalated into hard fighting. The Chinese choose to fight on, which ensures that the Japanese will still be prevented from concentrating on the Russians whom they see as the greater enemy.

In Germany the Blomberg–Fritsch scandal sees Hitler purge top-ranking army officers to maintain his unchallenged position, but this incident in February 1938 sows the seeds of discontent which will return to haunt the Führer.

On 12 March Germany invades Austria and announces that it is now to be considered a province of the Third Reich. A few weeks later the Czechs begin mobilisation amid fears that German troops are moving to their borders; France and Great Britain reluctantly back this action and warn Germany off.

Germany invades Austria

In September unrest flares in the Sudetenland, the area of Czechoslovakia where the majority of that country's German-speaking inhabitants live. These people have been pressing for union with Germany and are urged to action by a tirade from Hitler on 12 September. Although the Czech authorities quell the immediate rebellion, the British Prime Minister, Neville Chamberlain, flies to meet Hitler with a plan, which at this point has not been discussed with the French, to have those parts of Czechoslovakia ceded to Germany where the local populace votes for it. Hitler agrees, as reluctantly do the French. Then, seeing such acquiescence, the Führer asks for more. Chamberlain again visits him and returns from this trip with the wish to accept new terms that have been discussed, but finds himself outvoted in cabinet.

On 23 September the Czechs fully mobilise. Mussolini is urged to act as a go-between to persuade Hitler not to invade but this confirms the Germans' belief in Anglo–French timidity. Chamberlain and Daladier again go to Munich and accept German proposals presented to them by Mussolini as his, although they have been drawn up by the Germans. Before leaving, Chamberlain gets Hitler to sign a meaningless 'friendship' document which the British Prime Minister brandishes at reporters on his return home with the tragic assurance that it represents 'peace in our time'.

Munich conference

Czechoslovakia, forsaken by France and Great Britain, is invaded by the Germans. Its territory is broken up, parts being claimed by Poland (Techen) and Hungary (Ruthenia). In the east the Japanese discontinue action against Chiang Kai-shek so as to look at the larger picture and announce themselves masters of the Pacific region, a stance which confirms the worst fears of the American and British leaders.

Germany invades Czechoslovakia

On the night of 9 November the most overt indication of Jewish persecution in Germany to date is seen when much property is damaged by marauding mobs reacting to the murder of a German diplomat by a Jew in Paris.

During the spring of 1939 Great Britain and France send guarantees to Poland, Greece and Roumania as those countries feel the oppressive threat of expansionism by Germany and Italy. Hitler's demands become more vitriolic and his intransigence clear as he rejects mediation by President Roosevelt.

Conscription introduced in United Kingdom

By May conscription has been introduced in the United Kingdom, and the new Soviet Foreign Minister, Molotov, has talks with British and French leaders ahead of more formal meetings a few weeks later. The apparent power game played by the Stalin regime, whereby they will only join in a fight against Hitler in return for confirmed increases in power and influence in eastern Europe, disconcerts the British and inconclusive meetings continue through into August. Simultaneously with the dialogue in London and Paris, Stalin has been negotiating with the Germans and, on 21 August, an economic agreement between the two countries is signed,

Russo-German non-aggression pact

followed shortly by a non-aggression pact which allocates some disputed territories.

On 25 August Hitler issues orders for the invasion of Poland but cancels them when he is told of Mussolini's reluctance to commit forces to battle and word comes of a formal alliance between Great Britain and Poland.

During the remaining days of August 1939 diplomats scurry back and forth across Europe and the radio broadcasts a stream of suggestions and offers and counter offers in a frantic endeavour to stay Hitler's hand. But all comes to nought. At noon on 31 August the order to invade is given, German troops advance to the border and the Kriegsmarine and Luftwaffe make ready.

World War Two is but a few hours away.

1939

SEPTEMBER 1939

1 September The Order of the Day from German High Command states: 'The hour of trial has come. When all other means have been exhausted, weapons must decide. We enter the fight knowing the justice of our cause. We believe in the Führer. Forward, with God, for Germany!' There is no formal Declaration of War to the general public in Germany or to the world.

Schleswig Holstein fires opening shots of World War Two

The German naval training ship *Schleswig Holstein* opens fire on the Westerplatte, a spit of land on the Vistula estuary, which contains a Polish military garrison, thereby announcing the German invasion of Poland. The land forces which begin the incursion include two Army Groups under Field Marshals von Bock and von Rundstedt with more than 3,000 tanks and substantial air support. The latter begins early bombing raids on Polish airfields, though many of the Polish aircraft have been transferred to other sites. The Luftwaffe has more success with its Stuka dive-bombers in attacks against Polish troops on the ground; with no anti-aircraft guns the Poles are scattered and their defence role quickly nullified.

Great Britain and France immediately demand a German withdrawal but make no threats or promises of action. In Great Britain the evacuation of young children from London and other likely bombing targets is begun.

2 September The Germans are 'in' Poland. There has been little action of any consequence on the border, and the German advance is already showing unprecedented pace. Such is the speed of this first example of the 'Blitzkrieg' technique that the German tanks often get far ahead of their infantry colleagues and need to hold a position in order for the troops to catch up. The Polish news agencies claim that no great advances have been made by the invading forces, but the CinC, Marshal Smigly-Rydz is still under-estimating the power and pace of the Germans, believing that he still has time to deploy substantial defensive lines.

London and Paris are in constant touch to establish how to respond to the invasion. The British Parliament now rails against Chamberlain's ineffective passive stance with Hitler and the cabinet decides to send an ultimatum to Germany. Italy announces its intention to stay out of the war.

Britain and France declare war on Germany

3 September Hitler ignores the British communiqué and, at 11.15 a.m., Neville Chamberlain is obliged to announce to the nation that 'a state of war now exists between Great Britain and Germany'. It marks admittance of the failure of his appeasement policy. He forms a war cabinet with Churchill as naval minister and including Anthony Eden; these two have been the most outspoken against Chamberlain's tactics. By the afternoon, the French have also formally declared war; they are joined by Australia, India and New Zealand. In Poland, Cracow is all but lost and war minister Kasprzycki is ordered to prepare the defence of Warsaw.

The first RAF flight over enemy territory sees a Blenheim of 139 Squadron undertake a photo-reconnaissance mission.

4 September Where Polish defensive lines are formed they are no match for the rampaging German ground forces. The Polish air force is short of ammunition and many aircraft are destroyed on the ground.

No general mobilisation of the German forces at home has yet been ordered; no shots have yet been fired on the Western Front.

The British announce successful raids on the German naval bases at Wilhelmshaven and Brunsbüttel despite inclement weather and vigorous anti-aircraft fire. The report is countered by the Germans who claim no bomb damage and five of the twelve aircraft shot down.

The Germans announce that they are mining the western Baltic. In London, press agency reports confirm the torpedoing of the British liner SS *Athenia* with 1,400 passengers on board. The attack was mounted by *U30* whose captain took the blacked-out ship for an armed merchant cruiser. Embarrassed by the bad press the sinking brings, the Germans first blame the attack on the British themselves, and subsequently ensure that the relevant entry is deleted from the U-boat's log.

Athenia sunk

5 September An RAF Anson reconnaissance aircraft attacks two British submarines by mistake. Its depth-charges score a direct hit on the conning tower of HMS *Snapper*.

The first British freighter to be sunk is a small steamer, *Bosnia*, which is lost to Leutnant-zur-See Prien's *U47*. Later in the day *U48* sinks the armed merchantman *Royal Sceptre*.

First British freighter sunk

6 September The Polish defensive line between Czestochowa and Warsaw is broken. France makes an insignificant military move on vacated German sites on the Siegfried Line near Saarbrucken; in truth, neither Great Britain nor France do anything in early support of the doomed Poles.

South Africa declares war on Germany.

7 September Marshal Smigly-Rydz moves his HQ from Warsaw to the temporary sanctuary of Brest-Litovsk.

8 September German forces reach the suburbs of Warsaw. Many Polish troops are now cut off and cannot retreat or fight. Some pockets of resistance do still hamper the German advance, however, and 4th Panzer Division loses half its tanks in a short fight close to the capital.

German forces reach the suburbs of Warsaw

Okecie airfield, on the outskirts of Warsaw, is captured.

The Westerplatte garrison surrenders after days of naval bombardment and the landing of assault troops.

9 September The Army of Poznan enjoys some success against the left flank of General Blaskowitz's Eighth Army causing it to delay its move on Warsaw. It is one of the few occasions when Polish forces are assisted by their aircraft for here reconnaissance flights alert them to German troop movements.

10 September Field Marshal Gort takes the first large units of the British Expeditionary Force to France.

BEF crosses to France

More successes for the Poznan and Lodz Armies do not prevent the Polish military hierarchy from realising that the pace of the German advance is preventing any retreat or regrouping.

Canada declares war on Germany.

British submarine HMS *Triton* sights an unidentifed submarine and rams it. The stricken vessel sinks before it is discovered to be another British vessel, HMS *Oxley*, with a crew of fifty-four. Off the North Sea coast the British lay the first minefield in German waters.

11 September The futile resistance of the Poznan unit continues while elsewhere tens of thousands of Polish troops are being taken prisoner. Soon German reinforcements bring a halt to the Poznan effort and the drive for Poland can be continued in all areas.

The first meeting of the Anglo–French Supreme War Council is held.

The rapid deployment of mines in the English Channel prevents German naval incursions there.

13 September The last meaningful flights of the Polish Air Force are undertaken in an attempt to supply the besieged city of Modlin.

The French Navy suffers its first loss when the minelayer *Platon* detonates one of its own mines.

Battle of Bzura

14 September The Battle of Bzura begins when the Army of Pomorze launches a surprise offensive around Lowicz. Extra forces are pulled from Warsaw and Kielce by von Rundstedt, but the Polish General Kutrzeba keeps all these forces occupied for five days with doughty fighting and tough resistance. Elsewhere, however, the advance on Warsaw continues and the Polish military leaders begin to lose touch with their field officers.

U-boat *U39* attacks the aircraft carrier HMS *Ark Royal* but is sunk by depth-charges from three escorts.

15 September The German Fourteenth Army moves to cut off a possible Polish retreat into Roumania.

16 September Despite its parlous state, Warsaw refuses to surrender.

Soviets enter Poland

17 September As Polish resistance nears its death throes, the country is faced with a wholly new threat as two Soviet army groups march into eastern Poland with the clear intention of joining in on the benefits of victory, as already promised in the German–Soviet Non-Aggression Treaty of 23 August. The Polish government flees to Roumanian territory, and internment; their remaining operative aircraft follow the same route.

Polish government flees

Courageous sunk

U29 sights the carrier HMS *Courageous* off the Irish coast and launches three torpedoes. She is struck centrally and sinks quickly, together with her 48 aircraft. Her escorting destroyers had failed to alert her to the presence of the U-boat.

18 September Massive air raids and heavy artillery bombardment of Warsaw denote that Polish resistance has been brushed aside and the capital is about to be taken.

19 September Remnants of the brave Poznan and Pomorze armies – some 170,000 men – surrender. Other Polish forces cross into Hungary. The Soviet and German invaders meet up at Brest-Litovsk.

20 September Lublin finally falls.

U27 is sunk by the destroyers HMSS *Fortune* and *Forester*; her crew are rescued.

21 September The Roumanian Prime Minister Calinescu is assassinated by Fascist Iron Guards

22 September Polish forces in Lvov surrender to the Soviets

24 September Warsaw is blitzed from the air as the German ground forces prepare for an assault on the capital

25 September Warsaw is hit by 400 German aircraft dropping high-explosive and incendiary bombs. With its water pipes ruptured and its fire-fighters evacuated, the resulting fires cannot be quenched.

Warsaw bombed

The Germans introduce food rationing.

26 September The propaganda war opens up with the Germans claiming to have sunk the carrier HMS *Ark Royal*. A Junkers Ju 88 has certainly come close to bombing Home Fleet vessels and Göring, having been assured that the carrier has been destroyed, decorates the pilot as a result, but the truth is discovered when *Ark Royal* deploys in the South Atlantic a few days later in search of the German battleship *Graf Spee*.

27 September Warsaw surrenders; Polish resistance ebbs away. Hitler advises his military chiefs that an attack in the west will begin; there is opposition, mostly muted, but many army officers have not been consulted.

Warsaw surrenders

28 September Modlin, which has withstood mighty German attacks, finally surrenders.

29 September Poland is to be partitioned following a friendship treaty between Germany and the Soviet Union. The latter now begins to pressure the Baltic states into pacts which will enable their ships to use Baltic ports and so have control over the waters of the region, and access to more ice-free harbours.

Poland partitioned by Germany and Russia

30 September A Polish Government-in-Exile is set up in Paris. General Sikorski is nominated CinC of the armed forces.

Graf Spee, disguised as *Admiral Scheer*, sinks the British steamer SS *Clement*, the start of her campaign against merchantmen which will see her claim more than 50,000 tons of shipping. By now the greater part of Germany's coastal waters have been protectively mined.

OCTOBER 1939

1 October Winston Churchill, in a radio broadcast, declares that: 'Poland has been overrun by two of the great powers which held her in bondage for 150 years, but were unable to quench the spirit of the Polish nation ... Russia has pursued a cold policy of self-interest.'

Admiral Unrug and his 4,000-strong force on the Hela Peninsula give up an unequal fight but Polish mines do claim their only victim when the German minesweeper *M85* is sunk in Danzig Bay.

3 October Twenty-one countries of the American continent meet in Panama and set a neutrality zone ranging between 300 and 600 nautical miles off their coasts.

4 October The Polish air force fly their final missions. Its modest resources have caused more Luftwaffe casualties than had been suffered throughout the Spanish Civil War.

5 October The hunt for *Graf Spee* is begun by the British and French

6 October As the last Polish ground troops surrender, national losses can be totalled; they include 700,000 captured by the Germans and a further 200,000 by the Russians as well as great loss of life. More than 120,000 troops are believed to have escaped. The invaders have also had losses – the German more than 10,000 dead and the Russians several hundred. Numerical superiority has won the day and the pace of advance has been unprecedented.

Hitler, speaking in the Reichstag, expresses a desire for peace with France and Great Britain and states that his actions to date have had the sole aim of correcting the injustices of the Treaty of Versailles. He calls for a European Conference but this is rejected by the British and the French.

The German pocket battleship *Deutschland* sinks the British merchantman *Stonegate* within the US Neutrality Zone.

7 October The British Expeditionary Force completes its unopposed crossing to France.

The German battleship *Gneisenau* leads a Kriegsmarine move on Norway, hoping to draw British naval units within range of Luftwaffe bombers. The exercise meets with little success; the German air units have still to learn how to mount attacks at sea.

8 October A Dornier flying-boat becomes the first German aircraft to be shot down by a British aircraft when it encounters a patrolling Hudson over the North Sea. Near Landau, air combat sees five French Hawks vie with four Messerschmitt Bf 109s; two German aircraft are shot down.

Prien leaves Kiel in *U47*, heading for the British fleet anchorage in Scapa Flow on what is to be one of the most audacious naval missions in history.

9 October Hitler's Directive No 6 makes it clear that he will invade France via the Low Countries if that country and her ally, Great Britain, do not accept his moves for peace. The announcement demeans his own army hierarchy which continues to be kept out of much of the policy discussion.

10 October *Graf Spee*, flying a French flag, stops and boards the British steamer *Huntsman* and captures secret merchant vessel routing documents.

The hunt for *Graf Spee* begins

Hitler calls for European conference

First German aircraft shot down by a British aircraft

The latter's 'May Day' distress call had been intercepted by the triumphant radio operator of the German vessel.

Admiral Raeder urges Hitler to consider invading Norway to secure the harbours and anchorages so as to protect the vital iron ore traffic.

12 October Continuing negotiations between the Russians and Finns over the former's quest for more Baltic territory come to nought. The Finns have already mobilised their standing and reserve military units.

Chamberlain joins Daladier in rejecting Hitler's proposal of a conference to discuss the territorial disputes which he claims are at the heart of German moves to date.

Norway continues to feature in the war plans of Germany and Great Britain. Churchill urges the mining of Norwegian waters to disrupt German iron-ore shipping.

13 October Admiral Dönitz attempts his first 'wolf pack' deployment of U-boats, but without success. In the Orkneys, Prien, with masterly navigational skill, threads his way through the boom and net defences to enter Scapa Flow. Amazingly he remains undetected although surfaced until he reaches his first targets.

First 'wolf pack' deployment of U-boats

14 October At 0100 hours Prien's first torpedoes strike the battleship HMS *Royal Oak* in the bows; inshore there is no reaction while U47 reloads and repositions. At 0123 three more torpedoes are fired and soon the battleship is riven by explosions which finally raise the alarm; 883 members of the crew are lost. Prien escapes to the open sea. This is a heavy blow to morale; according to Dönitz the sombre British radio announcement is his first intimation of the success of the raid.

Royal Oak sunk

The Polish submarine *Orzel* is escorted into British home waters, having evaded German searchers during a remarkable 44-day passage.

16 October German bombers are lost over Scotland during the Luftwaffe's first attempt to hit the British fleets in harbour. Minor damage is suffered by the cruisers HMSS *Southampton* and *Edinburgh* and the destroyer HMS *Mohawk*.

17 October The victorious Prien arrives back at Wilhelmshaven to be welcomed by Raeder who promotes Dönitz to rear-admiral on the deck of *U47*. Prien and his crew fly to Berlin where he is decorated with the Knight's Cross of the Iron Cross by Hitler.

It is not all success for the U-boat fleet, however. During this month four of them are disabled in the English Channel, and from now on U-boats patrolling the North Atlantic are routed around the British Isles on passage to and from their home ports. The magnetic mine has come into its own as a hidden destroyer of surface vessels; British and German ships and aircraft lay thousands of them around harbours and shipping lanes.

18 October The Russians invade Estonia as part of their quest for control over the Baltic ports. Similar moves will soon be made on Latvia and Lithuania.

Soviets invade Estonia

19 October The German High Command plan for a Blitzkrieg drive to the west is completed. Its hasty compilation reveals weaknesses, and modifications will be made, but the ability of the Germans to read the French codes enables them to highlight weaknesses in the defensive lines at Sedan.

NOVEMBER 1939

1 November *Deutschland* is recalled from her patrol south of Greenland after an inauspicious mission. It will not be the last time in this war that the mere threat of the presence of a German capital ship is more potent than her performance.

USA alters its Neutrality Acts to facilitate arms sales to France and Britain

4 November The USA, by altering its Neutrality Acts, facilitates the purchase of weaponry through private companies provided that the purchaser transports the *matériel*; this excludes the Germans, but France and Great Britain take immediate advantage.

5 November In Germany opposition to Hitler's proposed invasion of Holland and Belgium escalates. General Halder, Chief of the General Staff, and his circle are rebellious, and a *coup d'état* is considered.

7 November The drive to the west is postponed by Hitler for the first of many times.

The first torpedo attack from a German aircraft narrowly misses two Polish destroyers off the east coast of Great Britain.

8 November The security of the British agents operating in Czechoslovakia and elsewhere is compromised by the capture and interrogation of MI6 officers, Stephens and Best, on the German–Dutch border.

Hans Frank is appointed Governor-General of Poland; his chief task will be to begin the persecution of the Jews there.

10 November Colonel Charles de Gaulle, concerned at the apathy of the French government, prepares a report urging more stringent preparations against invasion. His warnings are ignored.

The destroyer HMS *Blanche* is lost to a magnetic mine in the Thames Estuary

16 November Martial law is declared in Czechoslovakia in response to increasing unrest.

17 November A Czech National Committee is set up in Paris and will become recognised by Great Britain and France.

Eleven weeks into the war the U-boat fleets are given the 'green light' to attack any merchantman identified as French or British.

Hitler orders *Deutschland* to be renamed *Lützow* to avoid the possibility of a ship bearing his country's name being sunk.

20 November German seaplanes begin minelaying operations in the shipping lanes outside British east coast harbours.

21 November The destroyer HMS *Gipsy* is lost to a mine as she leaves

Harwich, and the new light cruiser HMS *Belfast* is damaged by a mine in the Firth of Forth.

23 November Hitler calls a halt to rocket development at Peenemünde, believing that victory against Poland has shown that the war can be won without such weaponry.

The German battlecruiser *Scharnhorst* sinks the British armed merchant cruiser *Rawalpindi* north of the Faeroes and escapes pursuit with her partner *Gneisenau*.

Rawalpindi sunk

25 November Hitler orders the U-boat arm to pursue a strategy for cutting off the United Kingdom's seaborne contact with other countries.

26 November Relations between Russia and Finland reach a new low. Spurious claims and counter-claims are traded.

29 November Soviet attacks on Finland begin. There is no formal declaration of war. The Finns have a minuscule army of about 30,000 men, a few old tanks and aircraft and little ammunition; they will capture more *matériel* in their few victories than by new manufacture.

Soviets attack Finland

30 November Finland is attacked on all fronts and Helsinki is bombed from the air. Hopelessly outnumbered and under-equipped, and without supportive allies, the Finns have only the climate and terrain on their side. In many instances the invaders encounter no opposition for days at a time.

Helsinki bombed

The Soviet Baltic Fleet joins the operation with the aim of controlling the Gulf of Finland. This stimulates Great Britain to move against the port of Narvik so as to free it for Allied use in supplying Finland.

DECEMBER 1939

1 December The Finns' fighting skill enables them to achieve some success against Russian tank forces and a Finnish fighter downs a Tupolev SB-2 bomber.

2 December Finland appeals for League of Nations backing for its case against Soviet aggression, but it will be some time before the League convenes its meeting.

Commodore Harwood with three British cruisers in the Falklands is alerted to the presence of *Graf Spee* in the South Atlantic by a radio message from the freighter *Doric Star* before she is stopped by the German vessel off the west coast of South Africa.

3 December The freighter *Tairoa* is sunk by *Graf Spee* but, again, a 'May Day' signal helps Harwood to plot the enemy ship's probable arrival time off the coast of South America.

4 December King George VI visits troops in France

The battleship HMS *Nelson* hits a German mine off the coast of Scotland and is out of commission for several months.

5 December The Soviet Seventh Army reaches the Finns' defensive

Mannerheim Line, but Finnish resistance continues to blunt the sharpness of their advance.

7 December Boarders from *Graf Spee* foil an attempt by the crew of the British freighter *Streonshath* to ditch Allied shipping route plans. In the North Sea German and British destroyers clash for the first time; HMS *Jersey* is torpedoed and very badly damaged.

8 December Vidkun Quisling, leader of the small Norwegian Nationalist Party, meets Hitler to discuss the possibility of a *coup d'état* in his country.

11 December The resourcefulness of the Finnish Army is demonstrated by its 9th Brigade managing to cut off the Soviet 163rd Division at Suomussalmi.

12 December The Finns capture equipment and inflict losses on Soviet Eighth Army

Commodore Harwood concentrates his light cruisers HMSS *Ajax* and *Achilles* and the heavy cruiser HMS *Exeter* off the River Plate with the intention of attacking Kapitän Langsdorff's *Graf Spee* on sight.

Battle of the River Plate   **13 December** Langsdorff spots their smoke and, taking it for destroyers escorting a convoy, makes straight for them and engages. After two hours *Exeter* and *Ajax* have been badly damaged by superior armament, but *Achilles* is virtually unscathed. The German ship is also damaged and makes for Montevideo for repair. *Exeter* heads for Port Stanley but Harwood follows *Graf Spee*. Once docked, Harwood is content to keep her penned-up until his force is strengthened by the arrival of the carrier HMS *Ark Royal* and the battlecruiser HMS *Renown*. Fooled by BBC radio broadcasts suggesting that they have already arrived, Langsdorff believes he is trapped and reports accordingly to Berlin.

German cruisers *Leipzig* and *Nürnberg* are put out of action by the submarine HMS *Salmon* in the North Sea.

14 December The Soviet Union is expelled from the League of Nations.

A German High Command press notice confirms that *Graf Spee* has 'received several hits and is currently in the port of Montevideo'.

15 December British sailors, survivors of vessels sunk by *Graf Spee* and released by Langsdorff when the ship arrived in Uruguay, report that they have been well treated by the Germans.

16 December Soviet Seventh Army mounts a 48-hour attack on the Mannerheim Line without success.

Uruguayan authorities insist that *Graf Spee* quit their port by 1700 hours next day.

Graf Spee scuttled   **17 December** With only forty crew aboard, Langsdorff takes *Graf Spee* to the entrance of Montevideo harbour and scuttles her with explosives rather than attempt to fight his way through the naval cordon which he believes surrounds him; in fact only the heavy cruiser HMS *Cumberland* has reached the area. The explosion shakes the city and a 20,000-strong crowd of onlookers.

18 December Wellington bombers on patrol and naval bombing missions are located by German radar and fighter interceptors are guided to the aircraft by radar and radio telephony. A bloody battle sees fifteen of the 22 British aircraft lost and, as a result, daylight bombing strategies are thoroughly revised to incorporate fighter protection; night raids become the norm for much of the war.

The German High Command gives the Uruguayan ultimatum to leave port as the reason why *Graf Spee* could not be repaired and made seaworthy and the explanation for the decision to scuttle the vessel.

19 December The German luxury liner *Columbus* is located by the destroyer HMS *Hyperion* off Norfolk, Virginia. Realising his plight, the commander, Kapitän Dahne, scuttles his ship by fire to become the 23rd such German casualty since the outbreak of hostilities.

20 December Captain Langsdorff commits suicide in Buenos Aires rather than accept capture by the Allies, and possibly because he had disobeyed the order not to engage enemy warships.

23 December The first Canadian troops arrive in Great Britain.

With great bravado, the Finns mount a counter-attack on the Karelian Isthmus but are severely punished for their nerve.

Canadian troops arrive in Great Britain

27 December The year draws to a close with the Finns still putting up stout resistance against the advancing Russians. Their tactics of isolating mechanised units before attacking them owes much to their skill in cross-country infantry manoeuvres and the inability of the enemy to adapt to the situation.

28 December Meat rationing begins in Great Britain.

The battleship HMS *Barham* is torpedoed by *U30* and put out of action for some months.

30 December The year ends with Germany extending the U-boat threat to all nations chartering or selling vessels to Great Britain. The first four months of the sea war have seen the German U-boat threat in the ascendance and Allied plans to counter it yet to have any significant effect.

1940

JANUARY 1940

1 January The U-boat threat to Allied shipping in the North Sea and Atlantic Ocean continues. This month sees more than 70 vessels lost, a total of 214,500 tons; it also records an escalation of mining activities and the degaussing (the elimination of a ship's inherent magnetic field by an electric current passed through a cable around the hull) programme is stepped-up.

4 January Hermann Göring is put in overall charge of German war industry.

6 January Bad weather across Europe has curtailed military flying in the early days of the year but on this day Finnish pilot, Jorma Sarvanto, and a colleague shoot down all seven bombers in a Soviet formation. Whilst Stalin is suitably alarmed by these and other losses, and dispatches 600 new aircraft to the region, the small Finnish force is also receiving British, Italian, Swedish and American machines and volunteers from several countries.

Finns receive aid

8 January Soviet losses mount in Finland: more than 27,500 men are lost at Suomusalmi. Few Russian troops are good skiers (training manuals accompany non-skiers on the battlefield!). General Timoshenko's arrival brings new order to the chaos, but the Finns are still achieving successes out of all proportion to their numerical strength.

End of the Battle of Suomussalmi

Food rationing is introduced in Great Britain; France shortly follows suit.

10 January A Messerschmitt Bf 108 courier aircraft, forced by bad weather to make an emergency landing in Belgium, is found to be carrying plans for the western offensive, and indicating that it will begin within the week. The British and French use this evidence in an attempt to get more willing co-operation from the Belgians.

German invasion plans discovered

14 January Under the guise of security needs, Hitler issues a statement saying that no one will learn more of a secret matter than he has to know to fulfil his duty. This edict enables even more of the inner workings of the political hierarchy to be kept from the military commanders.

15 January The Belgian government, confused by the incident of the 10th, protests to the Germans about the aircraft entering their air space; they fear that their country will become a battlefield yet again. The discovery of the German plans and the poor weather causes Hitler to abandon his invasion plans again.

The Finnish news agency reports, with some amusement, that captured Soviet war crates reveal more quantities of skiing manuals as yet unused; the Finns have needed no such aids for they are masters of the snow and have used it to their advantage to outwit the Russians.

19 January The acquisition of Soviet aviation fuel by the Germans continues to worry the Allies who now give serious consideration to a plan to attack the Soviet oilfields.

In the southern North Sea the destroyer HMS *Grenville* is sunk by a mine; many of its crew are lost.

21 January Another destroyer, HMS *Exmouth*, is lost, this time to a torpedo from *U22*.

26 January A memorandum submitted by de Gaulle to his military masters campaigns for a re-appraisal of the nation's approach to mechanised armed forces. It includes the statement: 'We began the war with five million soldiers yet our aerial forces are only now being equipped and our armoured vehicles are too weak and too few in number.' He states his expectation that 'the present hostilities are likely to expand considerably'.

27 January Hitler orders the planning for the invasion of Norway. At the same time, an Allied war council meeting in Paris agrees that an expeditionary force sent to Finland could be used as an excuse for occupying Narvik and keeping part of the force in the Norwegian port.

28 January The Finns enjoy a good day. The 9th Division has successes against the Soviet 54th Division at Kuhmo but has insufficient numbers to force home the advantage gained.

29 January French leader Daladier demonstrates calm or apathy, depending on the opinion of the listener. He says that total war 'still hesitates to break out' but gives the cause as the fighting prowess of his troops.

FEBRUARY 1940

1 February Japanese military expansionism is signposted by a huge budget devoting unprecedented sums to weaponry and training.

3 February The North-West Front, under Timoshenko, moves against the Finnish Mannerheim Line with extensive air support. The Finnish 6th Division defends capably.

5 February The Supreme War Council of Great Britain and France agrees to intervene in Norway and commit aid to Finland. They aim to land forces in Norway by 20 March.

11 February The Soviet 123rd Division breaks the Finnish defences on the Mannerheim Line close to Summa and holds its position despite a spirited counter-attack next day.

The Soviet Navy is restricted in its support of the Finnish action because the Gulf of Finland is icebound.

12 February *U33* is located while laying mines in the Clyde Estuary and sunk by the minesweeper HMS *Cleaner*. This minor success is made significant by the recovery of three wheels from an Enigma decoding machine.

Enigma code machine

13 February Soviet Seventh Army breaks through Finnish lines at Summa.

14 February The Germans announce that all British merchant ships in the North Sea will be considered vessels of war following a British decision that they will be armed.

Altmark incident

16 February After a long hunt, the German tanker *Altmark* is sighted off the Norwegian coast. She is known to be carrying hundreds of British prisoners from her time as a supply ship to *Graf Spee*. The destroyer HMS *Cossack* pursues her into Josingfiord only to withdraw after being assured by the Norwegians that she has already been checked and found to be unarmed. Her Captain Vian seeks instructions from London and is told by Churchill to return to the fiord and free the prisoners. After negotiations with the Norwegians fail, Vian manoeuvres towards the German vessel which runs aground while trying to force *Cossack* into the shallows. A British boarding-party fights its way aboard *Altmark* and brings off 303 prisoners; several Germans are killed and five wounded. The brazen nature of the raid and its complete success was much celebrated in Great Britain. Raeder was critical of the Norwegians for failing to maintain their neutral status, although *Altmark*'s Kapitän Dau had himself blatantly abused this neutrality by forcing the Norwegians to make the false report about their search of his vessel.

18 February The battlecruisers *Gneisenau* and *Scharnhorst* with the cruiser *Hipper* and two destroyers attack convoys between the UK and Scandinavia. The destroyer HMS *Daring* is torpedoed by *U23*.

21 February The Germans begin construction of Auschwitz concentration camp.

22 February General Gamelin produces a report (see 19 January) which pinpoints where and how oilfields in the Caucasus could be attacked.

Two German destroyers sunk by 'friendly fire'

An apparently 'friendly fire' incident sees the Germans admitting the loss of the destroyers *Leberecht Maass* and *Max Schultz* as they are hit by bombs dropped from aircraft flying so low that their German markings could be seen, though Allied reports suggest that the sinkings were caused by mines.

23 February A Russian rifle division is decimated by the Finnish Talvela Group, one of the Finns' few major successes of the war.

24 February The Soviets have lost much *matériel*, including their latest armoured vehicles, in the Finnish War.

MARCH 1940

2 March The passenger ship SS *Domala* is attacked by German bombers within sight of the Isle of Wight, the first such action in the English Channel.

3 March Poor performance by the Russians in Finland sees General Grendal, commander of 13th Army, dismissed. Soviet claims of large quantities of Finnish *matériel* captured amuses the Finns and others, these never having been available.

4 March German naval effort is now switched to Norwegian waters to support the planned invasion.

28

7 March Marshal Baron von Mannerheim recognises the hopelessness of the Finnish situation and urges negotiations. One-fifth of Finish forces have become casualties.

First U-boat sunk by an aircraft

11 March This day sees the first example of an aircraft sinking a U-boat when *U31* is attacked and sunk off Wilhelmshaven by a lone RAF Blenheim.

Atlantis, the first of a dozen German commerce raiders, puts to sea. These 'ghost' ships are to prey on merchantmen sailing without the protection of a convoy. Their 60,000 nautical miles range will see them in action in the Atlantic, Pacific and Indian Oceans.

12 March Finland cedes land to the Soviet Union in a treaty which ends the short war during which Finnish casualties exceeded 65,000 and the Red Army lost nearly 50,000 dead and three times that number wounded. Such was the strength of the Finnish resistance that the country earned a more amenable settlement than would have been the case had it given way to Soviet aggression. Using offensive tactics whenever possible and creating strategies which took full advantage of the climate and terrain, the Finns forced the Russians to learn lessons that would serve them well later on.

End of Russo-Finnish War

The summary of the air element of the Russo–Finnish conflict gives the former as having lost more than 680 aircraft and the Finns just 67.

First British civilian killed by Luftwaffe

16 March The first British civilian is killed when fifteen Junkers Ju 88 bombers attack the Grand Fleet's anchorage in Scapa Flow.

20 March The Royal Navy's Home Fleet returns to Scapa Flow. The waters between the North Atlantic and North Sea have now been heavily mined by the British.

The Allied plan to bomb Soviet oilfields is accelerated, the intelligence services in Great Britain being asked to provide aerial reconnaissance.

27 March Peter Fraser is appointed Prime Minister in New Zealand following the death of Michael Savage.

28 March Great Britain and France agree that neither will make a separate peace.

The Allied Supreme War Council agrees to mine Norwegian waters and to land troops near some of the larger coastal towns.

30 March A reconnaissance flight from an RAF base near Baghdad flies unmolested for several hours over the Soviet oilfields on the Bahu Peninsula.

APRIL 1940

3 April Intelligence reports received in London advise of a concentration of German troops and vessels in northern German ports, suggesting a readiness for a Scandinavian invasion. For this first amphibious operation of the war, the Germans will deploy thirty warships and the same number of U-boats plus many support vessels. As a consequence, the Allies choose to delay their Norwegian operation, leaving Hitler to land in Norway first.

5 April Another recce flight from Baghdad targets the Batum oil seaport on the Black Sea. This time the aircraft comes under fire but escapes. The resulting photographs are being examined in the UK next day and plans are made for a raid to be undertaken within weeks.

The Norwegians are advised that Great Britain and France reserve the right to act to deprive Germany of access to Norwegian raw materials.

6 April The German fleet sails for Narvik; among the ground forces embarked are specialist mountain troops.

Gernay Invades Denmark and Norway

7 April A large element of the Reich's naval resources are committed to Operation '*Weserubung*' (invasion of Norway and Denmark). The risks involved, including the passage through British-controlled waters, have been acknowledged, losses of up to 50 per cent of the forces engaged being considered acceptable. British airborne reconnaissance monitors the German ships at sea and in harbour. A British fleet leaves Scapa Flow and Rosyth but its initial route north enables the Germans to get to Norwegian ports unchallenged.

8 April A chance encounter between the destroyer HMS *Glowworm* and the heavy cruiser *Admiral Hipper* and two destroyers sees the former ram the cruiser before bursting into flames; *Hipper* is damaged but survives.

9 April The small Norwegian air force does not merit much Luftwaffe involvement in the invasion, other than tactical support of the land and sea strategies. Just two German divisions, under General Kaupitsch, are devoted to the invasion of Denmark; Copenhagen, is taken within twelve hours.

Bad weather keeps British naval patrols close in-shore, which enables the wallowing German ships to reach their Norwegian objectives. *Admiral Hipper* bluffs Norwegian coastal batteries and gets into Trondheim. Land-based gunners are blinded by the vessel's searchlights and the few that recognise the ship are knocked out when they open fire. The battlecruiser HMS *Renown* sights *Scharnhorst* and *Gneisenau* returning from Narvik and damages both vessels from 18,000 yards before they escape under a smoke-screen. A large bomber force from the 10th Air Corps attacks the British fleet off Bergen, sinking the destroyer HMS *Gurkha* and damaging the cruisers HMSS *Southampton* and *Glasgow*, and the battleship HMS *Rodney*. The first German naval losses of the Norwegian operation see the heavy cruiser *Blücher* and the torpedo-boat *Albatros* sunk by shore-based batteries, but the Kriegsmarine sink or capture ten Norwegian vessels. The port of Bergen is taken by the German light cruiser *Köln* when her 'English' radio message to the port authorities fools the Norwegians. By evening, all significant Norwegian ports are in German hands. Weak and ill-informed British naval decisions have eased the process for the Germans; their long passage could have been blocked or, at least, made more difficult, and poor weather is insufficient excuse for the failure.

Blücher sunk

10 April An advance for British naval aviation sees Blackburn Skuas sink the light cruiser *Königsberg*.

Königsberg sunk

11 April Radio Stockholm reports 'the largest sea battle of all time' as having taken place involving 150 Allied and 100 German vessels plus nearly 200 aircraft. The submarine HMS *Spearfish* torpedoes the heavy cruiser *Lützow* (ex-*Deutschland*) causing her to return to Kiel and putting her out of action for a year.

13 April Eight German destroyers are lost to Royal Naval numerical superiority in the Vestfiord of Narvik.

Battle of Narvik

14 April The first Allied troops land in Norway, at Harstad in the Lofoten Islands near Narvik.

15 April *U49* is sunk by the destroyers HMSS *Fearless* and *Brazen* and secret documents are recovered from the debris.

17 April German mountain troops in Norway are urged by Hitler to hold their perilous position for as long as possible.

18 April French troops land at Namsos and during the next few days are reinforced.

The British Ministry of Shipping announces the loss of 81 merchant ships since the outbreak of war.

27 April German bombers blitz Namsos, attacking the freighters landing supplies for the Allied forces. The order is given to evacuate the port.

MAY 1940

2 May The evacuation of Namsos is completed but the town has been destroyed by German bombing. The French destroyer *Bison* is blown up and the destroyer HMS *Afridi*, having rescued survivors of the French vessel, is sunk by Stukas.

3 May *Atlantis*, the commerce raider, gains the first prize for this class of vessel when her crew board and sink the British freighter *Scientist*.

5 May The submarine HMS *Shark* is captured by the Germans: having been damaged by a mine the previous day, she is 'confronted' by an Arado flying-boat which touches down and stands by the surfaced vessel until naval support arrives.

7 May Nearly 5,000 Polish mountain troops land at Harstad, taking Allied forces in the Narvik area well beyond 20,000 while the Germans can only boast some 5,000 men from mixed units.

8 May Timoshenko replaces Voroshilov as Soviet defence chief and, as a result, the lessons learned during the Finnish war are more quickly implemented.

9 May Hitler sets in motion the western offensive. Belgium, Luxembourg and Holland are to be invaded without warning or declaration of war. Army Group B will occupy Holland and Belgium and prepare to confront the expected Allied response; Army Group A is to break through to Liège

German Western Offensive begins

31

and cross the Meuse; Army Group C, made up of infantry troops without tanks, is to draw off as many Allied forces as possible on their route to the south. Confronting this advance would be the French, whose numbers are concentrated in the north-eastern sector of the country; the Belgian Army which, it is hoped, would hold its eastern border for a while; and the British Expeditionary Force which can claim no armoured divisions and only 310 tanks, mostly of outmoded design.

The Kriegsmarine, licking its wounds from the Norwegian venture, has little part in the beginning of this major campaign.

Churchill replaces Chamberlain

10 May Chamberlain resigns and is replaced as Prime Minister by Winston Churchill who immediately forms a war cabinet drawn from all political parties. At the outset of the parliamentary debate which has brought about his downfall, Chamberlain's government has had a majority (281 to 200) on the first vote but he accepts that this is not enough. He has not been as much at fault for the errors in the Norwegian campaign and elsewhere as others, including Churchill, but his decision-making is seen as weak and, of course, his poor judgement of Hitler stands against him. It has seemed initially that Lord Halifax (ardently pro-Hitler) would succeed as Prime Minister but his, and others', fears about a government leader being in the House of Lords brings his withdrawal and a clear path for Churchill.

Britain occupies Iceland

British troops occupy Iceland.

At the outset of their campaign the Germans can claim nearly 4,000 operational aircraft. The combined aerial strength of Great Britain, France, Holland and Belgium amounts to a little more than half that number. The Dutch and Belgian elements are effectively destroyed in the first few hours of fighting, but British and French losses of about 60 aircraft initially compare favourably with the Luftwaffe which loses more than 300 machines destroyed, 50 damaged, and 267 aircrew killed. Two airborne landings, using the wholly unsuitable Fiesler Fi 156 Storch aircraft, are undertaken by the Germans, close to Luxembourg in the south, and east of Sedan in the north. Some 400 troops are landed to block roads until the armour arrives.

Eben Emael captured

On the same day paratroops raid and capture the Belgian fort of Eben Emael, with its 1,200-man garrison, in a surprise move using gliders. It is already clear, just hours into the German advance, that the Belgian and Dutch armies will be unable to delay, let alone offer any significant defence against, the panzer Blitzkrieg.

One result of Churchill's elevation is the prompt use of bombers over Germany. Thirty-six take off for raids on Mönchengladbach on the night of the 10th.

11 May The Reich Press Office urges its officers in the field to report truthfully, without invention or sensation, and insists that descriptions of places and progress must match centrally distributed information.

British and French troops move into the Dutch Caribbean islands of Aruba and Curaçao to protect oil installations.

The Luftwaffe continues its dive-bombing raids and tactical support of the Blitzkrieg drive to the west. Few Allied flights are made in counter-attack against the German ground advances. Bridges are targeted too late and aircraft given hopeless tasks; one Belgian mission of nine aircraft misses all its target bridges on the Albert Canal and loses seven aircraft.

12 May Even the Germans are surprised by the lack of opposition, especially the lateness and ineffectiveness of flights attempting to hit bridges they have already crossed. The French Seventh Army confronts the Germans near Tilburg but is thrust back contemptuously.

British naval units open fire on the coast around Narvik ahead of French alpine troops landing and pushing inland.

13 May In the first heavy armoured battles in the west, divisions of XVI Panzer Corps inflict heavy losses on the numerically superior French at Tirlemont. The Meuse is crossed at Sedan and Dinant with General Guderian in the forefront at the former and General Rommel part of the advance at the latter. The 9th Panzer Division reaches strategic Dutch rail and road bridges just fifteen miles south of Rotterdam and, before the end of the day, moves on to the city.

Heavy French losses

Allied forces begin their moves on Narvik and Churchill makes his 'blood, toil, tears and sweat' speech.

14 May French tank forces fail to prevent the German armour blitzing across the Meuse.

In Rotterdam 900 civilians are killed when bombers disgorge their deadly cargo soon after surrender negotiations with the Dutch had begun. The flares which were fired to warn the flight to turn back were partially masked by smoke and more than half the aircraft failed to heed this late abandonment.

Rotterdam bombed

British flights against advancing German ground troops prove disastrous with many aircraft lost, few bridges hit and the momentum of the panzer forces barely affected.

Heavy British aircraft losses

15 May The Reich Press Office orders the German media to refrain from dismissing the ability of the British troops but urges emphasis of the failure of the command structure and the resultant rout of the Allied forces.

General Winkelman signs the Dutch surrender as French forces continue to be swept aside by German armour advances. Gamelin, Supreme Commander of these defensive forces, remains unmoved and is slow to respond even when Guderian reaches Montcornet, Field Marshal von Kleist forms bridgeheads over the Meuse and the French 1st Armoured Division is destroyed by XV Panzer Corps.

Dutch surrender

Unaware of the circumstances regarding the bombing of Rotterdam, Churchill and the Allies take it as an example of German callousness in its air warfare strategy and a reason to consider German cities as viable targets for the RAF. At this time Great Britain has barely one hundred serviceable long-range bombers, but, even so, Bomber Command still has to fight for its share of manufacturing funds.

The night of 15 May sees 99 RAF aircraft bomb oil and transport targets in the Ruhr to herald the commencement of the strategic bombing offensive. French fighters are also active, but although they continue to down enemy aircraft, their efforts do little to hamper German ground movement.

Air Marshal Dowding is being urged to send more fighter aircraft to France in support of the ground fighting but he defiantly argues that the force must be retained for a more fundamental defensive role. Had he lost this debate the result of the Battle of Britain might have been different.

A new class of U-boat, the Type IXA, makes its début with *U37*.

16 May British and French units are forced to retreat to their defensive lines at the Scheldt only days after advancing from them. The Germans press on to Cambrai and St-Quentin; the pace of their advance astonishes their own strategists who cannot believe that the French have not attempted to expose the extended German flanks. Gamelin and Churchill meet in Paris where the latter is dumbfounded by the absence of a planned response to the German thrusts.

The decision of the British to ban their merchant shipping from the Mediterranean will have wide-ranging ramifications. The route to Suez is extended by 20,000 miles and the loss of French ports in Africa will mean that Freetown, Sierra Leone, will be the sole west coast port of entry for supplies and troops.

President Roosevelt secures funding for a massive production of 50,000 military aircraft a year. Although the USA is not yet 'at war', he is preparing for the time when it will be.

17 May French Premier Reynaud tells his countrymen that its government is not leaving Paris. He rejects the claim that the Germans have reached Reims and admits only to heroic fighting by French forces against a broad pocket opened by the enemy across the Meuse. In a note to Reynaud, Churchill congratulates him on appointing the ageing General Weygand as CinC, Allied Forces in replacement of the ineffectual Gamelin; Weygand is brought back from duty in the Middle East.

The Germans walk into Brussels unopposed while de Gaulle leads a small force against the German units at Montcornet before being driven back by dive-bomber attacks.

The Stuka dive-bombers continue to have a devastating effect. Not only do they help cut a swathe through the countryside for the ground troops but they also knock out French armour deployed in the counter-offensive role.

18 May The Reich Press Office, continuing to guard against exaggeration, urges its officers to comment on the harshness of the battles and the tasks to be overcome. Cambrai and St-Quentin fall and General Reichenau walks his Sixth Army into undefended Antwerp. Reynaud makes fresh appointments, in addition to that of Weygand, to induce some urgency into the French war effort. Among these new men will be some who oppose Weygand's desire to fight on.

Tyler Kent, an American clerk at the US embassy in London, and Anna Wolkoff, a Russian emigrée, are arrested on spying charges. The American has provided scripts of conversations and correspondence between Churchill and Roosevelt for the woman to pass to Germany via the Italian diplomatic staff in London. The US Ambassador does not allow Kent to claim diplomatic immunity to avoid prosecution.

Spies arrested

A request by Churchill to Roosevelt for 40 vintage US destroyers is refused.

19 May Ten days after the Germans began their drive to the west, their Allied opponents are forced to consider the evacuation of the BEF from mainland Europe.

Lord Gort, CinC of the force, prepares for the eventuality; Admiral Ramsay, Flag Officer at Dover, is put in charge of the 'transport' which will be the core element of Operation 'Dynamo'.

20 May Guderian, whose vigour is a perfect match for the Blitzkrieg tactics, takes Amiens and Abbeville within the day. He moves faster than even the other panzer forces, rejecting any call to pause and regroup. The changes of personnel within the French command only serve to delay the necessary response to Guderian's advance.

21 May British tanks attack Rommel's 7th Panzer Division at Arras but are too few in number to improve on some early success. Weygand's attempt to co-ordinate a stronger Allied response is in disarray, not helped by Billotte's death in a car accident, but the efforts at Arras have enabled much of the French First Army and four British divisions to move back to Dunkirk.

Arras counter-attack

Raeder tells Hitler that, given its losses in the Norwegian theatre, he does not want to commit his navy to any invasion of England, viewing this as a short-term support role which should not be allowed to siphon off vessels and crews from larger tasks.

22 May The German forces are at the English Channel coast and sweep north to Boulogne and Calais. In Paris, Churchill accepts Weygand's plan to attack the German corridor but both men doubt its chances of success. The Germans are delayed near Arras by the first concerted Allied resistance, the better armed and heavily built British tanks getting the better of their opponents for a while; the delay means more troops can retreat to Dunkirk. In London parliament takes emergency powers to speed the war effort.

The RAF loses its last airfield in France, at Merville, and will now have to fly from its bases in the UK.

RAF loses its last French airfield

23 May Weygand's counter-offensive is postponed when Allied forces have to evacuate Arras. With Boulogne under fire and ever more Allied soldiers being enveloped by Germans at the coast, a seaborne withdrawal appears inevitable.

Göring's plan to support ground attacks against Allied troops running for Dunkirk are hampered when bad weather, low cloud and airfields too far from the fighting, limit the value of the Luftwaffe.

In England, Oswald Mosley, figurehead of the British Fascist movement, is arrested.

Germans halt advance on Dunkirk

24 May To Guderian's utter disgust, but based on a proposal by von Rundstedt, Hitler orders von Kleist to halt his advance into Dunkirk. The Führer has been assured by Göring that his Luftwaffe will take out the remaining encircled forces and so avoid the need for Hitler to risk his tanks in the flat, boggy fields in the area. Hitler's direct involvement in local strategy and tactics appals many of his commanders on the ground, but is destined to be repeated many times. The German pause allows the beleaguered Allied forces time to regroup. The evacuation has a chance of success.

Meanwhile, the Allies plan to capture Narvik, destroy its port, and then leave, despite the recent strengthening of air support in the area.

25 May Churchill asks Edmund Ironside, Chief of the Imperial General Staff, for a policy report on Gort and the BEF. A defensive withdrawal is now under hourly study. At Boulogne and Menin, Allied resistance is overcome and any thoughts of a counter-attack are abandoned.

General Guderian, in an address to his troops who have fought the Blitzkrieg campaign through Belgium and France, says: 'I asked you to go without sleep for 48 hours. You have gone for seventeen days. I compelled you to take risks ... you never faltered.'

Evacuation of troops from Dunkirk begins

26 May The order for the evacuation of troops through Dunkirk is given this evening; it will prove a daunting task and last until dawn on 4 June. Some 335,000 servicemen and civilians will be rescued by more than 700 assorted vessels of which 71 will be lost including six RN and three French destroyers, but others will be damaged so severely that they will be out of action for many months. Admiral Ramsay puts his plan into operation, and not before time as Dunkirk is now receiving a constant stream of retreating Allied forces and the Belgian Army's situation in the town is hopeless. German Army Group A bombards the town from the outskirts but does not attempt to enter it.

Allies capture Narvik

27 May The Allies take Narvik despite bad weather hampering the intended air support.

The most diverse armada ever assembled collects in ports along the English Channel coast; it includes pleasure boats from the holiday resorts, fishing vessels, cabin cruisers from the Thames manned by their civilian owners, and tugs and ferries from the ports. The Admiralty gives the go-ahead for Operation 'Dynamo'.

Belgians capitulate

28 May King Leopold of the Belgians agrees to capitulate as the evacuation from Dunkirk gets under way.

The steamer *Mona's Isle* is the first ship to arrive at Dunkirk. She comes under fire from coastal batteries but leaves again with more than 100 dead on board.

29 May Dunkirk is encircled by German artillery and, from above, is pounded by the Luftwaffe but the evacuation continues, with French troops now joining the exodus.

The destroyers HMSS *Wakeful*, *Grafton* and *Grenade* are lost on the Dunkirk run.

30 May Even though they now have clear weather, the Stukas are less effective around Dunkirk than Göring had expected. Their ability to hit land convoys and static targets is not matched when faced with the armada of vessels plying to and from the French coast.

While more than 860 vessels are employed on runs to and from the Dunkirk beaches, the German bombardment lessens and some units move back to prepare for action elsewhere in France.

31 May Roosevelt introduces his massive armament programme which will boost his country's position as a dominant military nation.

USA rearmament programme

The air battles over the evacuation beaches become more even with the Spitfire now on active duty; more than 68,000 men are taken off. The Stukas are quickly found wanting by the sleek, highly manoeuvrable British fighter.

The German Navy is hardly seen during the Dunkirk episode, but it has been busy during May with twenty Allied ships lost to mines and a further fifteen merchantmen to U-boats. On this day, E-boats *S23* and *S36* sink the French destroyer *Sirocco*.

JUNE 1940

1 June More Allied shipping is lost than on the preceding days of the Dunkirk evacuation and daytime sailings are postponed.

2 June The remaining French forces at the Dunkirk perimeter are driven back into the town but the Germans still fail to move into its centre. The evacuation area is now very small but boats still manage to get in and out. In Norway a further Allied evacuation gets under way.

3 June Although only two miles from the harbour, the Germans still do not prevent Operation 'Dynamo' from being all but completed. A late arrival of various French forces and civilians leaves just 40,000 to be captured. The last vessel to depart Dunkirk, the destroyer HMS *Shikari*, sails at 0330 hours with 338 men. Just six hours later von Kluge's Fourth Army enters the town.

Evacuation of troops from Dunkirk finishes

Elsewhere, Göring has transferred his bombers inland and begins a programme of bombing airfields and industrial sites around Paris.

4 June Churchill delivers his 'we shall fight them on the beaches ....' speech. Unstated but apparent in the words is his belief that France will fall and that Great Britain may be the lone opponent to Hitler in Europe.

When the Germans enter Dunkirk they capture the remaining French forces and much Allied equipment, but more than 350,000 men have got away, including more than 110,000 French. Some 80 vessels have been lost, including nine destroyers, and the RAF has lost 80 pilots. It has been a military exercise without precedent or parallel, but the Germans could, and should, have done more to prevent it. Some land commanders showed hesitancy, and the Luftwaffe was held back by poor weather and political vacillation; Hitler has shown such caution that his motives are questioned from this day on. From a point where the Germans could have captured a quarter of a million British troops, with the resulting effect on the morale of both sides, Hitler has now given Churchill the opportunity to deliver his 'we shall fight them' call for national resolve. All the more strange then that Hitler should order all church bells in Germany to be rung to announce the end of 'the greatest battle in world history' when he has chosen not to do battle with his opponents here but save his men and machines for the drive on Paris. It is argued that this decision will lose him the war.

The battlecruisers *Scharnhorst* and *Gneisenau* leave Kiel with orders to intercept the Allied evacuation fleet from Norway.

5 June As if to demonstrate the insignificance of Dunkirk, German forces now move on to the Battle for France. Regrouped French forces put up a good defence north of Amiens, but otherwise the Blitzkrieg campaign regains its energy. German Army Group B breaks the Weygand Line manned by 49 French divisions along the Somme and Aisne.

Daladier is dropped from the French cabinet and de Gaulle is promoted to Under-Secretary for Defence.

The Luftwaffe ace Werner Mölders is shot down by French aircraft. General Vuillemin pleads with the British to send him aircraft to help his cause; the fact that he is not ably using all his own machines would count against him even if the RAF had aircraft to spare.

Glorious sunk

8 June *Scharnhorst* and *Gneisenau* encounter the aircraft carrier HMS *Glorious* and her escorts HMSS *Ardent* and *Acasta*. The British ship, her Swordfish aircraft still on deck, is a sitting target. From a range of fifteen miles *Scharnhorst* scores direct hits and sinks her; the escorts attack the German ships but are also hit and sunk, though *Acasta* torpedoed and badly damaged *Scharnhorst* before going down. More than 1,500 naval and air force personnel are lost, but the engagement has prevented the German ships from getting at the evacuation convoy farther north.

Italy declares war on Britain and France

10 June Italy declares war on Great Britain and France, bringing to the battlefield 1,500,000 men including colonials, more than 1,700 aircraft and a worthy naval fleet of six capital ships, nineteen cruisers, 59 destroyers, 67 torpedo-boats and 116 submarines. Fuel is in short supply and many of the personnel poorly trained; the Italian High Command has no fixed strategy of its own and is not being included in substantial policy discussions with Germany. Mussolini has not planned his war in any way; he wants to emulate Hitler but has little idea of the strategic planning and vast military production that has brought the Germans to their present pre-eminence.

The Germans' occupation of Norway is complete, but at some cost. The naval high command knows that the exercise has been a strategic error, and has depleted their resources.

11 June The French government decamps from Paris to Tours.

French government quits Paris

The first air combat between the British and the Italians sees the RAF bombing the Italian base at El Adem in Cyrenaica and a reprisal attack on Malta a few hours later.

Churchill, meeting the French government in their new headquarters at Tours, is unable to generate the same fighting spirit there that he is instilling at home. He steadfastly refuses to send RAF squadrons to France, knowing this would reduce his own country's chances of survival. It brings to an end RAF sorties from bases in southern France.

12 June The Italian Navy records its first success when the submarine *Bagnolini* torpedoes the light cruiser HMS *Calypso*.

13 June Roosevelt continues his military expansion with huge funds being set aside for naval construction. Some surplus US weaponry is sent to the UK through the intermediary of a steel company.

14 June The Germans enter Paris. The French Seventh Army under General Frère leaves the city without fighting and von Studnitz leads the 87th Infantry Division in its triumphal entry march.

Germans enter Paris

15 June The German 71st and 76th Infantry divisions take Verdun. Guderian's forces link up with Dollman's Seventh Army to encircle and capture 400,000 French troops near the Swiss border.

Red Army units occupy Kovno and Vilna, bringing Lithuania under Soviet rule.

Soviets occupy Lithuania

16 June The Rhine is crossed at Colmar by von Witzleben's First Army. Reynaud resigns and his replacement, Marshal Pétain, proposes an armistice to Germany.

The Italian submarine *Provana* is forced to the surface and sunk by the French sloop, *La Curieuse*.

17 June Guderian reaches the Swiss border at Pontarlier. Allied troops evacuating the Atlantic coast of France in the troopship *Lancastria* are bombed by the Luftwaffe and 3,000 men are drowned. Churchill demands that this news be kept from the British people – and it was for some years. Despite this loss, some 192,000 troops are brought home from the north and west coasts of France.

Churchill makes his 'finest hour' speech.

18 June The Allies evacuate Nantes and St-Nazaire on the French Atlantic coast.

Allies evacuate Nantes and St-Nazaire

The relatively unknown Brigadier-General Charles de Gaulle broadcasts to the French people from London, pressing them to fight on in any way they can.

Hamburg and Bremen
bombed

The RAF bombs Hamburg and Bremen.

19 June General Hoth's XV Panzer Corps occupies Brest and General Stülpnagel's II Army Corps reaches Nantes.

20 June General Hoepner's XVI Panzer Corps, following the southern route, reaches and occupies Lyons. The French ask the Italians for an armistice.

Many French naval ships stay in port in compliance with a German message sent in the form of an official coded French government edict which insist that they do so; but many escape or are already in British or French colonial ports.

Italy attacks France

21 June Italy attacks France. Forces including Italian First and Fourth Armies attack the French Alpine Army and advance to Menton.

France signs armistice
with Germany

22 June France signs an armistice with Germany at Rethondes, in the same railway carriage in which the November 1918 Armistice was signed. It provides for occupation of the country north and west of a line through Geneva, Tours and the Spanish border so as to give the Kriegsmarine access to all French Channel and Atlantic ports. A minimal French army is to be permitted and the navy is to be disarmed but not surrendered. The occupied area is to be governed by a team with Pétain as its Head and Laval as Chief Minister. All remaining French forces are to surrender, though 38,000 assorted French and Polish troops from the 45th Army Corps cross into Switzerland and are interned. The armistice in effect reduces almost two million French people to the status of prisoner of war. At this point the Blitzkrieg to the west has seen the Germans lose 27,000 dead more than 111,000 wounded and 18,000 missing. The French have lost 92,000 dead and more than 200,000 wounded; the British Expeditionary Force has lost more than 68,000 men.

The western offensive has taught the German much, though they will not remember all the lessons. They have seen the movement of heavy armoured vehicles, and the battlefield tactics they could employ, significantly reduced by unhelpful terrain and the most modest of road obstructions; columns of such machines have also often been badly delayed by human traffic, in the form of fleeing refugees. With command of the air and

Lessons of Blitzkrieg

relatively light resistance, however, the Blitzkrieg technique has been proven; the pace of advance has been unprecedented and, indeed, caused its own, unforeseen logistical problems. But the success of the Battle of France may have proved to be the Germans' undoing for they expect future battlefields to be equally susceptible to these techniques and when this proves not to be the case some of its finest commanders will be found wanting, their one-dimensional approach not being effective in defence or retreat.

Furthermore, the rapid defeat of France has focused Allied minds. Had they been able to hold their ground for longer, old strategies might have been clung to and new equipment might not have been urgently demanded.

For the French, the last weeks have been a chastening experience. Their industry has broken all manufacturing records to keep the armed forces supplied, but political foresight and military resolve have been absent. It is indicative that their air force ends the Battle of France with more aircraft than when it started, thanks to that manufacturing spurt accompanied by the logistical failure to deploy what was available.

24 June The armistice between France and Italy is signed. In the minor skirmishes between the two countries the French, weakened and demoralised, have comfortably beaten off badly managed and ill-conceived Italian attacks.

Armistice between France and Italy

25 June In France hostilities cease. The fall has taken place with unprecedented rapidity and suggests that no other European country is safe.

In Gibraltar plans are put in hand to create Force H, a British naval unit which will seek to replace the French Navy in the western Mediterranean.

26 June The Soviets, with German intervention, persuade the Roumanians to secede areas of Bessarabia and Bukovina.

27 June The Pacific region enters diplomatic debate when British and Australian representatives urge the US Secretary of State, Cordell Hull, to make the necessary stand to deter Japanese expansionist threats. This more active role is discounted by Hull at this point.

28 June In London General Charles de Gaulle is recognised as leader of the Free French by Great Britain.

de Gaulle becomes leader of the Free French

30 June German forces land in the Channel Islands, the only part of the British Isles that they will occupy.

Dönitz visits Brittany to view the U-boat bases which he believes will hugely increase the potential of his U-boat fleet. Now freed from having to make passage north of the British Isles to reach the Atlantic, the U-boats will surely be able to impose his will upon the all-important shipping lanes to and from the USA. With occupation of Norwegian, Danish, Belgian, Dutch, and French ports, the Kriegsmarine is in a position to control the seas of northern Europe in which Great Britain now seems ever more isolated. Indeed, a surge of success has been seen in June, with Allied shipping of more than 350,000 tons being lost to the U-boats.

JULY 1940

1 July Vice-Admiral Somerville takes command of Force H, a group consisting of the carrier HMS *Ark Royal*, battlecruiser HMS *Hood*, and two battleships plus cruisers and destroyers. Its first action will be against the French who, though claiming that none of their vessels will be allowed to fall into German or Italian hands, are proving reluctant to take determined action to avoid this.

Force H established

3 July Force H stations itself outside the French naval base at Oran (Mersel-Kebir), Algeria. The commander of the French fleet there rejects suggestions that his ships should either come under the control of the Royal Navy or be disarmed and immobilised. The decision is taken in London that Force H should destroy the French ships by gunfire and air bombing but the execution of the order falls short of its desired result. Only one old battleship, *Bretagne*, is sunk – with the loss of many men – and a newer ship damaged by a nearby explosion. The battleship *Strasbourg* and five destroyers escape the harbour and, avoiding later attacks from the air, reach Toulon. The action, one of the more controversial of the early war years, causes much ill-feeling in France; it had been the first show of enmity between Great Britain and France since the Battle of Waterloo.

The First Sea Lord, Dudley Pound, and others are urging Churchill to take the Navy out of the eastern Mediterranean but he chooses to keep it there, perhaps because he is uncertain of how the current issue of the French fleet will be resolved.

Royal Navy seize French warships

Earlier in the day the Royal Navy seize battleships, destroyers, torpedo-boats, submarines, the submarine-cruiser *Surcouf* and one hundred other French vessels with some 5,000 personnel, at anchor in British Channel ports.

Italians enters Sudan

4 July The Italians move from Abyssinia into the Sudan, using two brigades to occupy one town, Kassala, which is garrisoned by two companies.

British attack French warships

Torpedo-bombers from the carrier HMS *Hermes* attack the new French battleship *Richelieu* at anchor. Churchill's determination to eliminate the French from any naval equation brings calls from Laval, Darlan and others to declare war on Great Britain. Meanwhile the Luftwaffe attacks a convoy off the Dorset coast, sinking five of the nine ships. A classified report from Germany's intelligence service says that the German population is not being affected in any way by increasing bombing raids, and that the RAF flights only increase the desire of the German public to see Göring's Luftwaffe unleashed against Great Britain.

5 July As a direct outcome of the British attack on the French fleet, Pétain's government in Vichy breaks off diplomatic relations with Great Britain.

6 July Aircraft from HMS *Ark Royal* attack the damaged French battleship *Dunkerque* at Oran. The French news agency reports that, as a result of attacks on the national fleet by the British, French naval officers have been forbidden to wear British medals.

7 July Italian aircraft attack British naval bases at Malta and Alexandria.

8 July Air and sea attacks on the French battleship *Richelieu* at Dakar have only partial success. The ship is hit but remains operational.

Action between the British and Italian fleets

9 July Force H is attacked by high-altitude bombers; fire from HMS *Warspite* in Admiral Cunningham's Mediterranean Fleet damages the Italian battleship *Guilio Cesare* in the first action between the British and Italian Navies.

10 July The Luftwaffe raids military targets in the South of England to test RAF fighter response and willingness to engage; the Battle of Britain has begun. At its outset the Germans see it as the precursor to invasion and the British as a 'last stand' to prevent this; at its completion Hitler will look eastwards for further expansion and the British will begin to plan the retaking of Europe.

Luftwaffe raids South of England

12 July British shipping in the Atlantic faces a new threat with the stationing at Bordeaux of the Focke-Wulf Fw 200 Kondor long-range bomber and reconnaissance aircraft. One of these sinks a trawler off the Irish coast.

13 July Hitler decrees that the German air offensive will begin on 5 August even though the Luftwaffe will not be ready by then. He also talks of the likelihood of having to invade Russia.

The Italians cross the border from Abyssinia into Kenya.

Italians enter Kenya

16 July Hitler's Directive 16, setting out the plans for Operation 'Sealion' – the invasion of England – gives no target date but stresses the importance of control of the air over the Channel. It will also entail the use of submersible tanks; tests begin on primitive designs. Of Germany's 1.2 million tons of shipping capacity at this time, more than half may be needed to transport the invasion force across the Channel.

In Japan, a new cabinet with Prince Konoye at its head includes General Tojo as Minister of War.

17 July With the imminent need to defend their cities against bombers from the UK, the Germans begin to plan the formation of night-fighter squadrons; initially these will be based on Dutch airfields to intercept incoming flights.

19 July In the Reichstag, Hitler gives what he says is 'a final appeal to common sense' to Great Britain. Meanwhile Roosevelt signs a 'Two-Ocean Navy Expansion Act' which calls for hundreds of new warships and thousands of naval aircraft.

The Italians lose their first large ship when the light cruiser *Bartolomeo Colleoni* is sunk by the Australian light cruiser *Sydney* and the destroyers HMSS *Hyperion* and *Ilex*.

22 July The Special Operations Executive (SOE) is created in Great Britain to train and activate people to act subversively against the German forces in occupied Europe. Run on a 'shoestring', this organisation will enjoy success well beyond what the numbers employed could be expected to achieve. The Americans will later establish the Office of Strategic Services (OSS) to perform a similar role and, on many occasions, to work in concert with SOE. Although established through a false premise, that 'fifth columnists' were behind the German expansionist successes, these services will be modified as the conflict evolves and come to practise subversive action many times more effectively than the Germans had ever thought possible.

SOE created

25 July A US decision to limit its exports of oil places an immediate and continuing problem with the Japanese who have come to rely on foreign supplies. Their stocks dwindle from this day and cause them to look to the Dutch East Indies and Malaysia.

31 July Hitler meets Raeder to disclose his plan to invade England on 15 September. From that meeting he moves into discussions with Field Marshal von Brauchitsch and speaks of his intention to attack Russia in the spring of 1941.

The month ends with Great Britain able to claim that the pace of fighter aircraft production, 1,200 machines since May, is closing the quantity gap between the RAF and the Luftwaffe.

AUGUST 1940

1 August Hitler's Directive 17 updates the plan for the invasion of England. The new target date is now 19–26 September, though this still assumes that the Luftwaffe will have gained air supremacy.

2 August The Chief of the German Ministry of Economics and Armament is requested to set a programme in train which will increase the army's strength to 180 divisions; this in preparation for the invasion of Russia.

Hitler orders
destruction of RAF

Hitler orders the 'destruction of the RAF and the British aircraft industry' and states that the necessary air offensive must start on 5 August. The significance of this is that it accords the Luftwaffe an independence of role and action that has not been permitted hitherto. Its 'offensive force', rapidly assembled in France, the Low Countries and Norway, will consist of almost 1,700 aircraft including bombers, fighters, Stuka dive-bombers and fighter-destroyers. Field Marshal Kesselring's Luftflotte 2 will play the major role because its bases are the closest to England; in support will be Field Marshal Sperrle's Luftflotte 3; General Stumpff's Luftflotte 5 will operate from Norwegian bases against sites in the English Midlands. At this point the Germans remain unaware that the fighters which will be ranged against them are controlled by ground radar, a crucial asset in the weeks to come.

British evacuate
Berbera

3 August The Italian Air Force contributes significantly to the offensive against British Somaliland. Within ten days the British have to evacuate the capital, Berbera, as there is no prospect of aerial back-up in the region.

5 August The German Eighteenth Army already has sixteen divisions in Poland. Even these forces will be dwarfed by the numbers called for by General Staff plans.

8 August The Head of British Secret Intelligence, Wing Commander F. W. Winterbotham, learns of Göring's orders for the air offensive against England. Dowding is alerted.

9 August The German plans for the campaign against Russia show Poland converted to a huge military base.

10 August Many British tanks are to be sent to the Middle East in support of the campaigns there. This despite the fear of a German invasion of England.

The intended opening day of Göring's air offensive, code-named the 'Day of the Eagle', is postponed for three days because of bad weather.

12 August Raids by Messerschmitt Bf 110s and Stukas on radar stations along the coasts of Kent, Sussex and the Isle of Wight fail to break the system. RAF HQ reports five German aircraft shot down and others damaged; the Germans report their air raid on Portland Harbour with vessels damaged and ground installations destroyed.

Luftwaffe raid radar stations

13 August Bad weather causes a brief delay to the first major action of what will develop into the Battle of Britain. The day still sees nearly 500 bomber sorties and twice that number of fighter sorties. A German press report suggests that a lessening of the fighting spirit has been seen in the British fighter pilots confronting the waves of Luftwaffe aircraft.

Battle of Britain begins

14 August Air action over England is again restricted by bad weather, but the RAF fly 700 sorties and down 45 Luftwaffe aircraft.

45 Luftwaffe aircraft lost

15 August More than 2,000 sorties over England mark this as the Luftwaffe truly at war; RAF Fighter Command deploys all three of its Groups for the first time. The propaganda war is at its height with Germany issuing no acknowledgements of RAF bombing raids against industrial sites or success in dogfighting over the Channel, preferring to assure Germans at home that Göring's forces are facing little opposition and recording great victories; the British newspapers and official government releases overlook the impact of some German raids, the heavy fighter escorts accorded to most incoming bomber formations, and the poor return from some of the high-risk bombing missions to the German heartland.

Aldertag: opening of decisive phase of Battle of Britain

16 August Some 1,700 sorties are flown by the Germans against military sites in the south and south-east of England. The RAF attacks the Fiat manufacturing plant in Turin.

17 August Hitler orders a total blockade of the UK; all vessels, including those of neutral countries, will be sunk without warning. Elements of the Mediterranean Fleet bombard Italian positions at Bardia and Fort Capuzzo

18 August Kenley and Tangmere airfields are severely damaged and other Surrey and Kent RAF stations hit by German bombers, but the Luftwaffe loses 71 aircraft.

19 August Using reactive rather than offensive patterns, the RAF is succeeding in confusing the Luftwaffe hierarchy and gaining advantages for itself. The Germans, expecting fighter confrontations, find instead selective heavy concentrations of opposing fighters interdicting their routes to and from target areas. The use of radar is enabling the RAF to concentrate its fighters where they are needed; fuel is saved, pilots are given the best chances of success, and the impact of the huge German bombing missions is reduced.

20 August 'Never in the field of human conflict was so much owed by so many to so few', thunders Churchill in a typically inspirational speech which implants the description of the RAF fighter crews as 'the Few' into British history. The same day sees the announcement that some air bases will be leased to the Americans.

Germans bomb
centre of London

24 August Through an accidental loss of course, a German bomber off-loads over the centre of London with some loss of civilian life.

The German battleship *Bismarck* enters service.

RAF bombs Berlin

25 August In a reprisal for the London bombing of the night before, the RAF attacks Berlin. Spectators at major sporting events in England on this Saturday choose to ignore air raid warnings and cheer the sight of RAF formations flying over the sports arenas.

26 August German High Command admits to RAF bombing raids on Berlin but denies any damage has been caused there or elsewhere. The United Press Agency, based in the city, claims, however, that ten heavy explosions were felt in the first few minutes of the raid. Reuters in London tells of damage caused by fires started by German incendiary bombs dropped in clusters.

Dönitz is able to employ his U-boat 'wolf pack' strategy when German intelligence intercepts the sailing plans for Convoy SC-2. At this time only the shortage of serviceable U-boats prevents him from playing greater havoc. The use of Asdic detection enables the Allied escorts to locate submerged U-boats, but the wolf packs carry a great threat; in August alone they sink more than 260,000 tons of shipping.

31 August Since mid-August the RAF and Luftwaffe have suffered combined losses of more than 800 aircraft, of which the German count is 467 fighters and bombers. The Germans have also lost more aircrew; their British opponents can bale out to safety and return to duty, the Luftwaffe personnel are usually taken prisoner.

SEPTEMBER 1940

USA provide Great
Britain with 50
destroyers

2 September The USA finally agrees to provide Great Britain with 50 veteran but essential destroyers in return for air bases in Bermuda, the West Indies and Newfoundland. This small move is an important step in Roosevelt's gentle moves towards a more active involvement in the Allied cause. The need for caution is essential if the American people are to be supportive.

4 September Hitler, stung by the bombing of Berlin on 25/26 September, orders an air assault on London. This ill-advised, reactive move gives the embattled RAF bases and their crews a respite from the raids of the past weeks. The back-room planning centres can also regroup and continue to develop their radar systems and air warfare strategies.

The USA issues a statement saying that Japan must refrain from aggressive moves in Indo-China.

5 September The change of Luftwaffe policy sees 60 tons of bombs dropped on London.

7 September More than 900 German aircraft attack London. Göring observes the sorties from the Channel coast at Cap Gris Nez. A new escort tactic sees fighter aircraft flying cover for the bomber formations. The German High Command reports a huge cloud of smoke from the centre of London to the Thames estuary. By this action the Germans effectively 'invade' England from the air, but within another ten days Hitler will have cancelled his plans for Operation 'Sealion', the full-scale invasion of England.

8 September A Reuters press release tells of a greyhound race meeting in London which continues after a bomb lands on the field during the event. Another report from the same agency speaks of many civilians being killed when a German bomb falls through the ventilation shaft of a London air raid shelter housing mostly women and children.

9 September The US government places contracts for a further 210 naval vessels.

Six French warships make a run for Dakar from their Toulon base.

12 September The Italians move into Egypt from Libya. Marshal Graziani can call on thirteen divisions while Great Britain's Western Desert Force, under General O'Connor, has only two.

Italians attack Egypt

The Channel ports of France, Holland and Belgium hold more than 1,000 assorted German vessels gathered for the cancelled invasion and are raided by the RAF. More than 80 barges in Ostend are sunk.

13 September The Italians move to occupy Sollum on the Egyptian coast as the weak British forces withdraw ahead of a more substantial stand farther east. The Italians use unnecessarily complex tactics and, despite their advance, are showing a lack of awareness of desert warfare strategies. British harassment of the Italian force continues to undermine resolve and morale.

14 September More RAF raids, this time a particularly heavy one on Antwerp, inflict great destruction on the German invasion *matériel*, but a Reuters News Agency report in London expresses the feeling of many when it notes that a German invasion is expected, and that the German Navy will play a large part.

15 September On the day which will come to be known as 'Battle of Britain Day', the RAF scrambles all its fighters for the first time. The Germans lose nearly 25 per cent of their force – 56 aircraft – for a British loss of 26; the Luftwaffe hierarchy is convinced that it cannot continue to bear such losses. It has failed to gain control of the skies, the invasion cannot proceed, and its first opportunity to function as a separate arm has

'Battle of Britain Day'

47

been a failure. It will change its strategy to night raiding, but the British have survived and the German advance to the west has been stopped at the English Channel.

16 September The Italians reach Sidi Barrani which they occupy and fortify while awaiting supplies. These are delayed by British naval attacks in the Mediterranean.

At sea, Fleet Air Arm aircraft from the carrier HMS *Illustrious* attack the port of Benghazi. Four Italian ships are sunk.

Invasion of England postponed

17 September Hitler announces the postponement of the invasion of England. By the time he comes to reconsider the chance will have been lost. In a revised plan for the invasion of Russia, General Paulus specifies lines of attack which will aim for Leningrad, Moscow and Kiev; this is the core of the final plan for Operation 'Barbarossa'. Nevertheless Hitler still has his shipbuilding industry working on invasion barges and trawlers rather than capital ships such as the battleship *Tirpitz* and the desperately needed new and repaired U-boats.

18 September The Italians remain at Sidi Barrani and leave the British to withdraw and regroup without harassment.

20 September Field Marshal von Bock takes command of the German troops on the Germans' eastern border.

Convoy HX-72

An Allied convoy, HX-72, is located and attacked by a U-boat wolf pack. Twelve of the 41 ships are sunk, Commander Schepke in *U100* causing havoc without being detected.

21 September The stations on the London Underground system have long been used by civilians sheltering from the German bombing. The government gives way to the inevitable and officially sanctions their use for this purpose.

22 September Churchill advises South Africa's General Smuts of the proposed move against Dakar and warns of the consequences to the Cape route if the exercise were to fail. The Japanese make a minor move into Indo-China.

The RAF bombs Berlin.

British and Free French attempt to capture Dakar

23 September The British and Free French, working together, launch Operation 'Menace', aimed at returning Dakar to Allied control. Cunningham and de Gaulle with about 8,000 troops and some warships face the Vichy government's forces which include the battleship *Richelieu* and other vessels. The three-day operation ends when the Allied force abandons the mission, on Churchill's orders, after the warships HMSS *Resolution* and *Barham* have been damaged.

26 September The Vichy government reacts to the Dakar incident by sending 54 bombers to raid Gibraltar. Officials there reporting the raid, over-estimate the number of aircraft involved, and claim that more than 300 bombs were dropped.

Hitler demonstrates his strategic naivete by under-estimating the value of the Mediterranean theatre to the war as a whole and rejects Raeder's plea to expend more resources there.

27 September A tripartite pact is signed by Germany, Italy and Japan. Its principal aim is to discourage the USA from pursuing a more active involvement in the war.

Tripartite Pact

30 September In a final daylight raid on England, the Luftwaffe lose 47 aircraft to the British twenty. The month has seen the Luftwaffe deliver more than 6,000 tons of explosive bombs and 8,500 tons of incendiaries on London. The German High Command decides to drain British morale and resolve by night bombing.

Luftwaffe switches to night bombing

OCTOBER 1940

1 October This month will see the fourth phase of the Battle of Britain with the Luftwaffe avoiding the losses of previous months and British ground defences proving ineffectual against the waves of night bombing raids. New anti-aircraft firepower will soon redress the balance.

The next few weeks will see bad weather in the Atlantic and rough seas will frustrate the charismatic, daring U-boat captains – such as Prien, Kretschmer and Schepke – after their late summer period of dominance.

4 October Hitler meets Mussolini to warn him against foolhardy solo military efforts. The Italians will need help in North Africa, though Il Duce rejects assistance at this point; the Führer would prefer them to fight to his direct orders rather than detract from his own strategic intentions by their own ineffectual actions.

5 October Instead of acting as a deterrent, the Axis' tripartite pact prompts the US government to activate some naval reserves.

6 October Hitler sends troops into Roumania to 'help re-organise the army'. His real object is to protect the oil fields

Hitler sends troops into Roumania

7 October In the heaviest raid on the German capital to date, thirty Wellington and twelve Whitley bombers drop fifty tons of high-explosive bombs on Berlin.

9 October Ever-increasing U-boat successes in the North Atlantic are forcing the British to strengthen the convoy protection, which removes some escort ships from anti-invasion work.

11 October In a radio broadcast Pétain suggests that the French people should revise their historic view of who is friend and foe among the European countries.

The port of Liverpool is bombed by the Luftwaffe.

Four Italian destroyers attack the British light cruiser HMS *Ajax*, but two are sunk and the others badly damaged.

12 October Hitler postpones Operation 'Sealion' until the spring of 1941. His priorities are now elsewhere and Göring has been unable to achieve the vital air superiority. The operation will never receive the go-ahead.

15 October Mussolini secretly plans to invade Greece despite the knowledge that it will infuriate Hitler. They expect it to be a short, sharp battle and believe it may repair their reputation in German eyes.

With the invasion of England postponed yet again, Göring turns to the night bombing campaign, with London, aircraft manufacturing plants and the Midlands industrial belt being top priorities.

18 October Anti-Semitism grows in France; Jews are removed from public office and high-ranking business posts.

20 October From East African bases, Italian aircraft attack oil fields in Bahrain and Saudi Arabia.

22 October Some 180 Italian aircraft gather in Belgium in preparation for their first sorties against England.

23 October Hitler meets General Franco in southern France. It is perplexing to many that Franco has failed to join the Reich cause and Hitler presses for a positive move from the Spanish leader. Vague assurances and uncertain proposals are all that Hitler leaves with, and the Spanish dictator, tired of conflict and short of resources after the Civil War, will remain on the sidelines of the great conflict. This will have undoubted effects on the progress of the war; the independence of Spain will enable Gibraltar to remain in operation and will close northern and southern Spanish ports to both sides during the war.

Admiral Scheer sorties

Undetected by British reconnaissance, the pocket battleship *Admiral Scheer* reaches the Atlantic via the Denmark Strait.

Italian aircraft attack Britain

24 October The Belgian-based Italian aircraft attack Harwich in a joint mission with Luftflotte 2.

25 October A British Air Ministry announcement demonstrates the diversity and numerical strength of the flying personnel available to it. Airmen from Poland, France, Belgium, Holland and Czechoslovakia are being deployed and still more are in training. The Eagle Squadron of American volunteers is also growing.

26 October The 42,000-ton luxury liner *Empress of Britain* is bombed by a Focke-Wülf Fw 200 off the Irish coast. Two days later an attack by *U32* will finally sink the vessel.

Italy invades Greece

28 October Italy invades Greece from Albania with 155,000 men. After becoming fully mobilised the Greeks can field 420,000 men and their forces are set back from the border region. For the first two days the invaders are hampered by bad weather which prevents any air support. An irate Hitler meets Mussolini at Florence but accepts that German forces can be made available if it means preventing the British from threatening the Roumanian oilfields.

29 October The British occupy the strategically important Mediterranean island of Crete and begin to mine the waters off Greece.

31 October The Italian submarine *Scire* arrives off Gibraltar with its 'cargo' of manned torpedoes. The mission, to attack the naval base, is a novel and daring one, but it meets with failure. None of the torpedoes is deployed successfully and in attempting to ditch one of the faulty machines it is left detectable to the British who promptly recover it for analysis. The design will become the master for British vessels of this type.

NOVEMBER 1940

1 November The Italians lose an aircraft to the Greek 1st Fighter Wing.

2 November In one of the more extraordinary aviation incidents of the war, Greek pilot Marinos Mitralexis, having run out of ammunition, rams his machine into a Savoia-Marchetti SM 79 bomber, lands his damaged fighter and promptly captures the crew who have parachuted to safety.

3 November The Greek II Corps forces a partial Italian retreat.

Hitler receives reports of Italian weaknesses in North Africa and is urged to send four panzer divisions to the theatre; he refuses, for the time being.

Italian retreat

4 November Unimpressed by the Italian forays, Hitler decides to invade Greece from Roumania, Bulgaria and Hungary. The Italians' attempt to replicate the German pace of ground advance has been found wanting; Hitler's belief in the Italians' fighting ability, never strong, is fast evaporating. The need to reinforce his numbers in Greece is obvious to Mussolini, but the logistical back-up to the invasion seems to have been the last thing in the minds of the Italian planners.

In North Africa, General Wavell has had his forces increased by the arrival of 7th Division plus Australian, New Zealand, Indian and Polish contingents. He believes that he can oust the Italians from Sidi Barrani in three days.

5 November President Roosevelt is elected for a third term.

Admiral Scheer sights Convoy HX-84 in the north Atlantic. She is engaged by *Jervis Bay*, an armed merchantman, in an unequal fight and then pursues the dispersed convoy and sinks five ships. One of the worst damaged ships, the tanker *San Demetrio*, is set on fire and abandoned only to be sighted and re-boarded by the remnant of her crew next day. Without navigational equipment, they manage to get the ship, and her oil, to the UK.

Admiral Scheer sinks 6 ships

9 November The British war effort is put in context when an inventory of available scrap iron from old bridges and railways is drawn up showing the availability of half a million tons, enough to build 7,000 tanks or 300 destroyers.

11 November The British Fleet Air Arm enjoys its finest hour with its raid on Italian shipping at Taranto. The Italian vessels were about to leave for an attack on Crete but are still in harbour when twenty Fairey Swordfish, flying in two waves and delivering their torpedoes from zero feet, achieve six direct hits to sink three battleships at anchor. The Italian High

British Fleet Air Arm attack Taranto

Command admits to only one ship being hit but the truth is that two, *Littorio* and *Caio Duilio*, are retrieved and repaired over the next six months but *Conte di Cavour* never sails again. Churchill announces to parliament that the raid has altered the balance of naval power in the Mediterranean; it has certainly disabled half the Italian battleship fleet and demonstrates the value of the carrier as a floating air base.

Greeks counter-attack

14 November The Greeks mount a significant counter-attack against the Italians, their I, II and III Corps driving the greater part of Italian Ninth Army back into Albania.

Coventry bombed

The Midlands city of Coventry is devastated by a German bombing raid. It is possible that British code-breakers could have given early warning of the raid, but, in any event, the fear of alerting the enemy to their ability to read the German code would render public evacuation regrettably unwise. The British night-fighters are unable to prevent the bombers getting through and ground defences claim only two enemy aircraft. In a mission lasting more than ten hours, nearly 1,400 bombs are dropped on the aircraft manufacturing plants around the city and the cathedral is severely damaged. The human cost of keeping the Ultra decoding secret is more than 500 dead and 865 injured.

16 November In reprisal raids for the Coventry bombing, the RAF attack Berlin, Hamburg, Bremen and other German and German-occupied cities, and a Beaufighter night interceptor shoots down a Junkers Ju 88 to record the first ever instance of an aircraft using its own airborne radar for such a task.

17 November Air Marshal Dowding is replaced by Sholto Douglas at RAF Fighter Command. The former is given a minor position controlling aircraft supply, paltry reward for one whose prudence and good sense during the year has proved a crucial factor in Great Britain's performance against the Luftwaffe.

British troops aid Greeks

21 November Further Greek Army drives see more Italian forces driven well back into Albania. In recent days the Greeks have been supported by the arrival of 7,000 British troops.

22 November The Greeks' III Corps to the east and I Corps to the west continue to drive the Italians back and break their border defences.

Roumania joins Axis

23 November Roumania officially joins the Axis when President Antonescu submits to German pressure during a visit to Berlin.

26 November German persecution of Jews becomes overt when a ghetto is created in Warsaw.

Fleet Air Arm aircraft from the carriers HMSS *Eagle* and *Illustrious* attack targets at Tripoli and Rhodes respectively.

27 November The numerical superiority of an Italian naval force off Sardinia fails to gain an advantage over a convoy of British vessels heading for Malta; both sides have one ship damaged but the convoy gets through.

DECEMBER 1940

5 December The Greek II Corps breaks into Albania, after heavy fighting with the Italian invaders who have retreated to the border area.

Greeks break into Albania

6 December In the first significant British land advance of the war, Wavell moves 31,000 men forward some 36 miles in Cyrenaica. Marshal Badoglio resigns as Italian commander-in-chief because of the continuing poor performance in Greece. He will play a part in Mussolini's downfall in 1943.

British desert advance against Italians

9 December General O'Connor, under Wavell's overall direction, moves the British units with their 225 tanks and 120 guns against General Gariboldi's Italian Tenth Army at Sidi Barrani and other strong-points. He is backed-up by artillery bombardment from the Royal Navy off the coast and by RAF attacks on enemy airfields. Sidi Barrani falls after two days, on 11 December, and British 7th Armoured Division promptly cuts off the Italian retreat route from Sofafi. The Italian forces are annihilated; almost 40,000 men are taken prisoner and the Italian sortie into the Libyan/Eygptian border area is foiled.

Italian efforts to halt their own retreat into Albania and go back on to the offensive come to nought despite reinforcements.

11 November Cunningham assists Wavell's moves against the Italian Army by bombarding Sollum.

13 December Hitler directs Field Marshal List's Twelfth Army to attack Greece from Bulgaria. In North Africa, a small British unit hurries into Libya to cut the western access to Italian forces at Bardia.

15 December British troops take Halfaya Pass on the Libyan border and now have a route through to central Cyrenaica. Italian Tenth Army has withdrawn to Bardia and reinforcements have been brought to Tobruk and the defensive line inland from Dernia.

17 December The British capture Sollum and other border positions south of Bardia to where the retreating Italians have fled.

18 December Hitler issues an edict stating that the Soviet Union is the ultimate target for the Third Reich; Operation 'Barbarossa' will take place. He has typically modified the campaign plans presented to him by the army; the advance on Moscow is given lesser importance. The Blitzkrieg tactics, proven in Poland and France, will, it is predicted, wrap-up the campaign in three to four months. The starting date is set for 15 May 1941. Armament production will now have to concentrate on the needs of the army; Raeder, not surprisingly, is appalled and repeats that the need to secure the Mediterranean should be given equal prominence.

The battleships HMSS *Warspite* and *Valiant* bombard the Albanian port of Valona where Italian supplies are being landed.

19 December The Italians, facing reversal after reversal in all their military actions, appeal to Hitler to send an armoured division to North Africa without delay.

Italians defeated

23 December Anthony Eden becomes British Foreign Secretary; Lord Halifax becomes Ambassador to the USA.

24 December Becoming outnumbered by the Italians in their drive into Albania, the Greeks are beginning to slow down and more Italian counter-attacks are encountered.

In a rare rebuff, the heavy cruiser *Admiral Hipper* is driven away from a 20-ship convoy en route to Sierra Leone by its especially strong escort vessels.

Italians plea for German help

28 December Now the Italians, in a direct plea from Mussolini to Hitler, ask for German help in Albania. The Führer declines to become involved, having committed himself to drives into Greece via other routes. Also, he is becoming restless with Italian failures and has no desire to be dragged down by their sub-standard performance.

29 December President Roosevelt gives a radio address stating that America should be 'the arsenal of democracy', and, by doing so, effectively announces a full-hearted support for the Allied cause.

Large scale incendiary raid on London

For a second night London suffers awesome bombing raids. The proportion of incendiaries used ensure that large-scale fires are started across the central City area.

30 December The Greeks now commit only their II Corps to the advance in Albania. After heavy fighting and losses on both sides, the units take Kelcyre and Italian resistance is further undermined. At this time the Greek and Italian forces confronting each other in Albania are of similar numbers, but the Greeks are beginning to have logistical problems.

Feverish activity by the German armaments industry has seen more than 1,000 tanks and even more heavy artillery weapons built in just a few months. The British, with barely 200 tanks remaining after the Dunkirk débâcle, are having to concentrate on quantity rather than quality, with the result that little technical advance is looked for as the quest for numbers of vehicles is pursued. Away from the European theatre, US production is in overdrive and turning out large numbers of vehicles in quick time.

The fearful bombing suffered by the United Kingdom during the last three months has not dealt the morale-crushing blow that Hitler has expected; furthermore, his bombers will have to cause much more indus-trial damage in order to make the raids a strategic success. On RAF Bomber Command raids against Germany there have been few attempts at interception by the Luftwaffe and the anti-aircraft fire has been sporadic and ineffective.

1941

JANUARY 1941

1 January The Luftwaffe build-up in the Mediterranean has reached the point where its 270 bombers and 40 fighters pose a very real threat to the under-strength RAF units there.

British naval officers are urged to search all captured vessels for encoding machines and related paperwork. The British are improving their deciphering standards by the day, but are encountering problems with the naval Enigma-M codes, which they are destined to spend another year cracking.

2 January The USA announces plans to build 200 utilitarian freighters – the 'Liberty ships'.

3 January Australian forces arrive in North Africa to replace the Indian Division which has been transferred to the Sudan. The new forces attack Bardia, the Italian stronghold, and take almost 40,000 prisoners on this first day.

4 January The Greeks begin to falter against the Italians who now outnumber them.

5 January Bardia falls and the remaining Italian forces withdraw to Tobruk. In the raid on the fortress the Allied casualties have been kept below 500; the Italians have had 40,000 men and much equipment captured.

6 January In their pursuit of the Italians, Wavell's men reach Tobruk and begin its encirclement. At this point there are 25,000 Italians with 220 guns and about 70 tanks in the town.

7 January Unknown to Göring, who is absent on one of his increasingly frequent hunting trips, Hitler places the work of I Wing of 40 Bomber Group, operating with Fw 200 Kondors out of Bordeaux, under the control of Dönitz so as to weave its work into naval reconnaissance needs. Göring is annoyed but cannot persuade Dönitz to defer implementing the edict.

8 January More than 60 per cent of the new US budget will be spent on defence.

A bombing raid by Wellingtons on Naples harbour records hits on the Italian battleships *Giulio Cesare* and *Vittorio Veneto*.

9 January Hitler agrees to send a panzer force to Libya to support the struggling Italian forces.

10 January The first discussions in the US Congress on the vital Lend-Lease Bill brings considerable opposition. Those ranged against the proposals include Charles Lindbergh and Joseph Kennedy (both dedicated pro-Nazis). Debate and agreements between Russia and Germany continue in spite of the latter's plan for invasion. The countries agree on a shared programme of raw materials and machinery.

The carrier HMS *Illustrious* returns damaged to Malta after an attack on a convoy by 60 Stuka and Heinkel He 111 bombers. She has been hit six times by huge bombs. The destroyer HMS *Gallant* is damaged by mines off Malta and later beached in Grand Harbour. The arrival of new German air power in the region prompts the British to send eighteen more fighters to the Mediterranean.

11 January Realising that Germany has to do more in the Mediterranean theatre, Hitler orders the creation of the Afrika Korps.

More Stuka success in the Mediterranean sees the cruisers HMSS *Southampton* and *Gloucester* attacked en route from Malta to Gibraltar. The former is lost during an attempt to tow her to port.

12 January British aircraft from Malta attack German and Italian airfields in Sicily. The aircraft there pose a serious threat to HMS *Illustrious* which is undergoing repairs at Malta.

14 January The German commerce raider *Pinguin*, in a strange act of piracy, attacks an Arctic whaling fleet and takes fourteen ships as prizes, including one with 22,000 tons of whale oil aboard.

16 January The inevitable attack on *Illustrious* is mounted by 80 Stuka dive-bombers. Ten are shot down, but the carrier, the cruiser HMS *Perth*, and some harbour installations are hit.

18 January There are further raids on Malta harbour and airfields on the island.

19 January In a meeting with Mussolini at Berghof, Hitler confirms his readiness to attack Greece if the British engage there. The Italian leader, unwilling to acknowledge the poor performance of his forces in almost every campaign in which they have taken part hitherto, rejects the offer of German help in Albania but acknowledges that German involvement in Africa is essential. The Sudan-based British forces move against the Italians in Eritrea and quickly take Kassala.

Another raid is launched against HMS *Illustrious*.

21 January The attack on the fortress of Tobruk is begun by Australian 6th Division in O'Connor's British XIII Corps. A sector of the Italian position is bombarded and broken. The attackers are supported by naval bombardment from British vessels offshore.

22 January The remainder of the Italian garrison at Tobruk surrenders. More than 27,000 prisoners are taken and much equipment. Italian forces are also falling back in Eritrea.

23 January The patched-up *Illustrious* leaves Malta at best speed for Alexandria.

24 January The Italians retreat after a short battle with British 4th Armoured Brigade near Mechili and their forces are now split between here and Derna on the coast. Australian troops head for the latter; the Italians are in desperate need of more men, equipment and strong command.

US Secretary of the Navy Frank Knox advises Secretary of War Henry Stimpson of the possibility of an attack on Pearl Harbor. The Commander of the Japanese Fleet, Admiral Yamamoto, has indeed already discussed

Hitler and Mussolini confer

British invade Eritrea

Allies capture Tobruk

such an attack with colleagues and it is considered risky but feasible.

26 January The Italians are allowed to withdraw from Mechili.

27 January Roosevelt gets further warning of a possible attack on Pearl Harbor, via the US Ambassador in Tokyo. The CinC Pacific Fleet, Admiral Kimmel, is assured by the Navy's intelligence services that there can be no truth in the suggestion.

29 January The 'Europe First' option for Allied war strategy is raised at a Washington meeting between British and American representatives. It is agreed that, in the event of war in Europe and the Pacific, Allied policy should be to defeat Germany first. The co-operation shown at this meeting is taken further by a US visit to the UK in March when naval bases and airfield sites are evaluated.

Italians retreat in North Africa

Further Italian regression is seen as Derna is vacated and they retreat along a perilous coastal route. In East Africa, Allied forces cross from Kenya into Somaliland in preparation for the drive against the Italian sector there.

31 January The minesweeper HMS *Huntley* is sunk by German aircraft in the eastern Mediterranean.

FEBRUARY 1941

Italians retreat in Eritrea

1 February British forces take Agordat in Eritrea and their Italian opponents withdraw to the hills near Keren. General von Funck reports to Hitler after a visit to Libya and spreads alarm about the parlous state of the Italian forces there.

The heavy cruiser *Admiral Hipper* leaves Brest for a campaign against shipping in the Gibraltar convoy lanes. She will attack Convoy SLS-64 on 12 February. The US Navy creates the Atlantic Fleet under command of Admiral King with the remit to build up convoy protection and U-boat hunting capabilities.

2 February Wavell and O'Connor decide to dispatch 7th Armoured Division on an inland route to Beda Fomm in order to cut off the rapid withdrawal of the Italians along the coastal route.

The carrier HMS *Illustrious* is to be replaced by HMS *Formidable* in the Mediterranean and aircraft from the latter are sent to raid the harbour at Mogadishu even before the vessel takes up her new duties. *Illustrious* will sail to the USA for full repairs.

Scharnhorst and Gneisenau sortie into Atlantic

3 February Operational plans for the invasion of Russia are presented to Hitler by Army chiefs.

Admiral Lütjens leads the battlecruisers *Scharnhorst* and *Gneisenau* into the North Atlantic to engage convoy traffic.

4 February The British dash across Cyrenaica reaches and takes Msus. Full support is lacking, but speed is important if the Italian retreat is to be arrested. In East Africa British forces attack the Italian defensive lines at

Keren. The Italian forces number 30,000 in this area and are able to repulse many British attacks.

5 February The first British units reach the North African coast at Beda Fomm in time to engage the retreating Italians and take 5,000 prisoners; the British have no heavy tanks, only light armour. The Italians are aware of the Australians following along the coast road behind them in a pincer movement.

6 February The Australian troops occupy Benghazi and push on behind the Italians making for Beda Fomm where the British blocking force is struggling to prevent increasing numbers of Italian troops from getting through.

7 February The Australians continue to chase the Italians towards Beda Fomm where the hopelessness of their position is dawning on the Italian commanders. Surrenders are not long in coming, with 25,000 additional prisoners being taken plus guns and tanks. Although the Allied force now lacks serviceable vehicles and has suffered 555 dead and 1,400 wounded, its modest numbers have decimated an Italian group five times larger.

Italians in full-scale retreat

Following von Funck's report a week before, plans are put in hand for a German operation in North Africa.

8 February The first German troops and equipment bound for North Africa embark at Naples. They will reach Tripoli without encountering resistance.

Lütjens' battlecruiser group harries Convoy HX-106 but does not attack because of the presence of the battleship HMS *Ramillies*.

9 February Although there is little Italian resistance to prevent him advancing farther, Wavell is now ordered to supply troops to the Greek theatre, East Africa and Palestine. Not for the first time, this capable commander is being asked to do too much with too little; the North African campaign stops short of the total success it might have been.

In an attack on Genoa, Livorno and La Spezia harbours, the battlecruiser HMS *Renown*, the battleship HMS *Malaya*, and aircraft from HMS *Ark Royal* encounter no opposition and sink five ships and damage eighteen.

Genoa, Livorno and La Spezia raided

A unique raid of combined air, surface vessels and U-boats sees *U37* sight Convoy HG-53 and call the heavy cruiser *Admiral Hipper* and bomber aircraft to the scene. Five ships are lost to raids from Fw 200 Kondors.

10 February The formalisation of Great Britain's change of policy over North Africa is confirmed when Churchill advises Wavell that assistance to the Greeks is to be given high priority. The British are now having to cultivate the support of smaller countries in the sensitive war zones and are being urged by the Americans to consider the Balkans as a preferred region to take on the Germans.

The first ever paratroop action mounted by British forces features a surprise assault on the aqueduct serving Taranto. The entire unit is captured while escaping to their submarine. Although the channel is put out of action, it is fully operational again within days.

First German units
arrive in North Africa

11 February Troops of the German 5th Light Division land at Tripoli and await their commander.

Admiral Hipper returns to Convoy HG-53 and sinks another ship.

12 February General Rommel arrives in North Africa. Although nominally under the command of General Gariboldi, his strength of character and superior battlefield ability will soon be brought to bear. The man who will become known as the 'Desert Fox' has already enjoyed success in Europe; a good reputation is about to become one of the most feared of the war.

In the Soviet Union, General Zhukov is appointed Chief of the General Staff.

Another convoy, SLS-64, falls victim to *Admiral Hipper*; unescorted, it loses nine of its vessels sunk or severely damaged.

13 February The carrier HMS *Formidable*, en route to her new station in the Mediterranean, attacks Massawa to prevent the dropping of further mines in the Suez Canal by German aircraft.

British advance in
Somaliland accelerates

14 February British advances in Somaliland accelerate; 22nd East African Brigade takes Kismayu with the support of vessels from Force T, including the carrier HMS *Hermes*.

17 February Turkey is effectively lost to the Allied cause when pressured by Germany to sign a friendship treaty with Bulgaria; the agreement allows German troops to operate inside the country. Yugoslavia is still holding out against joining the tripartite pact; they favour the assistance of the Allied nations.

19 February Orde Wingate's Gideon Force is joined by Emperor Haile Selassie in sniping attacks against the numerically stronger Italian forces in East Africa.

Anthony Eden meets Wavell and General Alan Cunningham in Cairo to discuss British involvement in Greece.

20 February A convoy carrying supplies and an anti-aircraft unit docks in Tripoli to support the German forces there. Next day German vehicles are seen operating in North Africa for the first time.

22 February *Scharnhorst* and *Gneisenau* get among a dispersed convoy and sink five ships. The German vessels refuel at sea and move south-east towards the coast of West Africa.

23 February The Greeks accept what they are assured is a minimum force of 100,000 men and equipment for the expected German attack. Decisions on the campaign strategy are not so quickly arrived at; this dilutes the value of the British move.

In East Africa, Cunningham's forces enjoy some success and press on towards Mogadishu.

24 February The British destroyer HMS *Dainty* is sunk in Tobruk harbour by German dive-bombers.

Allies take Mogadishu

25 February Mogadishu is taken and valuable supplies captured. The British have averaged 75 miles in each of the previous three days.

Prien's *U47* chases and finally closes on Convoy OB-290, sinking three of the vessels.

Off Tunisia, a single torpedo from the submarine HMS *Upright* sinks the Italian cruiser *Armando Diaz*.

26 February Anthony Eden fails in an attempt to persuade Turkey to the Allied side.

Once again *U47* is active. She calls in Fw 200 attacks on OB-290 and eleven ships are sunk in the most successful air raid on Allied shipping to date.

MARCH 1941

1 March Bulgaria becomes a full member of the Tripartite Pact. The Free French, aided by the Long Range Desert Group, enjoy some success in south-east Libya.

Bulgaria joins Tripartite Pact

Increasingly active in a supporting role, the USA forms a force of three destroyer units to assist the Atlantic Fleet.

2 March German forces move into Bulgaria.

4 March Hitler now exerts pressure on Yugoslavia to join the tripartite pact. Prince Paul tends to prefer the Allied cause but is not convinced of support from that source.

As the first Allied troops land in Greece, the tactics they will employ there are now seen to be ill-defined; Greek troops are found to be pursuing different aims from those that the new Commander of the British forces there, General Wilson, is planning.

Allied troops land in Greece

The controversial Lofoten Raid by British Commando units sees 215 German prisoners taken when the naval teams land on the Lofoten Islands off the north-west coast of Norway. The success of the operation, which involves more than 500 men from Nos 3 and 4 Commandos, causes the Germans to react violently against the local population; they may have been incited by the message from a British Commando leader who sends a note from a captured telegraph office, 'Dear Adolf Hitler. You said German troops would meet the English wherever they landed. Where are your troops?' Although the Germans were able to destroy much of their Enigma coding equipment, some valuable wheels from the machine are recovered.

British Commandos raid Lofoten Islands

6 March Churchill forms the Battle of the Atlantic Committee which will meet weekly to ensure the availability of ships, men and repair facilities matches the requirements of that theatre.

U70 and *U99* join Prien's *U47* in pursuit of Convoy OB-293. As they engage they are disturbed by the corvettes HMSS *Camelia* and *Arbutus*. *U70* is forced to dive and is destroyed by a depth-charge.

7 March Closing the large OB-293 convoy again, Prien's *U47* is depth-charged and sunk by the destroyer HMS *Wolverine*.

61

8 March As was the case a month before, the battlecruisers *Scharnhorst* and *Gneisenau* locate a convoy, this time SL-67, but do not attack because of the presence of the battleship HMS *Malaya*.

9 March Mussolini appears in person to observe the Italian offensive against Greece from Albania. His presence does not improve the tactics used which are cumbersome and antiquated.

British advance into Abyssinia

10 March The British have advanced with great pace since taking Mogadishu and are into Abyssinia before they encounter any Italian resistance.

Lend-Lease Bill passed

11 March The all-important Lend-Lease Bill is passed in Washington. Although it will prove to have massive implications for Great Britain's long-term economic indebtedness to the USA, it does not hugely alter the balance of military hardware at the moment of its signature – the immediate benefits are more of the fuel and food variety – but its significance at this juncture is the demonstration of whole-hearted support by the US administration for the Allied war effort.

13 March Hitler issues the Directive for the invasion of Russia.

15 March President Roosevelt assures Great Britain of 'aid until victory' in a Washington speech, separating himself from the many would-be isolationists in American politics.

Once again Lütjens' battlecruiser group causes mayhem among a dispersed merchant convoy; sixteen ships are sunk. A British naval force from Aden arrives at, and takes, the port of Berbera before the forces it has brought to the East African theatre move inland. The Italians try to mount counter-attacks against British and Indian divisions farther inland.

16 March After Prien's loss earlier in the month, the U-boat fleet is dealt a further blow by the sinking during convoy battles of *U99* and *U100*, commanded by Kretschmer and Schepke respectively; the former is rescued and taken prisoner. The loss of his vessel marks the first successful use of radar by surface units against U-boats. The success of the U-boats will never again rise to the level achieved by these commanders and their colleagues.

The German luxury liner *Bremen* is set on fire and destroyed while camouflaged in Bremerhaven awaiting use as a troopship. Initially believed to be the work of raiders, the arsonist is later said to have been a young boy avenging a punishment. Whoever the culprit is, the liner's fate is the breaker's yard.

19 March German High Command repeats its requirement to Rommel that he limit his activity to supporting the Italian forces in North Africa. He is to wait for 15th Panzer Division to arrive, though his superiors do not plan to 'release' the Desert Fox even then.

The German approaches to Yugoslavia reach an impasse and the country is given an ultimatum to join the Axis powers within the following five days or face the consequences.

Another first is recorded for US co-operation when the battleship HMS *Malaya* is sailed to New York for repairs after being damaged in a convoy attack by *U106*.

20 March The Royal Council in Belgrade is showing signs of being prepared to sign up with Hitler; four ministers resign as a result.

Vessels from Force H leave Gibraltar to intercept *Scharnhorst* and *Gneisenau*. The German ships benefit from intelligence warnings and evade the British vessels.

22 March Following days of successful advance and little resistance, the Allied forces in East Africa take Babile Pass.

Avoiding all British attempts to locate and engage them, *Scharnhorst* and *Gneisenau* regain French waters having sunk 22 ships of 115,600 total tonnage. This level of performance obscures the fact that the damage could have been so much greater had the U-boat fleet been enlarged and better maintained.

Scharnhorst and Gneisenau have sunk 22 ships

24 March Rommel begins to exert some influence in North Africa and the Allied forces there, depleted by numbers having been sent to Greece and having only previously faced ineffective Italian units, are unable to prevent German forces taking El Agheila. General Neame, commanding the Allied troops, has only older tanks whereas Rommel has brought new equipment. The Desert Fox will choose to use his advantage and act independently, contravening the instructions he has had from German High Command and ignoring the line of command through his Italian superior.

Rommel begins advance in North Africa

25 March The Slavs sign the tripartite pact which brings the people on to the streets to show their disapproval. The Germans have agreed to accept Yugoslav sovereignty and not use the country as a military route for their troops, though such promises count for little.

Off the coast of Crete, the Italian destroyers *Crispi* and *Sella* begin a mission which will see them launch six explosive-laden assault boats at British targets in Suda Bay. The vessels, set on course by their one-man crews before they dive overboard, break through the protective barriers and reach their targets. The heavy cruiser HMS *York* is hit and sunk in shallow water together with a tanker.

The Ultra code-breakers at Bletchley Park have deciphered details of a planned Italian naval operation in the northern Mediterranean.

26 March This day sees the start of the Battle of Cape Matapan when the Italian fleet is drawn out into the Aegean to disrupt British movements to supply Greece. The mission has been stimulated by Luftwaffe pilots filing faulty reports which suggest that they have hit and weakened the Mediterranean Fleet. The commander, Admiral Iachino, has a battleship, six heavy cruisers, two light cruisers and thirteen destroyers.

27 March A coup in Yugoslavia sees 17-year-old King Peter II replacing Prince Paul and the Regency Council. General Simovic, who has led the uprising, becomes head of the new government. Hitler's response is to order the invasion of the country to take place alongside the moves into Greece, delaying the Russia invasion if necessary.

The Italians are suffering increased casualties from the Allied advance in East Africa. The British forces are closing on Addis Ababa.

In Washington a meeting of US and British general staffs continues to back the 'Europe First' policy whereby if the US enters the war the defeat of Germany would remain the top priority.

Iachino's force moves to engage a British supply fleet of four light cruisers and four destroyers sailing from Piraeus, but Admiral Cunningham also has three battleships, a carrier and nine destroyers en route from Alexandria.

28 March In a masterpiece of understatement, the Reich's press chief advises in his daily notice: 'Yugoslavia is not kindly disposed toward Germany. When you report recent events there ... make this somewhat clearer but without taking on the form of a threat.'

Battle of Cape Matapan

The British fleet approaching from Piraeus engages some of Iachino's cruisers at long-range and the Italians retreat, unsure of the British strength. Swordfish from HMS *Formidable* score hits on the battleship *Vittorio Veneto* and the cruiser *Pola*; the former is slowed, the latter stopped before eventually sinking. As the Italians return to assist their stricken vessels they are tracked by the British on radar and three cruisers and two destroyers are sunk by close-range fire without response. The entire operation brings only one British aircraft loss and the Italians, ruing the German assurances of secure seas which lured them from port in the first place, lose five precious warships and close to 3,000 men.

30 March The widely dispersed and minimal Allied forces in North Africa find Rommel advancing from El Agheila towards Mersa Brega.

This night sees an extensive RAF bombing raid on *Scharnhorst* and *Gneisenau* in the harbour at Brest; it is unsuccessful but the number of aircraft involved – 109 – indicates the desire of the British to cripple these vessels.

Rommel briefly halted

31 March Rommel engages in fierce battles with British 2nd Armoured Division and is briefly halted. The 15th Panzer Division lands in Tripoli to support Axis movements in the region.

APRIL 1941

1 April The British reluctantly withdraw from their substantial position at Mersa Brega. They move back into the inhospitable wastes of the Cyrenaica plateau.

General Platt leads the British forces into Asmara, the capital of Eritrea. There is a coup in Iraq led by Nationalists who are opposed to the British presence in the country. Troops will be sent from India to protect Great Britain's oil interests.

2 April Rommel leads his rampaging forces by diverse routes across Cyrenaica, watching their progress from the air. He faces weak British forces which have been surprised by the suddenness and pace of the Axis advance. Wavell seeks to improve the situation by recalling the convalescing O'Connor.

Rommel's advance continues

4 April Rommel is now advancing along three set lines with a mixed force of Italians and Germans taking Benghazi on the coast, another struggling through difficult terrain inland and a third, farther south, racing towards Mechili.

5 April Yugoslavia is invaded by the Germans.

6 April The German news bureau reports: 'At 5.30 this morning the German government announced that it felt compelled to order the Wehrmacht to march into Greece and Yugoslavia last night, with the aim of driving Great Britain out of Europe once and for all.'

Germany invades Yugoslavia and Greece

The German move on Yugoslavia gathers momentum with bombing raids on Belgrade and the advance of List's Twelfth Army from Bulgaria; Greece is also bombed. The widely dispersed units of the Yugoslav Army are unable to mount much resistance and, with huge numbers of aircraft committed to the campaign, the Germans hold great advantages over General Wilson's small force in Greece where a few RAF aircraft and British and Anzac troops are trying to support the battle-weary and ill-equipped Greeks. The latter, in their frontier positions on the Metaxas Line, are the first to feel the German attacks.

For their first air raids in Yugoslavia the Luftwaffe flies from bases in Austria and Roumania and its bombing of Belgrade kills 17,000 civilians. The Italian Air Force is virtually excluded from this theatre despite the numbers it could have brought to the campaign; it will shoot down four aircraft but lose five.

In North Africa, O'Connor returns but does not replace General Neame; he intends to act only as an adviser, which is what Wavell has spoken of while expecting the former to take control. In the event, both are captured by a German patrol. The Allies will especially rue the loss of O'Connor, a highly regarded strategist.

Generals O'Connor and Neame captured by Germans

Allied progress in East Africa sees Addis Ababa taken and the Italian forces retreating still farther.

Allies capture Addis Ababa

A German air raid on the port of Piraeus causes the British ammunition ship *Clan Frazer* to blow up and other ships to be sunk; damage to the port is considerable and Admiral Cunningham reports it as a serious blow to the operation of his Mediterranean Fleet. Off the French Atlantic coast *Gneisenau* is hit by a British torpedo-bomber. Returning to Brest, she will be hit again during a British air raid on 10 April. *Gneisenau* and *Scharnhorst* will be under repair until May.

7 April While the Allies are defending Mechili south of the Cyrenaica hills, the coastal town of Derna is overrun by Axis forces. The defence of

Mechili and an attempt at a breakout sees 2,000 British troops captured; the loss of Derna includes extensive food and fuel supplies which the Germans promptly use to advance further.

The German advance across Yugoslavia continues without great delay and the Greeks seek to reinforce their border defences in Macedonia rather than concentrate the Aliakmon Line north-east of the Vermion Mountains.

In a change of tactics, German bombers fly missions from the French Channel ports against sites in Scotland. The Luftwaffe is being increasingly taken in by dummy installations and the jamming of their radio navigational aids. Dozens of mock airfields litter the countryside complete with dummy aircraft and simulated runway lighting. They are also fooled by the scattering of flares which the German bomber pilots think are signals from their own pathfinder aircraft.

8 April The German First Panzer Group follows the earlier units into Yugoslavia via Bulgaria.

Allies capture Massawa

In East Africa Massawa falls to the Allied forces and a large number of Axis merchant vessels is confiscated in the port. The decision is taken to move 4th Indian Division from Eritrea to Egypt to supplement the forces there. In North Africa, Mechili finally falls and now Tobruk is Rommel's main target.

Germans capture Thessaloniki

9 April In Greece the Metaxas Line collapses and Thessaloniki falls to the Germans. Elsewhere, the invading forces are already at the Monastir Gap, leaving the British and Greek commanders no option but to reform at the Aliakmon Line.

The German Second Army is now in Yugoslavia. The country has been invaded by German, Italian and Hungarian forces.

10 April Zagreb falls and some Croats defect from the Yugoslav Army to join the Germans.

Rommel commits a small force to an early, testing raid on Tobruk.

The RAF again attacks the two German battlecruisers in Brest harbour. This time *Gneisenau* is hit above the waterline.

11 April The rape of Yugoslavia continues with Italian forces moving down the coast and inland towards Ljubljana, German units crossing the Roumanian border and heading for Belgrade and the Hungarians aiming also for the capital via Novi Sad.

Tobruk cut off

In North Africa, Tobruk is now totally cut off; British artillery and Australian infantry combine to hold off German attacks.

12 April Belgrade, in the knowledge that other German forces are closing in from the north, surrenders to von Kleist .

In North Africa, Fort Capuzzo and Sollum fall to the Germans.

13 April The Allied forces in Greece have retreated from the Aliakmon Line to the area around Mount Olympus but now have to move again, to a shorter line near Thermopylae.

Stalin greatly improves his chances of defending Russia from German invasion by signing a neutrality agreement with the Japanese which will release vital forces from Siberia.

14 April Before they have fully departed their Mount Olympus positions, Allied forces are attacked by the fast advancing German units. Wavell, in a position which is deteriorating by the hour, chooses to cancel the sailing of Australian and Polish reinforcements from Egypt, and by so doing effectively sacrifices Greece to the invaders. This is not so unwelcome to the Greek government as one might have thought because it fears that its territory would be ravaged by a drawn-out battle. The Allied withdrawal continues.

Allies withdraw in Greece

16 April The election of Ante Pavelic as head of a Croat republic heralds the opening of an awesome campaign of murder and mayhem between the Roman Catholic Croats and Orthodox Serbs, nearly half a million of the latter facing death rather than conversion to Catholicism.

A German and Italian convoy bringing fresh forces and supplies to the Afrika Korps is attacked and sunk by four British destroyers. More than a third of the German troops are rescued.

17 April The Chief of the Air Staff receives a critical memo from Churchill complaining that the failure of Bomber Command to damage German naval activities out of Brest is a major problem.

The Italian force which has taken the Dalmatian coastal route through Yugoslavia enters Dubrovnik.

19 April The first British contingent arrives in Iraq following the coup there. They land at Basra.

British troops enter Iraq

Wavell meets General Wilson and the Australian commander General Blamey in Athens. Although they are prepared to fight on, both they and the Greek government accept that evacuation is the preferred option.

In East Africa the Italians fall back from their positions near Dessie after pressure from 1st South African Brigade

Men from No 7 Commando land near Bardia to disrupt the supply line to the Afrika Korps.

20 April Allied forces still in action in Greece continue their withdrawal south of Thermopylae.

21 April The Greek Army is surrendered to List and nearly quarter of a million men become prisoners of war.

Greek Army surrenders

Under direct instruction from Churchill, three battleships from the Mediterranean Fleet shell Tripoli. An earlier Churchill proposal to block the harbour there by sinking the battleship *Barham* at its entrance had been rejected.

24 April Having held off the German advance, the evacuation of the Greek royal family and Allied troops to Crete can begin.

Allies evacuate to Crete

25 April Hitler orders an airborne assault on Crete.

Reuters News Agency in London reports that the 'new battleship *Prince of Wales* is so constructed that it cannot be sunk ... [it] is the strongest battleship in the world.'

26 April The Germans attempt to interfere with the evacuation of Greece by moving into the Peloponnese. They occupy Corinth and will shortly move on to Athens. The British Mediterranean Fleet provides six cruisers, 20 destroyers and 30 other ships from the southern beaches to bring the troops off the Greek mainland

27 April A transport ship and two destroyers from the evacuation force are bombed off Nauplia; there is much loss of life.

General Paulus arrives in North Africa to effect some German High Command control on Rommel whose early success in the theatre has not masked the fact that he has disregarded most of the instructions issued from Berlin. At his insistence, moves against Tobruk are halted and, instead, precedence is placed on a small reconnaissance force entering Egypt and setting up positions in the strategically important Halfaya Pass

28 April More than 50,000 troops and civilians have been evacuated from Greece. Axis forces have blitzed through Greece and Yugoslavia in less than a month. The debate as to whether the exercise has increased German confidence ahead of the move on Russia, or that the brief delay it has caused to the Eastern Front being opened has outweighed this advantage, will go on for a long time.

Germans attack Tobruk

30 April Now General Paulus allows a further attack on Tobruk and a heavy bombardment from artillery and Stuka dive-bombers is mounted. Subsequent raids are mostly repulsed.

MAY 1941

British forces attacked by Iraqis

1 May The British force in Iraq comes under attack and it is clear that British operations there will be contested.

2 May The German 15th Panzer Division is at Tobruk and Rommel can contemplate a full raid. His early efforts are still being resisted.

At Habbaniyah the airfield being used by the British is attacked by Iraqi forces, but the ageing training aircraft there are rapidly deployed and repel the raid.

Siege of Tobruk begun

4 May Impasse at Tobruk; the siege has begun. Rommel, discouraged by the lack of movement his latest attacks have produced, chooses to hold his strong encircling position. In a situation reminiscent of the World War One battlefields, trenches are dug and little action takes place other than some night sniping.

5 May Emperor Haile Selassie returns to Addis Ababa amid scenes of great jubilation.

The Allied troops at Tobruk are supplied by the first of regular night visits by a destroyer.

6 May The British hold their positions in Iraq with greater ease and are reinforced by the arrival of 21st Indian Division at Basra.

Operation 'Tiger', the Allies' daring attempt to sail a supplies convoy the length of the Mediterranean, begins when five transports and their escorts pass Gibraltar. Two more convoys leave Alexandria for Malta and the whole of the Mediterranean Fleet becomes involved in escort duty.

7 May The German weather ship *München* is captured near Iceland in a mission specifically designed to obtain the secret papers on board which will hasten the understanding of the Enigma coding machines.

In the Mediterranean, a detachment of the Allied fleet shells Benghazi harbour, sinking two ships.

8 May A total of 359 RAF bombers launch a night attack on Hamburg and Bremen.

The career of the most successful German commerce raider *Pinguin* comes to an end near the Seychelles when she is sunk by fire from the heavy cruiser HMS *Cornwall*. The raider has sunk or captured 32 ships.

German commerce raider *Pinguin* sunk

The Mediterranean convoys come under air attack and engage the Italian aircraft.

9 May In a reprisal for the Hamburg raid the Germans attempt to hit the Rolls-Royce aircraft engine factory in the East Midlands. Radio Berlin reports extensive damage but the truth is that just a few farm animals are killed in the bombardment. German raids do, however, damage some airfields in other attacks on the 8th and 9th.

More code-books and an entire Enigma cipher machine are obtained when *U110* is boarded and captured during a convoy raid. The notes recovered also give the future plans for the battleship *Bismarck* and her supply ships. The capture of this U-boat will be kept secret – she sinks from the effects of depth-charge damage while under tow – but post-war commentators will agree that this event has a major bearing on the progress of the sea war for the rest of 1941.

10 May Rudolf Hess, deputy leader of the Nazi Party and long-standing confidant of Adolf Hitler, undertakes an extraordinary flight to Scotland in an attempt to make contact with the Duke of Hamilton, a friend from a meeting at the pre-war Olympics. Hess appears to believe that there exists an anti-Churchill, anti-Communist caucus in Great Britain which would work with Germany. The mission is quickly disowned by the German hierarchy.

Rudolf Hess flies to Scotland

German bombers assault London in what turns out to be the final heavy mission of the Battle of Britain. More than 500 aircraft drop high-explosive and incendiary bombs which result in many fires and cause more than 3,000 casualties including many dead. Some 27 German aircraft are lost. In the preceding ten months approximately 50,000 metric tons of bombs have been dropped on the UK, but the Battle of Britain has been lost, and with it has gone Germany's chance of winning the war. Partly because of their lack of long-range fighters and heavy bombers, but also because of the eventual mastery of the RAF fighter squadrons and their tactics, the Germans will regard this as first significant turning-point in World War Two.

11 May German bombing missions again target British air bases, though many are again in fact dummy installations

Important Allied convoy arrives in North Africa

12 May Operation 'Tiger' is completed with just one vessel lost to a mine. Equipment including 238 tanks and 43 Hurricane fighters set out, and all but 57 tanks arrived. The Malta convoys will become a feature of the Mediterranean theatre.

13 May Martin Bormann succeeds the disgraced, and absent, Hess.

14 May Italian morale in East Africa, already very low, is made worse by the ferocious involvement of Ethiopian guerrillas on the Allied side.

15 May Wavell, with the replenishments brought by Operation 'Tiger', plans a move against the German positions in the Halfaya Pass. Under the command of General Gott the force reaches and takes Halfaya.

16 May The 8th Panzer Regiment arrives to confront Gott's force and the British troops are obliged to withdraw. Rommel is using anti-aircraft guns as tank destroyers and doing so effectively.

German aircraft raid Crete

The Germans mount concerted attacks on the island of Crete ahead of their planned landing there.

17 May A news agency report in London announces that more than 10,000 US citizens are already fighting under the British flag, mostly with the RAF but a few with de Gaulle's Free French.

Bismarck sortie begins

18 May Admiral Lütjens sails the battleship *Bismarck* from Gdynia in consort with the heavy cruiser *Prinz Eugen*. Two supply ships and five tankers are stationed in the Atlantic, and scouting ships are sent out in advance of the main vessels to search for suitable prey.

19 May The Duke of Aosta surrenders with 7,000 Italians at Amba Alagi. Some 80,000 remain in East Africa.

German assault on Crete

20 May The full German assault on Crete commences with air attacks followed by paratroops dropped on the four airfields. They suffer heavy losses. Some 23,000 troops and 600 aircraft are deployed. The British and Greek forces are short of equipment and firepower but know the Germans are coming; they will outnumber them considerably. The Mediterranean fleet is offshore preventing any German arrivals by sea. The German side of the mission begins well but is then hit by delays in the flights of the aircraft bringing more troops, by heavy ground fire against those who do land and loss of communication between many of the constituent parts of the invasion. Towards the end of the day, the withdrawal of New Zealand units from Maleme airfield gives the Germans an unexpected foothold.

President Roosevelt expresses outrage at the loss of the US merchant ship *Robin Moor* to gunfire from a U-boat in the Atlantic.

The military attaché at the British embassy in Stockholm alerts London that *Bismarck* has put to sea, though without complete evidence.

21 May In Crete the Germans develop their position at Maleme, enabling troops to be flown in.

The battleship HMS *Prince of Wales* and the battlecruiser HMS *Hood* leave Scapa Flow to intercept *Bismarck* which has now been positively identified by a reconnaissance aircraft.

22 May Admiral Tovey leads the battleship HMS *King George V* and the carrier HMS *Victorious* to join the hunt.

Off Crete, British ships prevent German convoys from reaching the island, but the battleship HMS *Warspite* is damaged during other actions and two cruisers and a destroyer are sunk; one of the cruisers is HMS *York* which had been brought to Suda Bay for repairs, having been damaged some time before. Admiral Cunningham, in Alexandria, receives faulty reports that the ships off Crete are short of anti-aircraft ammunition and orders their withdrawal.

23 May Mountbatten's 5th Destroyer Flotilla bombards Maleme airfield on Crete but loses HMSS *Kelly* and *Kashmir* while pulling back.

In the Denmark Strait, the cruisers HMSS *Norfolk* and *Suffolk* spot *Bismarck* so the German battle group sails beyond the Arctic Circle to hamper the shadowing British vessels. *Prinz Eugen* damages her propulsion mechanism in the heavy ice.

Bismarck located

24 May HMSS *Hood* and *Prince of Wales* engage *Bismarck* and *Prinz Eugen*. *Hood* is soon sunk and *Prince of Wales* breaks off, having been damaged. Only three of *Hood*'s 1,416 crew are saved; the vessel's quick demise is put down to the penetrative gunfire of the German ships and its own weak, antiquated armour, but a shell from the German battleship may have hit an ammunition store. *Prince of Wales* is, by comparison, very new and some of its equipment goes into action untested and with some crew inadequately trained to use it. Tactically, the offensive moves used by the British ships did not give them their best chance of success. *Bismarck* has not gone unscathed and Lütjens heads for Brest and repairs, so prompting a hunt for his ship which the battleships HMSS *Rodney* and *Ramillies* join. During the night, aircraft from HMS *Victorious* are flown off and *Bismarck* is hit once. Elsewhere, the hunting pack is increased when Force H leaves Gibraltar with the battlecruiser HMS *Renown* and the carrier HMS *Ark Royal*. The perceived threat posed by *Bismarck* has never been understated and, now, all effort is put into eliminating her from the sea war.

Hood sunk

25 May Fighting intensifies on Crete. Galatas is the scene of bitter action and control of the town changes hands several times.

Lütjens, believing that he is still being closely shadowed, keeps radio silence for much of the day and only when he breaks it are the British able to trace his ship. Even then the opportunity to engage her is missed by faulty interpretation of the tracking information.

26 May Consideration is given to a withdrawal from Crete.

A flying-boat locates *Bismarck* closing on Brest and it is clear that Force H, and particularly the aircraft from *Ark Royal*, represents the best chance of preventing her from reaching that port. In bad weather these aircraft

Bismarck relocated

first attack the cruiser HMS *Sheffield* in error, but later a flight of Swordfish score two hits on the German battleship which affect her steering gear and bring her almost to a stop. Further attacks that night by torpedo and from the British battleships are inconclusive.

27 May Wavell agrees to evacuate Crete. In North Africa, Rommel retakes Halfaya Pass and strengthens his position there.

Bismarck sunk

Now a 'sitting duck', *Bismarck* is engaged by *Rodney* and *King George V* and, within a couple of hours, is completely disabled, leaving her defenceless against the torpedoes of the cruisers HMSS *Norfolk* and *Dorsetshire* which finish the job, forcing her crew to scuttle the great ship.

28 May Retreating British troops and the Heraklion garrison are taken off by sea only for several of the vessels to be damaged or sunk. The effort to hold Crete has been expensive for the British, the Royal Navy in particular, but the Germans have lost more than half their men and more than half of the 493 Junkers Ju 52 aircraft deployed.

JUNE 1941

Allies evacuate Crete

1 June The cruiser HMS *Calcutta* is sunk while assisting the Crete evacuation. More than 18,000 Allied troops have been taken off, but a further 17,000 have been taken prisoner; the Germans record 7,000 causalties including many dead. It has proved a hollow victory; its significance in the overall war plan is minimal and it turns Hitler against large-scale airborne actions which could have helped his cause in other theatres.

In Iraq, the British enter Baghdad.

5 June British Blenheim aircraft raid Aleppo airfield in Syria where Italian aircraft stand ready for action.

In the first days of this month the Allies enjoy some success against German supply ships. In 72 hours the Germans lose the tanker *Belchen*, a reconnaissance ship, *Gonzenheim*, and another tanker, *Gedania* before, on this day, the tanker *Egerland* which is scuttled before it can be captured by the heavy cruiser HMS *London* and the destroyer HMS *Brilliant*. These events cause the Kriegsmarine to change its policy and limit the long-range missions it can undertake.

British invade Syria

8 June After their successful sortie into Iraq, the British invade Syria. There is little resistance from the Vichy French forces there despite their numbering in excess of 45,000. The British are joined by Free French forces. The invasion brings the British and French naval forces into conflict.

9 June Luftwaffe units begin their moves to forward positions close to the Soviet border.

The cruiser HMS *Leander* arrives with six destroyers off Syria to support the action there, and the destroyer HMS *Janus* exchanges fire with the French destroyers *Valmy* and *Guépard*.

12 June A British cruiser rescues valuable secret documents from the German supply ship *Friedrich Breme* before her crew can scuttle her.

13 June A campaign against Jews by the Vichy French sees 12,000 interned.

A valuable strike in Trondheim Fiord is made by an RAF Beaufort on the pocket battleship *Lützow* which has to return to dock; she will be out of action until early 1942.

15 June The British mount Operation 'Battleaxe' aimed at relieving Tobruk. Wavell is not in favour of the offensive and is proved right as moves against Halfaya and Hafid Ridge are repulsed; only a small offensive at Capuzzo records any success. Rommel watches defensively as the British lose too many of their limited number of tanks on this first day. *[margin: Operation 'Battleaxe']*

16 June The British lose the initiative as Halfaya remains in German hands and neither 7th Armoured or 4th Indian Divisions enjoy any success.

A French supply ship, leaving Toulon with ammunition for the Syrian theatre, is sunk by torpedoes from a British aircraft.

17 June Wavell notifies Churchill of the failure of 'Battleaxe' after Rommel takes the offensive against the weakened British units.

Hitler sets the start date for the invasion of Russia as 22nd of the month.

19 June Vichy French troops enjoy some success near Damascus when they defeat an Indian battalion. *[margin: Vichy French successes]*

20 June An opportunity to attack the US battleship *Texas* in what the Germans class as an operational area is declined by U-boat Headquarters.

In Moscow, an air unit is set up for the defence of the capital; it is one of the few concessions to imminent danger of attack which the Soviets allow themselves.

22 June Operation 'Barbarossa' commences without any formal declaration of war. In this, his greatest gamble of the war so far, Hitler achieves the principal advantage in battle – surprise. Remarkably, for all the planning, cancellations, industrial construction and troop movements, and warnings received from other countries, the German move comes as a shock to Stalin, and Soviet forces come second-best in every early action. The Germans begin the campaign with more than150 divisions headed by generals who have cut their teeth in the Blitzkrieg campaigns in Poland and France; they have excellent air support from more than 2,700 aircraft and can boast more than 7,000 heavy guns and 3,300 tanks. *[margin: Germans invade Russia]*

Logistic support is another matter entirely and, because of a shortage of heavy motorised transport, more than half a million horses will be employed; the rail network in Russia runs to a different gauge and must be converted before German stock can be used. The German Navy will not play a large part in 'Barbarossa'; it has lost many ships including *Bismarck*, has a number of others under repair, including *Scharnhorst* and *Gneisenau*, and more vessels, such as *Tirpitz*, not yet ready for action.

Facing the invasion will be less than three-quarters of the Red Army divisions; the rest are elsewhere in the country. Only one in four of Russian tanks are battle-ready and many of the aircraft are antiquated or poorly armed in comparison with the German machines. Even so, the Germans enter the campaign uncertain of the total Soviet strengths and unaware of the results of Stalin's purge of the Army before the war.

Where the Germans can draw on their land war successes in the Low Countries and France, the Soviets have only their sub-standard performance in Finland on the record. The lessons they have tried to learn from Finland have caused the Russians to retrain hastily and gloss over some weaknesses. Because of their lack of readiness for the invasion – the Red Army is not even mobilised for war, their units in the west of their territory are not set up in a sensible, defensive pattern or even stationed near strategically sensitive points. In short, the Soviets are barely prepared for an exercise on their western border, let alone a full-scale invasion by a battle-hardened army.

The German plan is for Field Marshal von Leeb's Army Group North to head for Leningrad; Field Marshal von Bock's Army Group Centre to move on Smolensk; Field Marshal von Rundstedt's Army Group South to advance on Kiev. Von Bock has 51 divisions and the invaluable Generals Guderian and Hoth; he is earmarked to support the flanking thrusts of the other Groups after taking Smolensk. No move will be made on Moscow until all three Groups have met their first objectives. This strange piece of direction from Hitler is controversial for it raises the historical vision of failing to reach the ultimate goal before the onset of the Russian winter. Perhaps Hitler believes his plan to be superior to that of the Emperor Napoleon, or perhaps he refuses to be influenced by the French failure of a previous era. Whatever the case, it is this edict which is a chief cause, if not the only one, for the operation falling short of its Moscow objective. The weather is against the Germans from the outset, not just the severity of the winter when it comes.

1,200 Soviet aircraft have been disabled

The first day of 'Barbarossa' begins in the hours of darkness with ground and air strikes. By midday 1,200 Soviet aircraft have been disabled and some German units have advanced more than 40 miles. Not surprisingly, Heinz Guderian is at the forefront of the fastest push; his men will cover almost 300 miles in the first week.

23 June The Luftwaffe prevents the Soviet Air Force from playing any significant part in defending home territory on this second day, although the Soviets claim that thousands of missions have been flown. Hoth and Guderian make ground and only the southern area sees resistance worthy of the name.

Convoy HX-133

In the Atlantic a pack of ten U-boats with thirteen escort vessels assembles to attack Convoy HX-133 . Five merchantmen are lost, but *U556* and *U651* are sunk.

24 June Vilna and Kaunas fall to the Germans who get their first sight of the KV1 Soviet tank which proves able to withstand their anti-tank guns.

Convoy HX-133, which has had four escort vessels, is to be given another nine from other missions.

25 June The French submarine *Souffleur* is torpedoed and sunk by its British equivalent HMS *Parthian* and a French tanker en route to the Middle East is immobilised by British torpedo-bombers. In the Atlantic, another German weather ship is captured together with maps and cipher papers.

26 June Soviet submarine strength is damaged by the hasty evacuation of their base at Libau in Latvia.

29 June Hoth and Guderian join up near Minsk. Finland has declared war on the USSR and joint German and Finnish actions in the Karelian Isthmus distract some Russian units.

Finland declares war on Russia

Convoy HX-133 loses five ships and two U-boats are sunk in this large escort versus submarine action.

30 June On the Eastern Front, Lvow is taken by Army Group South and other troops get closer to Kiev.

Churchill replaces Wavell with General Claude Auchinleck. The new CinC, Middle East will eventually receive the support his predecessor was denied, including the early appointment of Oliver Lyttleton as a resident Minister of State in the Middle East; indeed Wavell has suffered constantly from being asked to undertake impossible tasks with sparse resources. Wavell takes Auchinleck's post as CinC, India.

Army Group North takes Riga

JULY 1941

1 July The RAF attacks Brest harbour and hits *Prinz Eugen*, causing much damage and killing 60 of her crew.

2 July While Hoepner's Fourth Panzer Group makes good progress beyond the river Dvina, farther south German Eleventh Army links up with Roumanian Third and Fourth Armies for significant advances. The wet and boggy conditions they are facing are hampering the Germans elsewhere, with commanders reporting it as the only cause for lack of advance.

3 July Stalin appeals for every effort to stave off the invaders. In this first broadcast since the Germans crossed the border, he uses the 1939 Pact with the Germans as evidence of his preference for peace.

In East Africa the last Italians surrender after a wasteful and damaging campaign which has brought no permanent benefit.

Last Italians surrender in East Africa

In Syria the Vichy defence of the fort at Palmyra ends with a surrender to Allied forces.

5 July The first formal Soviet defence lines are quickly breached by German Sixth Army near Zhitomir while, in the north, the German forces have reached the Dnieper.

7 July Churchill sends a letter of encouragement to Stalin in which he speaks of 'utterly unprovoked and merciless invasion of the Nazis'. He adds that 'the longer the war lasts the more help we can give', suggesting that Stalin must fight his own battles while Great Britain attends to its own priorities. By this time, however, the Soviet defenders have been pushed back between 200 and 400 miles from their first positions; the Baltic states, White Russia and the Ukraine are severely threatened.

Having already begun air and sea patrols from bases in Newfoundland, the USA now relieves Allied forces from Iceland.

8 July Hitler, enthused by his early successes, urges von Leeb's Army Group North to move on to Leningrad with all haste; the Führer sees the city as a psychological prize of equal rating to Moscow and believes its capture will destroy Soviet morale even before Moscow comes under threat.

Soviets lose more than 40 divisions

9 July In the first weeks of the German advance the Soviets have lost more than 40 of their operational divisions. The Germans have reached Smolensk and encircle it.

10 July Four Italian divisions leave their home bases for service on the Eastern Front in a pallid attempt to show their continuing role in the Axis power bloc.

Vichy French sign armistice in Syria

11 July General Dentz defies instructions from his Vichy French superiors and signs an armistice with the Allies in Syria.

First Panzer Group is fifteen miles from Kiev. A new format for Red Army control sees General Voroshilov taking command in the north, Marshal Timoshenko in the central west sector, and Marshal Budenny responsible for the South-west Front.

William 'Wild Bill' Donovan is appointed by Roosevelt to head a new non-military intelligence agency which, in time, will become the Office of Strategic Services (OSS) in the style of the British Special Operations Executive (SOE). The move does not please J. Edgar Hoover at the FBI who sees his team as capable of taking responsibility for tracking possible German sympathisers in the USA.

12 July The British and Russians sign an agreement which forbids either of them to make a separate peace with Hitler and allows for increased mutual assistance. Bombs fall on Moscow for the first time.

In North Africa, General Bastico replaces Gariboldi as CinC, but will find that Rommel disregards him as he did his predecessor.

14 July The harbour and shipping at Suez is damaged by a Ju 88 bombing raid.

15 July A rare Soviet counter-attack near Lake Ilmen gives the forces defending Leningrad time to prepare for the German move on the city. The Soviets deploy their Katyusha M-8 rocket-launchers for the first time; the existence of these highly secret weapons was known to very few.

16 July Finnish attacks around Sortavala and Lake Ladoga cut off some Soviet forces in the west.

Hitler meets Bormann, Göring and Rosenberg and places the latter in charge of ridding new Reich territories of Jews and communists and of instilling the German code into the civilian population.

18 July In a cabinet reshuffle in Japan, the hawkish Matsuoka is removed in order to strengthen the caucus which favours discussions with America over oil resources and is not eager to side with Hitler.

19 July Guderian is infuriated by Hitler's demand that he and his forces detour to join the battle for Kiev when they have taken Smolensk. The tank commander, knowing that Moscow is under-prepared for the offensive the Germans can mount, wants to aim straight for the capital.

In London, the BBC begins broadcasts which will encourage, and help direct, the resistance movement against the German occupiers in France.

The USA again increases its role in the protection of Atlantic convoys by stationing P-40 fighters, flying-boats and more destroyers in Iceland.

21 July Moscow suffers its first full air raid, by 127 aircraft. The Soviets claim that their night-fighters and anti-aircraft guns bring down seventeen German aircraft; the Germans report fires across the city.

Operation 'Substance' is mounted in the Mediterranean, to get supplies through to the increasingly besieged Malta. Force H from Gibraltar is again charged with protecting the seven merchant vessels and has the battleship HMS *Nelson*, three cruisers and nine destroyers added to its resources for the exercise.

Operation 'Substance'

22 July The Malta convoy is located by Italian aircraft, but Italian warships do not put to sea because the authorities are apparently unaware of the nature of the supplies being brought to the island .

23 July Italian air attacks set fire to the destroyer HMS *Fearless* and damage a cruiser and three other destroyers from the 'Substance' convoy. *Fearless* is later scuttled.

24 July The convoy reaches Malta with only one merchantman damaged. The Italian fleet has failed to stop this vital supply convoy; poor intelligence about the nature of the mission is to blame.

The Japanese make immediate plans to occupy bases in Indo-China which are finally conceded to them by the Vichy French government.

In harbour at La Pallice, *Scharnhorst* is attacked by Halifax bombers and put out of action for the rest of the year. Already out of action are *Prinz Eugen* and *Gneisenau* so the German naval threat from French Atlantic ports is now minimal.

25 July The entire length of the Stalin Line has now been breached by German forces. Despite some successful local counter-attacks, the Soviets have failed to defend this fortified north–south line.

Stalin Line breached

The Italian X Flotilla undertakes a raid on Grand Harbour at Malta using assault craft and manned torpedoes. The mission, daring but doomed, sees all the boats lost and more than thirty of the crewmen killed or captured.

26 July Great Britain and the USA join in freezing Japanese assets in their countries; Japan retaliates with the same action. When similar moves are made in the Dutch East Indies 48 hours later, the Japanese at a stroke loses 90 per cent of their fuel supplies and most of their foreign commerce.

President Roosevelt appoints General MacArthur to command US forces in the Philippines and orders that that country's army be incorporated into the US Army for the duration of Japanese militancy.

Smolensk cut off

27 July At Smolensk the Russians are cut off by German pincer moves.

30 July Japan apologises for an attack by their bombers which damages the US gunboat *Tutiula* in Chungking.

Aircraft from the carriers HMSS *Victorious* and *Furious* attack German shipping near Kirkenes and Petsamo in Norway; almost 25 per cent of the aircraft are lost.

31 July A re-organisation of the Afrika Korps sees General Crüwell in overall charge with Rommel commanding the new Panzer Group Afrika.

AUGUST 1941

USA puts complete oil embargo on Japan

1 August A complete embargo on oil and aviation fuel from the USA pushes Japan closer to war in order to secure supplies from other sources.

On the Eastern Front the Germans repel various Russian attacks against their rear positions and raise the pressure on Vitebsk and Orsha.

2 August The American Lend-Lease plan is extended to the Soviet Union.

3 August The British CAM ships, merchant vessels converted to carry fighter aircraft and a catapult mechanism with which to launch them, claim their first success when a Hurricane from HMS *Maplin* shoots down an Fw 200 Kondor in the North Atlantic. Such aircraft would normally try to make for land after a flight, but could ditch alongside the mother vessel and be hoisted aboard.

Smolensk falls

5 August Smolensk falls. It has been defended by 700,000 troops of whom nearly half have been taken prisoner.

6 August The Japanese government makes proposals to the USA in an attempt to regain an oil supply.

The Soviet Air Force bombs Berlin in the first of several such missions throughout August. The raids are minor and do not achieve anything other than showing that Soviet aircraft are flying and can get through German air space.

8 August Six weeks into its Eastern campaign, the German Army is beginning to feel the effects of its own Blitzkrieg technique. It is losing more and more tanks, logistic support is finding the weather and terrain against it, and the enemy is showing greater resolve than expected. The battlefield commanders, whose mastery of the earlier actions in Poland and the west has been complete, are finding it less easy to cope with the counters and sniping attacks mounted by the defending forces, and the Führer's constant interference from a distance does little to raise their spirits.

9 August At a meeting in Newfoundland, Churchill and Roosevelt trade views on the state of politics and war in Europe and the Far East. They decide to invite Stalin to a three-handed conference and to warn Japan off any adventurous or militant moves on the British or Dutch territories in Malaya or the East Indies. The conference cements the working relationship between the two statesmen, but also – and crucially – among their respective staffs.

Churchill and Roosevelt meet at Placentia Bay

12 August Hitler adjusts the agenda for the Eastern Front. He confirms that Army Group Centre, including Guderian's units, must divert to assist other forces, Army Group North must aim for Leningrad and Army Group South begin its move into the Crimea.

Nearly 5,000 Australian troops are brought out of Tobruk and replaced by 6,000 from a Polish brigade. A cruiser, two destroyers and two minelayers support the mission which lasts some days.

The heaviest raid on Berlin to date sees 82 metric tons of bombs dropped on the city. So many German aircraft have been transferred the Eastern Front that the RAF is facing less opposition in its flights over occupied Europe.

15 August Severe sandstorms are limiting activity in the Western Desert. These, and a temperature which tops 100 degrees every day, makes the region a uniquely testing combat area.

The RAF is encouraged to try a daylight raid on a power-station near Cologne, believing the Luftwaffe strength en route to be insufficient to have an impact; in the event, one fifth of the bombers are brought down.

16 August German Eleventh Army occupies the important Soviet naval base at Nikolayev, promptly capturing a heavy cruiser, four destroyers, submarines, gun boats, ammunition and repair facilities.

Nikolayev falls

17 August The Japanese are sent the warning agreed at the Newfoundland conference.

18 August The Soviet forces in the south begin to withdraw behind the line of the Dnieper.

20 August The commander of the US air force units in Hawaii furnishes a report on the nature of any attack the Japanese might make on Pearl Harbor and requests many more aircraft so that effective reconnaissance can be mounted.

21 August The Germans cut the rail link between Leningrad and Moscow.

A convoy from Iceland to Russia is attempted for the first time; it will reach Archangel at the end of the month without enemy interference.

First Arctic convoy to Russia

23 August German forces begin to converge on Kiev. Several German commanders would prefer to be making straight for Moscow, leaving Kiev to be dealt with by follow-up forces.

24 August Aircraft from HMS *Ark Royal* attack Tempio airfield in Sardinia. The Italian battleships *Vittorio Veneto* and *Littorio* venture out but do not engage.

25 August Hitler confirms the plan – his plan, and one contrary to the wishes of his commanders on the ground – to concentrate on the drives to Leningrad and the oil-rich Caucasus, leaving Moscow until later. He is told that the campaign, whichever scheme is followed, cannot be completed by the end of the year so any move against Great Britain will have to be delayed until 1942; this is grudgingly accepted.

British and Soviet forces move into Iran to protect their oil supplies; there is little opposition. Axis merchant ships are seized in various Gulf ports.

British Force K begins Operation 'Gauntlet', with two cruisers, and the liner *Empress of Canada* as troopship which arrive off Spitzbergen. The troops are ferried ashore by lifeboats to destroy mining centres. They complete their work without detection by the Germans; indeed German aircraft steer clear of the area because of low cloud reports broadcast by the invaders from the weather station at Spitzbergen. The Germans remain ignorant of the operation for a further ten days.

26 August The Russians bomb Tehran and British forces occupy the Abadan area.

27 August The Germans make a major move to seize the Baltic port of Tallin.

U-boat surrenders

South of Iceland *U570* surrenders when she surfaces directly beneath a Hudson bomber. She will be taken to the UK for evaluation before being modified for Royal Naval service and re-appearing as HMS *Graph*.

An attempted assassination of Laval and a German newspaper man near Versailles is used as an excuse by the Vichy authorities to round up anyone opposing their regime.

28 August The Iranian government resigns and the new regime order a ceasefire so that they can start negotiations with the British and Russians.

Allies occupy key points in Iran

29 August Fighting ends in Iran. The capital is to be left unoccupied but Russian and British troops will guard key points.

SEPTEMBER 1941

1 September Leningrad is now within artillery range of the German forces.

The US Navy continues to increase its patrols in the Atlantic and begins patrolling the Denmark Strait.

U-boat attacks US destroyer

4 September The US destroyer *Greer* is advised by air reconnaissance that a U-boat is nearby. The aircraft drops depth-charges and the U-boat, *U652*, believing it to have been attacked by the warship attempts to torpedo it. In the event, neither vessel is damaged but the Americans use the incident to test their skill in presenting war events to the world media. The US Navy virtually enters the Battle of the Atlantic when Roosevelt shortly gives the order that all enemy ships found in waters which the USA deem important to their national defence be attacked. Strangely Hitler does not react to this edict with a change of policy against American shipping, which is currently off-limits to his U-boat fleet.

6 September Although the US Ambassador in Tokyo is urging Roosevelt to work with Prince Konoye rather than suffer the military regime which might replace him, he shows no sign of assisting the Japanese leader to get oil supplies which might keep the hawks at bay. At an Imperial Conference Konoye is persuaded to prepare for war and to be ready for military action by the middle of October.

In the first operational retreat by German forces since the outbreak of the war, troops are forced to cede ground near Yelnya and stand by while that town is recaptured by the Soviets. Just a few weeks after diverting his forces from the drive on Moscow, Hitler now decrees that it must proceed, as Operation 'Typhoon', by the end of September.

Hitler decrees that all Jews in occupied Europe must wear a Star of David on their clothing. By now the Auschwitz concentration camp is fully operational.

8 September In the first British use of American B-17 Flying Fortress bombers, two are lost and three badly damaged in an aborted mission over Norway. This sets many British officials against the aircraft which goes on to become the star of the US Eighth Air Force's deployment in the UK.

10 September Guderian has pushed the Soviet forces back on his drive to Kiev and von Kleist's First Panzer Group is on the move again as it breaks out from its bridgehead over the Dnieper at Kremenchug.

12 September Von Kleist and Guderian's forces link up and by so doing isolate more than half a million Soviet troops. German Second Army is closing on Kiev from the north.

Half a million Soviet troops isolated

Further relief activity begins at Tobruk with troop transports ferrying in new units and evacuating men from the earlier garrison force over a period of ten days.

15 September Leningrad is cut off from land contact by German moves around Lake Ladoga. The siege will become the longest and cruellest of the war.

Leningrad cut off

Hitler re-activates rocket development at Peenemünde which he himself had had shelved. The swift development and production of what will become the V-2 rocket is given priority over aviation and naval needs.

16 September With the Shah of Persia showing little inclination to remove Axis nationals from Iran, the Allies occupy Tehran; the Shah abdicates in favour of the Crown Prince.

Allies occupy Tehran

17 September The Germans are at the outskirts of Kiev.

The Canadian Navy is now assisting the US Navy in convoy protection in the Atlantic; the latter are increasing their participation almost daily and attending convoys between Newfoundland and Iceland.

New U-boats are coming off the production and testing lines to enter service with a new group operating in the North Atlantic.

18 September Another convoy en route for Tripoli and the Afrika Korps is attacked. This time the troopships *Oceania* and *Neptunia* are torpedoed by the submarine HMS *Upholder*. Most of the troops aboard are rescued.

Kiev falls

19 September Kiev falls after six weeks of fighting around its perimeter. Although Soviet loss of life may have reached half a million, the Germans have also lost close to 100,000. Official German High Command releases will later claim 665,000 Russian prisoners have been taken together with more than 884 tanks and 3,718 guns.

In Yugoslavia, the two leaders of resistance, Tito and Mihailovic, meet in an attempt to pool resources but each has his own agenda and the two men do not trust each other. Further meetings will be held, without success, and soon the rival groups will begin fighting each other instead of the common enemy.

First escort carrier success

20 September An aircraft from the escort carrier HMS *Audacity* shoots down a Fw 200 Kondor which is harrying Convoy OG-74 in the first successful action from one of these vessels.

The Germans create the Baltic Fleet to prevent the departure and operation of Soviet ships from Kronstadt. This new unit includes the battleship *Tirpitz*, the heavy cruiser *Admiral Scheer* and assorted escort vessels.

24 September The first of the German U-boats to enter the Mediterranean passes Gibraltar. Within weeks half the German submarine fleet will be in this theatre, but it will prove a far from ideal hunting-ground. Most of the likely operational areas are within range of land-based aircraft, and in these waters, so much calmer and of a different density from those of the Atlantic, a U-boat fifty feet down can often be seen from above, which is twice the visibility of other areas. Another major convoy 'Halberd' leaves Gibraltar for Malta; it comprises nine transport ships and escorted by three battleships, one carrier, five cruisers and eighteen destroyers.

Soviet forces in the Crimea isolated

25 September Soviet forces in the Crimea have been isolated from supplies by German advances. Air support enables the Germans to initiate fresh attacks.

26 September The battle east of Kiev is over, the Soviet South-west Front having been hammered by numerically superior German forces. The success causes Hitler to disbelieve the pessimistic predictions of his generals about the time needed to complete 'Barbarossa'.

The 'Halberd' Convoy brings out an Italian fleet of two battleships, six cruisers and fourteen destroyers.

27 September Field Marshal von Manstein's Eleventh Army takes Perekop, the northern land access to the Crimea.

Heydrich replaces von Neurath as German Governor of Bohemia and Moravia. Within the first hours in his new role he will impose martial law.

The Italian ships steaming to intercept the' 'Halberd' Convoy fail to make contact. The battleship HMS *Nelson* receives minor damage from a hit by an Italian torpedo-bomber.

28 September A meeting begins in Moscow which finally brings the Moscow meeting main anti-Axis nations together at a high level. The chief negotiators are Max Beaverbrook as Churchill's representative, Averell Harriman from the USA and Foreign Minister Molotov for the Soviets.

The 'Halberd' Convoy reaches Malta with the loss of just one transport. The 50,000 tons of supplies keeps the beleaguered island from a very real threat of starvation.

29 September Heydrich arranges the arrest of Czech Prime Minister Elias as part of his repressive regime which is causing much antagonism.

The sailing of convoys from the UK and Iceland to Archangel begins. The short life of the Baltic Fleet is ended when the Germans establish that the Soviets are not planning to deploy the ships from Kronstadt.

30 September His responsibilities in the Kiev battle now over, Guderian is allowed to move north and resume his advance on Moscow. In the south von Kleist too shows his taste for pressing on from Kiev by advancing towards the Donets and the Sea of Azov. The Soviet adventure has already taken its toll and the German Army finds itself with nearly 15 per cent of its starting strength lost; more than half a million troops are dead, wounded or missing.

OCTOBER 1941

1 October The Moscow meeting ends with a joint declaration guaranteeing increasing help for the Soviets from the other nations.

2 October Operation 'Typhoon', the code-name for the German attack on German attack on Moscow begins Moscow, is officially begun. Needless to say Guderian has taken a two-day start on everyone else, but he is followed by a huge force including Third and Fourth Panzer Groups and Second, Fourth and Ninth Armies. These ground troops can be assured of air superiority and they have more men and land armour than the forces which currently stand in their way. In a telling press release the TASS agency reports the first snow of the season around Leningrad and a consequent decrease in German attacks.

In Australia, Robert Menzies' Country Party loses power to the Labour Party led by John Curtin. Menzies, so loved and respected in Great Britain for his whole-hearted support in the war to date, has come to be seen by the voters as too acquiescent towards London and unconcerned with matters closer to home.

3 October German attacks on Kharkov and Kursk in the south have already begun and Hoepner and Hoth are breaking through around Roslavl and Smolensk; General Breith's 3rd Panzer Division takes Orel.

4 October Guderian's progress towards Orel and Bryansk shows no sign of slowing and large numbers of Soviet forces are close to being cut off in this region. Elsewhere, Hoepner and Hoth are also advancing.

6 October Large pockets of Soviet forces are cut off by the pace of the German advance. Von Kleist's units reach the Sea of Azov.

8 October The weather worsens on the Eastern Front; snow has already fallen in parts of Russia and now heavy rain begins to hinder the pace of the German attacks as much as any opposition the Soviets can put up. The home forces are defending strongly at Vyazma and Bryansk but 600,000 are destined to be captured there.

To the south, towards Tula and Kaluga, and in the north around Rzhev and Kalinin, German ground forces face only minor delays on their Blitzkrieg push forwards.

Soviet Eighteenth
Army destroyed

10 October General Zhukov returns to Moscow from Leningrad to organise the defence of the city. In battles around the Sea of Azov, General Smirnov is killed when his Eighteenth Army is destroyed by units of Army Group South.

12 October The Germans take Kaluga and are able to walk into Bryansk from which the Soviets have withdrawn.

In another two-weeks' operation to alternate forces at Tobruk, some 7,000 fresh troops are brought in and a greater number collected in a series of daring naval runs to the port. A minelayer is lost to a Stuka attack during the action.

13 October Vyazma falls to the Germans and the isolated Soviet pocket in the area is close to submission.

14 October To the north-west of Moscow, the Germans are at Kalinin; the central push hurries on from Vyazma and southern drives include a run for Tula. If these advances continue at this pace the capital's days are surely numbered.

16 October The first signs of public concern are shown in Moscow and government and party officials are seen leaving the city. Elsewhere, Odessa is evacuated and most of the departing men and ships reach Sevastopol.

Tojo replaces Prince
Konoye

In Japan Prime Minister Prince Konoye resigns and is replaced by the militant General Tojo. He takes control of the ministries of war and home affairs and surrounds himself with 'hawks'.

Pétain orders the arrest of Daladier, Reynaud and Blum; these former prime ministers are charged with complicity in the defeat of France.

US destroyer *Kearney*
sunk

The US destroyer *Kearney* is torpedoed and sunk with the loss of eleven men while on convoy duties with British, US and Canadian ships.

19 October Three defensive lines are being hastily built around Moscow; Stalin declares a state of siege but announces that he will stay in the city despite most of his government having decamped to safer areas. The German troops advancing on the capital are now facing appalling weather with tanks and trucks becoming bogged down in a morass of mud.

Malta is reinforced with more aircraft brought from Gibraltar, and two cruisers and two destroyers are en route to augment naval strength there.

22 October The Americans have agreed that two Japanese passenger ships can sail from Japan to Hawaii, unaware that they will be used to chart the route of the Pearl Harbor fleet. The first leaves from Yokohama with two experts on US aviation and submarines aboard.

23 October An important redefinition of Soviet command sees Zhukov take charge of the northern sector of the defensive line and Timoshenko the southern.

One of the Japanese liners reaches Honolulu and the welcoming Japanese Consul-General is given sealed orders which request the urgent mapping of the military installations around Pearl Harbor.

24 October Kharkov falls to German Sixth and Seventeenth Armies.

Kharkov falls

The destroyer HMS *Cossack* is torpedoed by *U563* and sinks two days later.

25 October The battleship HMS *Prince of Wales* sails for the Far East.

27 October The father of British Commando development, Admiral of the Fleet Sir Roger Keyes, is replaced by the younger Captain Lord Louis Mountbatten. The new man converts Churchill to the policy of mounting smaller, less costly raids as opposed to Keyes' preference for large-scale operations with their attendant cost and logistical problems.

28 October Poor logistic support, boggy ground, human fatigue and freezing overnight temperatures begin to hinder the German forces heading for Moscow. Guderian tries but fails to take Tula.

30 October The worst weather of the autumn halts the German forces, but winter frost will soon bring harder ground and a chance to move the tanks forward.

German progress halted

31 October The US destroyer *Reuben James*, serving with Convoy HX-156's escort, is sunk by a U-boat with the loss of 115 men.

US destroyer *Reuben James* sunk

NOVEMBER 1941

1 November The second Japanese liner which has sailed for Hawaii arrives in Honolulu to report on the situation the Japanese will find there if they decide to attack.

2 November A French convoy of freighters and passenger vessels en route from Madagascar is captured off Cape Town by a British cruiser force.

3 November Kursk falls to the Germans.

Kursk falls

5 November The Japanese make inadequate concessions in a new peace attempt. Their plans and discussions are being tracked by US code-breakers.

6 November The US Navy is patrolling the Atlantic coast of South America for the Allies and a first success comes with the seizure by the cruiser *Omaha* of a German blockade runner, *Odenwald*, carrying rubber from Japan.

7 November Churchill tells Stalin of the pressure he is putting on the Japanese.

The RAF raid Berlin with 169 aircraft, 21 of which are lost. Bomber Command has not let up on its nightly raids on this and other German cities despite worsening weather and increasingly effective air defence.

Berlin Bombed

8 November The Italian destroyers *Fulmine* and *Libeccio* are sunk during a night battle between an Italian convoy and vessels from naval Force K out of Malta. The Italian cruiser and destroyers do not fire when the convoy is attacked; all the transports in the convoy are sunk.

Yalta falls

9 November In the Crimea, Yalta falls to German forces.

10 November Admiral Nagumo orders his Pearl Harbor invasion fleet out of Tokyo. The vessels leave separately and observe strict radio silence.

12 November On the Eastern Front General Halder chairs a meeting with his front-line commanders and discloses his plan for the final push on Moscow. Three panzer groups and three infantry armies will be deployed; the plan does not enjoy their whole-hearted support.

13 November The carrier HMS *Ark Royal* is badly damaged by a U-boat attack while transporting more aircraft to Malta. She turns back to Gibraltar.

Ark Royal sunk

14 November *Ark Royal*, under tow to Gibraltar, loses the battle to keep afloat just 25 miles from her base and has to be abandoned to sink.

Offensive against Moscow re-opons

15 November The new offensive against Moscow gets under way as heavy frost hardens the boggy ground; the temperature remains well below zero day and night. Converging attacks from the north and south are planned; Third and Fourth Panzer Groups will handle the former, Guderian's Second Panzer Group the latter. Not best prepared for fighting in such conditions, they are hopelessly short of manpower and efficient equipment to cope with this the worst of Soviet winters. Frostbite, inadequate provisions, injured personnel, faulty equipment, and vehicles rendered useless by oil freezing in the bitter conditions are just some of the problems with which the German commanders will have to contend.

The Russians are in not much better shape; they will seek to hold the advance as best they can until reinforcements arrive from Siberia. They will allow some German progress where it is not too harmful, but will concentrate their forces in primary positions and set delaying ambushes where possible. At least they are used to the weather.

16 November The Germans are still rampaging through the Crimea but they have yet to face the defences of Sevastopol.

17 November Ernst Udet, a German flying ace from the 1914–18 war, personal friend of Göring's and head of the Office of Air Armament at the outbreak of war, commits suicide. He has been sidelined for some months after his poor performance in administering the uprating of the Luftwaffe and has been unable to come to terms with the adverse criticism. His death is reported as accidental and he is given a hero's funeral.

Operation 'Crusader'

18 November Operation 'Crusader', a new British strategy in North Africa, is begun in heavy rain with a move by XXX Corps from Egypt into Libya. The Allied forces, now commanded by General Cunningham and designated Eighth Army, have nearly 600 cruiser and light tanks plus those held within Tobruk. At this time the Germans are believed to have some 400 tanks though the majority are of Italian or older German design. The Allies can claim three times the number of German aircraft in the region. The Allies are aware of an imminent German attack – Rommel is planning for 21 November even though convoys of German supplies have not got through for some weeks – and their early move catches the Desert Fox by surprise; he is on the way back from a meeting in Rome. Haste means that the Allied plan is not as well thought through as it could have been, but this first day sees them advance unchallenged to Gabr Saleh.

In the drive for Moscow, Guderian's units struggle against fresh Soviet troops who have arrived from Siberia and his advance is halted. *Advance on Moscow halted*

The Japanese submarine fleet becomes active, a force of eleven boats moving into the Hawaii and other Pacific areas.

19 November Allied achievements in North Africa are mixed. The 4th and 22nd Armoured Brigades suffer reverses in engagements with German and Italian units respectively, but 7th Armoured Brigade reaches Sidi Rezegh without mishap. The day sees 40 British tanks lost.

A brutal head-to-head naval action off Western Australia sees the Australian light cruiser *Sydney* lost with all hands in a brief confrontation with the German raider *Kormoran* which also sinks after a fire. This daylight sinking of a cruiser by an armed merchant ship is unique. *Sydney* and *Kormoran* sink each other

20 November In North Africa British 4th Armoured Brigade again suffers losses, but moves are under way to break out from Tobruk. Rommel is now aware of the strength of the Allied operation and begins to react with typical determination.

21 November The first attempts to break out from Tobruk come to nought when 7th Armoured Brigade cannot move on from Sidi Rezegh to assist because of German tank attacks there which reduce the British unit's tank count to 21. *Attempts to break out from Tobruk fail*

The needs of the German forces in North Africa brings an increase in Axis convoy activity in the Mediterranean. Two are attacked from air and sea and escorting cruisers are hit.

On the Eastern Front, Rostov falls to the Germans after a fierce battle. *Rostov falls*

22 November The Germans gain a numerical superiority over the Allies in North Africa, at least in respect of tank strength, after a day of hectic fighting around Sidi Rezegh which sees 4th, 7th and 22nd Armoured Brigades all coming badly out of the confrontations. New Zealand troops have joined the Allies in the area, as part of XIII Corps.

While being flown to Berlin to attend the funeral of Ernst Udet, the fighter ace Werner Mölders is killed near Breslau when his aircraft, at low altitude because of engine trouble, hits a factory chimney .

The hugely successful German raider *Atlantis* is sunk by the cruiser HMS *Devonshire* off the coast of West Africa. The Royal Navy is increasingly effective in its pursuit of German shipping because of improved code-breaking techniques. *German raider Atlantis sunk*

23 November A combined German and Italian charge at Sidi Rezegh has limited success and loses the attackers both men and tanks. The Allies are stung by the attack and Cunningham is struggling to devise effective strategies in a military situation which is alien to him. His hesitancy will mean a call for Auchinleck to impose his tactical skill on the campaign. The New Zealand Division has a good day when it captures the Afrika Korps HQ and valuable communications equipment.

German troops are within 35 miles of Moscow on its north-west approaches but progress has slowed.

Germans withdraw from Rostov

24 November Field Marshal von Rundstedt contravenes a direct order from Hitler when he withdraws from the captured city of Rostov as he becomes aware of Soviet counter-attacks on the rear of his formation. It is a defining moment for attackers and defenders alike.

Rommel, in a move more notable for its intended pace and daring than its strategic value, begins a drive towards the Egyptian border, believing he can rout the under-strength Allied forces on the way. His progress is much slowed, however, by effective harrying attacks against his formation which becomes too dispersed because of the pace at which he heads the drive.

25 November In North Africa the Germans continue to mount wasteful attacks which do nothing to prevent the Allied brigades regrouping.

On the Eastern Front, the pincer movements to envelope Moscow are going well, but the Germans have yet to confront the expert winter troops arriving from Siberia to supplement the Soviet defences.

Barham sunk

While serving with a group from the Mediterranean Fleet in action against an Axis fuel convoy heading for Benghazi, the battleship HMS *Barham* becomes the only Allied battleship to be sunk in the open seas by a U-boat when she explodes after being torpedoed by *U331*. The convoy loses two freighters.

26 November Rommel ends his misguided attacks around Capuzzo and Sidi Azeiz and tracks back towards Tobruk where the New Zealand Division is reasonably fresh and ready to move in support of the besieged town. At this time British air superiority in the region is a major deterrent to German success.

In what they consider a final diplomatic move, the US government calls upon the Japanese to quit China and Indo-China and recognise Chiang Kai-shek; promising in return to negotiate new trade benefits. While this message is being relayed to the Japanese Nagumo's carrier force is already sailing for Pearl Harbor.

Germans re-occupy Rostov

27 November The Germans occupy Rostov for a second time, but in the Moscow sector it has become clear that Guderian cannot advance further without fresh troops and supplies. The charismatic commander continues to mount modest, sniping attacks but gains no ground.

Relief of Tobruk

New Zealand forces link up with troops from the Tobruk garrison at El Duda.

The Italian adventure in East Africa finally ends; Mussolini will never see his 'Roman Empire' ambitions realised. The surrender documents are to be signed on the 28th.

28 November In North Africa Sidi Rezegh continues to be the scene of heavy fighting as the Germans strive to separate the New Zealanders from the troops at Tobruk.

Rostov is again evacuated by the Germans who suffer heavy losses in the débâcle.

Germans withdraw from Rostov again

29 November A German unit under General Reinhardt manages to cross the Moscow–Volga Canal but cannot achieve continuing success against the fresher troops joining the Soviet ranks from Siberia.

The Japanese government decides to reject the final American offer; Japan will go to war.

30 November The Germans lose men as they force a New Zealand brigade to abandon the attempted link-up with the Tobruk garrison.

After his performance at Rostov, von Rundstedt is relieved of his command and is replaced by General von Reichenau. This is another case of German commanders proving less capable when the Blitzkrieg pulse begins to falter and of Hitler failing to back the judgement of previously efficient field commanders.

Reichenau replaces Rundstedt

Japanese naval moves are noticed by British units in Borneo.

Eighty-four RAF bombers from a force of 129 reach Hamburg to drop 138 tons of bombs. While the Soviets are proving able to relocate much of their production out of range of the Luftwaffe, the Germans are unable do so, and their manufacturing output is beginning to feel the effects of the British attacks.

A Whitley bomber makes the first successful use of air-to-surface vessel radar to locate, bomb and sink *U206*.

DECEMBER 1941

1 December The remaining New Zealanders at Sidi Rezegh are forced to retreat but the Germans are losing men of all ranks and are tiring fast because of the pace set by Rommel. The ability of the Allied convoys to get through the Mediterranean to supply Eighth Army, and the comparative failure of the Axis route is beginning to influence tactics and performance. Although the Desert Fox has regained his complete encirclement of Tobruk, he is so short of supplies that his troops are in no condition to press home their positional advantage.

2 December Now the German forces near Moscow can begin to feel the Napoleonic jinx; they can see the city, almost touch it, but are unable to make a concerted move to reach it. Von Kluge responds to Hitler's urgings and tries to advance, but the freezing cold and biting winds play havoc with the health and morale of all ranks; the defenders have the natural

89

strength which comes from the knowledge that they are protecting their capital city. The valuable air superiority enjoyed by the Germans is rendered useless by the constant sub-zero temperatures which make the forward airfields inoperable. Von Bock has already told Hitler that his men are close to complete exhaustion.

The Japanese naval force heading for Hawaii receive the coded message that peace negotiations have failed and the Pearl Harbor raid is to proceed, the attack date set for 7 December. The ships are battling through severe storms.

The battleship HMS *Prince of Wales* and the battlecruiser HMS *Repulse* have arrived at Singapore.

Rommel's forces stretched

3 December In North Africa despite the poor supply situation, Rommel continues to stretch his forces too thinly. His ability to contest at the major points of conflict is being compromised by his eagerness to become involved in every skirmish.

4 December The Japanese fleet refuels at the limit of its range. The Emperor's declaration of war is read to all crews. Midget submarines are already in position ten miles south of Pearl Harbor with orders to enter the shipping channel and destroy torpedo nets and block any US fleet departure. In the event the submarines fail in this mission and do not return.

Advance on Moscow ends

5 December Faced with the imbalance of convoy performance in the Mediterranean, Hitler orders Kesselring's Luftflotte 2 from the Eastern Front to that region. He has also agreed that the drive on Moscow be halted and that the forces there regroup and await reinforcements of men and equipment.

Soviets counter-attack

6 December Along the full length of the Moscow sector the Soviets mount significant counter-attacks against the stalled German formations. These plans are led by their creator, Marshal Zhukov, who believes that he can cut through and isolate many of the German divisions. The Soviets have troops fresh to the battlefield and can boast some new tanks; the Germans are tired, frozen, ill-equipped and poorly fed. Furthermore, their once superior air power has evaporated, the winter weather having removed many aircraft from active service.

The disclosure that a Japanese agent in Honolulu has been asked to report on the dispositions of the US fleet there is disregarded in Washington because similar requests have been made for other sites. Japanese ships are now en route to Malaya and the Philippines.

7 December The decoding of the Japanese reply to Roosevelt's appeal to the Emperor to consider peace is completed; it is established that it is effectively a declaration of war. A comedy of errors and omissions follows as delay upon delay on this Sunday morning means that a warning message to the officials in Hawaii does not reach the HQ in Oahu until almost midday. Remarkably, the Japanese embassy in Washington is also blissfully unaware of the urgency with which it has to get the official reply into the hands of Secretary of State Cordell Hull; it does not reach him until 2.30 p.m., though he already knows its contents because of the successful decoding. The British are likewise kept from the news for another three hours until their ambassador in Tokyo is given a copy of the message, as is the US Ambassador.

Early in the morning the Japanese send a final air reconnaissance flight over the harbour and the carriers turn into the wind and increase speed.

Just before 8 a.m. the main base of the US Pacific Fleet at Pearl Harbor is taken completely by surprise by 184 Japanese aircraft from the six carriers *Akagi*, *Hiryu*, *Kaga*, *Shokaku*, *Soryu* and *Zuikaku*, racing in at low altitude. The aircraft include torpedo-bombers, dive-bombers, high-altitude bombers and fighters.

Pearl Harbor attacked

A second attack by 171 aircraft, mostly torpedo-bombers, follows. Although these attacks are very effective – all eight US battleships are hit and five sink, three cruisers and three destroyers are lost and 2,403 men killed and 1,178 injured – three US carriers that will play a major role in the approaching Pacific war are absent from the harbour, and Admiral Nagumo fails to send a third wave against the oil storage tanks which have yet to be hit. It may be that he thought the job had been done because the entire scene is obscured by dense smoke, and in fact eye-witnesses believe that the oil tanks at Hickam Field air base must have been hit so black is the cloud emanating from there.

The raid has been a triumph of secrecy; the Germans are as astonished by it as the Americans and British. An assessment of the action shows the air component to have performed superbly and its efficiency is a tribute to its commanders. The reluctance to send off a third strike, and the complete failure of the underwater mission are the only negative aspects of the operation in the Japanese view. The Americans have been caught cold when they should not have been; from the moment they knew that Japanese carriers were at sea they should have shown a greater level of alertness. Indications of the possibility of such an attack have been coming in practically daily, but this intelligence has not been correlated or updated on an hourly basis. Until the strike was a matter of hours away, Washington, Hawaii and other stations have all failed to read the signs that should have increased preparedness and given a chance of defence and retaliation. Whereas the Japanese do not appreciably assimilate all that could be learned from the episode, the Americans will uprate their intelligence services, enforce greater liaison between army and navy, protect their assets more effectively and put the entire might of their industrial capacity into top gear.

For this attack, in addition to the carriers, Nagumo had had in consort two battleships, two heavy cruisers, destroyers, tankers and other support ships. After the attack the Allies were left with three US carriers and two vulnerable British vessels at Singapore as their only capital ships in the region.

The mastermind of the audacious Pearl Harbor bombing, Admiral Yamamoto, retains his scepticism as to Japan's ability to win a war against the Americans, but Japan enters the conflict with considerable forces. The Army has 51 divisions, some of which have been active in China and Manchuria; the Navy has ten battleships, ten carriers, 36 cruisers, more than 100 destroyers and some 63 submarines. The airborne strength, carrier and other naval, plus the Army's, totals 2,500 combat aircraft. The national intention is to secure sufficient territory in Malaya and the East Indies to make the Japanese self-sufficient in raw materials, and of a geographical size that will bring regional power and international influence.

The military strategy Japan intends to pursue consists of an advance into Malaya and a move on to Singapore, the taking of Burma and the Philippines, and the seizure of Hong Kong, Guam, Wake and the Makin Islands. Later phases will include Borneo, Sumatra and Java. All this to be achieved before the USA can re-organise and re-equip its forces.

In concert with the attack on Pearl Harbor, the Japanese have already raided or bombed Guam, Wake and Midway.

A German news bureau report demonstrates the softening of resolve in the Moscow sector when it concedes that the weather is determining the progress of the war. It speaks of temperatures of 35° below zero and snow-storms, and complains that motor vehicles and weapons cannot function in such conditions.

Rommel pulls back

In North Africa, Rommel decides to forego further attempts to attack Tobruk and retires to the Gazala line. It is an orderly movement and he takes along some 9,000 prisoners.

Allies and USA declare war on Japan

8 December Great Britain and other Commonwealth and Allied nations join the USA in declaring war on Japan, though Roosevelt does not include Germany and other Axis nations in his announcement. China declares war on Japan, Germany and Italy.

Japanese attack Philippines

The Japanese mount air attacks in the Philippines and send a small force ashore on Bataan Island to take out the garrison there. The air raids knock out many American aircraft on the ground. The Japanese are confronted by General MacArthur and his mixed force of about 110,000 local troops and 20,000 Americans which is ill-equipped in terms of weapons and battle experience and is dispersed among various island garrisons. His plan to use his aircraft to delay the Japanese while he and his forces retreat into the Bataan Peninsula to await reinforcements is nullified by Pearl Harbor and the loss of so many of his own aircraft.

Japanese landings in Malaya and Thailand

Other Japanese landings have taken place in Kota Bharu, Malaya, and Singora and Patani in Thailand. British opposition, under General Percival, is limited to three divisions and some fortress troops and many of these are guarding other vulnerable sites. The RAF has more than 150 aircraft there, but a good number are lost on this first day.

The Japanese 38th Division attacks Hong Kong which is defended by a mere five British battalions and a few guns. General Maltby mounts some defensive actions to ease his retreat to a position at the neck of the Kowloon Peninsula.

The Japanese also begin air attacks on Wake Island and occupy Shanghai including the small US garrison.

Shanghai falls

HMSS *Prince of Wales* and *Repulse* sail from Singapore.

On the Eastern Front, Soviets forces are enjoying successes outside Moscow and in the Leningrad area. Hitler has ordered his troops to forego offensive action and regroup for defence.

In the Tobruk area Rommel is down to 40 tanks before his withdrawal. Now he is absent while Eighth Army regains communication with the fortress which has been besieged since April.

9 December The Soviets are now retaking towns around Moscow and Leningrad. The latter is still suffering the siege of the city; very few supplies have got through and many of the inhabitants are still dying.

The Japanese take Bangkok and land more troops in Malaya and Thailand.

HMSS *Prince of Wales* and *Repulse* turn away from Japanese landing sites in Malaysia when enemy aircraft are spotted; they have no British aircraft to protect them. They head for Kuantan after reports of Japanese landings there, on the assumption that the necessary fighter cover will be provided.

10 December The Japanese continue to make landings: they occupy Tarawa, Makin and Guam. They also mount air attacks on Luzon and the naval base and weapons store at Cavite. Landings follow on Aparri and Vigan. A small British force which has moved into Thailand finds a stronger than expected Japanese contingent facing it and its attack is not successful.

A Japanese submarine unsuccessfully attacks HMSS *Prince of Wales* and *Repulse*, but reports their position. Within hours the ships are bombed and sunk by 90 Japanese aircraft, which reduces British naval presence in the Pacific region to zero. More than 2,000 crew members of the ships are reported as having been rescued.

Prince of Wales and Repulse sunk

11 December Hitler declares war on the USA and, in doing so, effectively sacrifices any chance of winning his war. The USA responds by its own declaration against Germany and Italy, and Congress empowers its armed forces to operate anywhere in the world.

Hitler declares war on USA

In Russia Guderian is being forced back by the hour and many German units are beyond mounting any resistance.

Within minutes of the US declaration of war a Lockheed P-38 Lightning shoots down an Fw 200 Kondor over the Atlantic.

A force of 450 marines sink two Japanese destroyers during an attempted landing on Wake Island. The Japanese are forced to withdraw.

12 December The Philippines suffer further air attacks and 2,500 Japanese troops land south of Luzon.

After Pearl Harbor Roosevelt has told Churchill, 'We are all in the same boat now!' and the British premier sails the stormy Atlantic in HMS *Duke of York* for the Arcadia Conference with the President.

13 December Although Rommel is able to beat off British attacks around Gazala, he accepts that the position cannot be held and begins a difficult retreat to El Agheila.

British forces have to withdraw in Hong Kong and from the Victoria Point air base in Burma.

Two Italian fuel convoys bound for North Africa are intercepted and sunk by British and Dutch ships.

14 December The Italian battleship *Vittorio Veneto* is hit by a British submarine while protecting a Benghazi-bound convoy and two of the transports are sunk by a British submarine, causing the mission to be abandoned. The cruiser HMS *Galatea* is sunk by *U557*.

Convoy HG-76 sails from Gibraltar to the UK, covered by the carrier HMS *Audacity* and twelve other escorts. The group will be attacked by twelve U-boats but will sink five and bring down two German bombers; the carrier, however, will be lost as well as a destroyer and two of the merchantmen.

15 December Soviet counter-attacks retake Klin and Kalinin north-west of Moscow.

Japanese efforts to land a force on Hong Kong island are repulsed.

16 December Japanese forces land at three points in Burma and set fire to oil stores; the British and Dutch forces withdraw.

British forces also retreat from Penang as many additional Japanese forces land in Malaya. A series of delaying actions are fought as the withdrawal continues to Gurun and south of the river Perak.

The Italians begin another convoy to North Africa with a cover of four battleships, five cruisers and 21 destroyers; Admiral Iachino is in command.

17 December The Germans begin their attacks on Sevastopol as if ignorant of the turn of the tide in other Eastern Front sectors.

Following the Pearl Harbor fiasco Admiral Kimmel is replaced as CinC, US Pacific Fleet by Admiral Nimitz.

Reuters reports the British Governor of Singapore as stating that 'further unpleasant surprises may still lie in store; but it is certain that Singapore will not fall to the Japanese'.

In the Mediterranean the First Battle of Sirte is fought when Iachino's convoy encounters an Allied convoy to Malta protected by Force K warships from Malta and Admiral Vian's Force B from Alexandria. The commanders concentrate on covering the merchantmen entrusted to them so the initial skirmishes do not amount to much.

The cruiser HMS *Dunedin* is sunk by a U-boat in the Atlantic.

18 December Having lost a cruiser and a destroyer to mines and the other cruiser damaged, the British convoy arrives at Malta, and the Force K ships leave to look for Iachino's convoy. In the harbour at Alexandria three Italian midget submarines slip through the open net defences and cripple the battleships HMSS *Queen Elizabeth* and *Valiant*. Both vessels settle in the shallow water.

Queen Elizabeth and *Valiant* crippled

19 December Hitler reacts to the dire news from the Eastern Front by assuming the role of CinC of the Army. His treatment of skilled battlefield generals has always been dismissive and from now on their views will not be solicited and seldom listened to. His strategy for the Eastern Front will be modest withdrawals to defensive positions that can be supplied by the Luftwaffe. He will use the perceived failure of traditional military minds to strengthen the activities of the Waffen SS which will lead to deprivations for the main army units.

The Japanese finally achieve positions on Hong Kong island.

20 December The Germans at home see evidence of the setbacks on the Eastern Front when Goebbels makes a public appeal for winter clothing. Now, even the offensive-minded Guderian is retreating with his Second Panzer Army.

Admiral King is appointed CinC, US Fleet. Although Washington-based, he will have a major impact on the war through his ready acknowledgement of the value of naval aviation and his support for the 'Europe First' strategy despite his pressing concern for the Pacific theatre.

22 December Churchill, Roosevelt and their principal advisers meet in Washington to confirm the plan to defeat Germany first and establish a command structure which will get the best out of the combined forces of the Allies. More US forces will be based in the UK and the bombing offensive against Germany will continue.

Wake Island is again bombarded from the air and a larger invasion mounted. Some 200 men do get ashore and after a fierce battle with the garrison, they will secure a surrender. The reinforcement unit en route to the island is still some distance away when it falls.

23 December In North Africa the Axis forces hurriedly leave Benghazi.

Axis evacuate Benghazi

The Japanese land in Sarawak and mount the first air attacks on Rangoon

24 December A major Japanese initiative sees a landing of some 7,000 men near Luzon in the Philippines. MacArthur has formed his forces into defensive lines to the north, but now knows that the reinforcements, which were part of his plan, will not arrive in time to support him.

25 December Both Guderian and Hoepner are so depleted of heavy armour that they cannot resist the Soviet offensives; their unheeded pleas for more men and equipment fuel a dispute with Hitler and Guderian is relieved of his command and sent back to Germany. It is shabby treatment for one who, in the advance at least, has proved himself a masterful battlefield leader.

Hong Kong falls to the Japanese.

Hong Kong falls

Axis forces continue
withdrawal in North
Africa

MacArthur's forces face an attack on their positions by the River Agno.

The Axis forces continue their withdrawal in North Africa as the Allies reach Benghazi and Agedabia.

26 December The situation in the Crimea is one of mixed fortunes. Whilst the Germans continue to batter Sevastopol there are surprise Soviet landings at Kerch which threaten German Eleventh Army positions.

A force of 260 British Commandos lands in the Lofoten Islands to destroy the fish-oil factories there

27 December Another 600 Commandos land elsewhere in the Lofotens to destroy radio installations and capture or sink various merchant ships and patrol craft.

28 December The Germans gain ground in their battle for Sevastopol and anticipate taking the city within days.

In North Africa 22nd Armoured Brigade suffers serious losses as the Germans turn and fight.

29 December German Eleventh Army has to break off at Sevastopol to tackle the increased Soviet landings in the Crimea. The expected capture of Sevastopol is delayed.

The Reuters agency in Singapore issues a report stating: 'The Japanese are launching a three-pronged attack against Singapore ... Japanese troops have all received special training in jungle warfare.'

American forces in
the Philippines retreat
to the Bataan
Peninsula

30 December The retreating American forces in the Philippines are now at their last defensive line on the Bataan Peninsula. It is imperative that this position be held so that reinforcements can come through Manila to Bataan.

31 December On the Eastern Front as the year draws to a close, the Soviets are undoubtedly in the ascendant even though their losses so far would have been catastrophic for any other national force. Apart from *matériel*, including some 20,000 tanks and 30,000 guns, the human cost has been huge; more than five million casualties and three million taken prisoner. The Germans have been held and then driven back by Soviet resolve aided by the climate, and will take time to regain fighting spirit and battle-field strength. The ravages suffered by both sides means that neither is yet in a state to dominate to the point of final victory, but of the two national leaders Hitler is surely the most damaged. He has fallen short of Moscow, just as Napoleon had before him, and must now see that the glittering prizes of Great Britain and the USSR have both eluded him, though he will continue to speak of ultimate success.

In North Africa, Rommel is back where he began his first advance, at Mersa-el-Brega on the Gulf of Sirte. Cyrenaica is re-occupied by the British but both sides are aware that this can only be a temporary state of affairs while Rommel has the spirit, firepower and personnel for the fight. He certainly has superior tanks at this point, though the Allies have a greater number, but he is fighting with minimal supplies and captured *matériel*.

1942

JANUARY 1942

1 January Twenty-six nations agree to combine their resources to defeat the Axis powers and hold a united line against any alliances or peace moves proposed by this common enemy. The Arcadia Conference at Washington sows the seeds of what will become the United Nations.

Germans cut off in Crimea

In the Crimea the Kerch Peninsula is cut off by Soviet forces despite their lack of air cover, which makes this action costly in casualties.

2 January In North Africa the Bardia garrison falls to the Allies

Units of Japanese 48th Division occupy Manila and MacArthur's forces set a defensive line along the route into the Bataan Peninsula; some leave for Corregidor.

4 January Air attacks from new Japanese bases in Thailand pressure 11th Indian Division which is seeking to hold its line on the river Slim in Malaya

5 January Marshal Zhukov finds himself suffering from the same interference from above as is being inflicted on his German counterparts when Stalin overrides his wishes and insists on an all-out offensive against German Army Group Centre. The early achievements this brings will cover up the sparse resources Zhukov has at his disposal.

6 January The British advance in North Africa reaches Mersa Brega and El Agheila

7 January President Roosevelt proposes a budget which will fund the production of 125,000 aircraft, 75,000 tanks, 35,000 guns and 8 million tons of shipping by the end of 1943.

The 11th Indian Division is badly mauled by Japanese tanks and infantry in Malaya.

8 January Wavell, again finding himself at a fighting front with limited resources and an impossible remit, orders a withdrawal to defensible positions south of the river Muar in Malaya.

9 January West and north-west of Moscow there is fierce fighting between the advancing Volkhov and Kalinin Fronts and the desperate German forces.

In the Philippines MacArthur's defensive line in the Bataan Peninsula comes under pressure.

Japanese enter Dutch East Indies

11 January The Japanese move into the Dutch East Indies with a triple advance strategy which will take in Borneo, Sarawak, Sumatra and Java, and Bali and Timor. The Japanese plan to move from island to island, knocking out enemy aircraft on the ground and then delivering seaborne troops who will make good the airfield, or build a new one, ready for flights to the next objective. The landing at Manado in Celebes is reinforced by paratroops and marks the first airborne operation in the Pacific.

The US carrier *Saratoga* is attacked by Japanese submarine *I6* close to Hawaii.

12 January The Australian divisions fighting in North Africa are to be moved closer to home to counter the Japanese threat, and 7th Armoured Brigade is also to vacate the North African theatre. Rommel, emboldened by the arrival of some new tanks, is planning a counter-offensive.

Kuala Lumpur is occupied by the Japanese.

A US steamer is sunk by *U123* off New York. The U-boats operating off the east coast of America enjoy what amounts to peacetime conditions; neither shipping nor coastal towns are blacked-out, buoys are lit, and there are no sophisticated anti-submarine defences in place.

13 January The Japanese inflict damage on the American/Filipino defences on the east side of the Bataan Peninsula.

U-boats of the larger, 740-ton design, are now operating off the USA's eastern seaboard and gain early successes against the shipping there which is, at this time, unused to the militant threat and the counter-measures required to combat it. There is some dispute between British and American naval officials about the absence of convoy protection which the British believe is a proven case.

15 January The Japanese move into Burma.

16 January In Russia the dismissal of Field Marshal von Leeb from command of Army Group North means that all three leaders of the main battle formations have been sacrificed, together with more than thirty other senior ranks. It is the price they pay for not achieving the final goal of Operation 'Barbarossa' and of showing what Hitler perceives to be timidity in the face of Soviet counter-attacks.

An American press agency in Washington reports that: 'It seems certain that the submarines cruising off the port of New York are German.'

17 January The isolated German garrison at Halfaya finally falls and more than five thousand German and Italian troops are captured.

The first U-boat attack on an Arctic convoy sees a destroyer and a merchantman sunk by *U454*.

18 January The Soviet counter-offensives are enjoying success in the region around the Sea of Azov and in the central sector where the Germans have been pushed back to within 60 miles of Smolensk. There is still some success for the German moves in the Crimea. The plight of many German units keeps the Luftwaffe in the air as a supply source rather than as an attacking force; it also keeps more aircraft in this region than is desired and deprives other theatres of air support.

19 January Fierce close-quarter fighting and Soviet paratroop drops see the recapture of towns in the central sector and the retreating Germans having to protect their rear positions because of partisan sniping attacks stimulated by the airborne deployments.

20 January At the Wannsee Conference in Berlin, Heydrich presents his plan to Hitler for his 'Final Solution' which will see all European Jews sent to extermination camps. The department of the SS which will

Japanese invade Burma

Soviet counter-offensives

99

implement the plan, which the Führer approves, is headed by Adolf Eichmann.

Rommel's attacks again

21 January The topsy-turvy nature of the war in North Africa is demonstrated by Rommel's new offensives there which puts the over-extended British forward bases on the coast and inland under immediate pressure. A reduction of RAF and Royal Navy activity in the Mediterranean has enabled more Axis convoys to reach their North African ports. The island of Malta is suffering almost daily bombardment by the Luftwaffe.

The Japanese increase their air raids on Singapore where their Zero fighters are proving very capable. Farther north, Allied forces are driven into retreat south of the river Muar.

General Joseph 'Vinegar Joe' Stilwell is appointed Chief of Staff to Chiang Kai-shek.

22 January Hitler tells Admiral Fricke, chief of German Naval High Command, that Norway is a vital war zone and that he is to deploy twelve of the newest Type VII U-boats against any Allied invasion. This prevents Dönitz from deploying them in US waters.

23 January The Japanese land in New Britain, Borneo, New Ireland and the Solomons.

British reconnaissance flights identify the battleship *Tirpitz* at anchor in Aasfiord, fifteen miles east of Trondheim. This will cause the British to be cautious about the number of convoys allowed on the Arctic route east from Iceland at any one time.

25 January Rommel's rapid advance in North Africa continues with a significant mauling of British 2nd Armoured Brigade near Msus.

British withdraw to Singapore.

In Malaya Wavell approves a withdrawal of the British forces to Singapore.

26 January The first permanent bases for American troops in the UK are established.

27 January Soviet forces have now pushed Army Group South back into the Ukraine and threaten its main supply base.

Rommel retakes Benghazi

29 January Rommel retakes Benghazi and moves on around the coast, pushing the British back to the Gazala Line, a chain of substantial field emplacements west of Tobruk. .

30 January US positions on the Bataan Peninsula are under increasing threat and the Japanese make amphibious landings in the area.

FEBRUARY 1942

1 February Vidkun Quisling is appointed head of the Germans' puppet government in Norway.

In North Africa the Allied forces have to withdraw from Gazala; Derna will follow within two days.

US naval forces, under the command of Admirals William 'Bull' Halsey and Frank Fletcher attack Japanese naval bases in the Marshall and Gilbert Islands.

The Hydra cipher key, used by U-boats in their coded messages, is replaced by Triton; there is also a more advanced Enigma M 4 machine in operation. The British cryptanalysts will not succeed in cracking parts of the Triton key before the end of the year.

4 February General Percival, now in Singapore with his troops from Malaya, and Wavell reject Japanese urgings to surrender. They hope continuing reinforcements will be sufficient to hold the Japanese while other units can be brought from elsewhere.

7 February In a brief, speedy move, typical of his career to date, Rommel reaches Gazala after having reclaimed most of the territory he had lost to the British. The British 1st Armoured Division has been worst affected but the morale of Eighth Army and its officers has been dented. Considering the imbalance of convoy supplies during the previous twelve months, the Germans have performed admirably in this rapid action. *Rommel reaches Gazala*

8 February The Japanese make a night landing in the north-west of Singapore island.

The German armaments minister Fritz Todt is killed in an air crash and is succeeded by Albert Speer who quickly galvanises tank production in particular.

10 February Allied troops at Singapore are misdirected to a defensive line deeper than necessary while the Japanese gain a foothold on the island.

11 February They try a last counter-attack but heavy losses force them to withdraw to the outskirts of Singapore city.

Hitler's belief that the Allies are planning to invade Norway becomes a phobia; he must have every available warship to prevent it. He tells Raeder that if *Scharnhorst* and *Gneisenau* cannot be made ready he will use their guns as coastal artillery. Much to his disgust the battlecruisers have been besieged in Brest harbour for almost a year. They now make a run for a home port in a daring race up the English Channel, escorted by well over 100 assorted vessels, from destroyers to torpedo-boats, with air cover from more than 170 fighters. *The Channel Dash*

12 February The Channel Dash is not detected by the Allies until mid-morning by which time they have already passed Le Touquet. The British fail to stop the ships, but *Scharnhorst* is severely damaged by a mine at the mouth of the Scheldt, and *Gneisenau* has been damaged by shellfire and will have to be docked when she arrives home; there she will be crippled by a bombing raid. The embarrassment this German move causes the Allies is offset by the fact that it is easier for them to control the movements of these ships when they are in German ports. The Dash is successful because of the failure of Allied coastal radar to locate them; this, in turn, is caused by German radar jamming equipment of whose existence the British are as yet unaware.

101

Soviet attacks slowed

13 February On the Eastern Front the Germans are receiving reinforcements and more consistent supplies, and Soviet attacks are being slowed.

A message from General Percival to Wavell reports: 'Enemy within 5,000 yards of the front, which brings the whole of Singapore within field artillery range ... would you consider giving me wider discretionary power?'

14 February Wavell's reply urges him to maintain the toughest possible defence and ends: 'Fully appreciate your situation, but continued action is essential.'

The controversial Area Bombing Directive to RAF Bomber Command requires attacks to be directed at damaging 'the morale of the enemy civilian population and, in particular, of the industrial workers'. In effect this reduces the requirement for bombing accuracy and asserts that public support for the war effort will diminish if personal property as well as the place of work is hit.

Singapore surrenders

15 February General Percival surrenders Singapore to General Yamashita to bring to an end a very sorry episode for the British. They have lost 138,000 men to their opponents' count of fewer than ten thousand. The Japanese have been better led, have shown astute fighting tactics and completed in two months what they expected would take three. The British have been left short of numbers, equipment and air support.

16 February U-boats are active in the Caribbean, shelling shore installations and sinking oil tankers.

19 February General Gamelin and former prime ministers Reynaud and Blum are put on trial by the Vichy French; the trial is never concluded because the defence arguments turn the heat on the Vichy authorities to a degree which prompts them to abandon the case.

The German press is criticised by the Reich Press Secretary for publishing stories about Churchill which are too positive and may cause the German population to believe in his leadership. It is urged to stress that he is a liar and is conducting the war like an amateur.

Japanese carrier aircraft attack the northern Australian port of Darwin. Japanese forces land on Bali

21 February A Japanese news agency reports that 200 tanks and 10,000 motor vehicles have been captured in the occupation of Singapore.

22 February Air Marshal Arthur Harris is appointed chief of RAF Bomber Command. Never a supporter of precision bombing, 'Bomber' Harris will resuscitate the bomber crews' morale and use the force to 'invade' Germany until ground forces can go on the counter-attack in Europe later in the war.

MacArthur is ordered to leave the Philippines and will do so within a few weeks.

24 February Increased airborne supplies to the German forces on the

Eastern Front enable them to delay the Soviet advance and defend their positions for longer periods.

Admiral Halsey in the carrier *Enterprise* leads a US force to attack Wake Island.

27 February An Allied fleet of five cruisers and eleven destroyers from four nations attempts an interception of a Japanese invasion force heading for Java and, in the Battle of the Java Sea, is severely mauled. The Japanese deploy their torpedoes effectively and their ships are scarcely damaged; their mission is delayed by only 24 hours and the Allies lose two cruisers and three destroyers. — Battle of the Java Sea

28 February British Commandos, who include a radar scientist among their number, drop by night on a radar installation at Bruneval near the French Channel coast. Under his direction the vital components are dismantled and taken off by waiting boats. This, the most important British airborne raid of the war to date, causes the Germans to fortify other installations in such a manner as to make them readily identifiable.

In North Africa the British are using the lull to bring in *matériel*, chiefly more effective anti-tank guns. They still have fewer troops than the Axis divisions but have more tanks and artillery. — Lull in North Africa

MARCH 1942

1 March The US begins an internment programme for Japanese-Americans.

In the Crimea the Soviet forces now begin to match their colleagues in other theatres; the Germans are now being pushed back everywhere.

U-boat operations off the US eastern seaboard increase; two-thirds of the U-boat strength is deployed in the Atlantic, much of it targeting US merchant shipping.

The Japanese make three landings on Java meeting little opposition.

2 March In the north of Burma the Chinese forces begin to feel the pressure of an all-out Japanese push. The 'Flying Tigers', a tiny force of veteran air volunteers under the command of retired American officer Claire Chennault, do their best to support the defence of Rangoon but now retreat to an RAF base at Magwe.

6 March Within hours of arriving in Rangoon to organise counter-attacks against the Japanese, General Alexander sees the first attempts fail and is obliged to order the evacuation of the city. — Rangoon evacuated

The battleship *Tirpitz* leaves Trondheim with three destroyers to mount her first raid against merchant shipping. Her nearest targets, Convoys PQ-12 and QP-8, do not spot the battleship because of bad weather.

7 March Having been forced to quit Rangoon, Burma's only seaport of any size, the Allies will now have to obtain supplies via the overland route from India.

The Japanese land in New Guinea.

A Reuters report in Malta claims that the Axis air raids since Christmas 1941 have killed 300 people and destroyed 4,000 houses.

9 March The Dutch authorities in Java have been evacuated and General Ter Poorten surrenders with 100,000 Allied troops.

10 March The US carriers *Yorktown* and *Lexington* arrive off New Guinea to send aircraft against Japanese naval units in the area.

MacArthur leaves Philippines

11 March General MacArthur finally leaves the Philippines with the celebrated assurance: 'I shall return.'

12 March The Japanese are now firmly in control in the Solomon Islands but US presence in the Pacific is growing daily; US troops land in New Caledonia to construct a base there.

15 March In a Memorial Day address, Hitler assures his listeners that the Soviet Army will be destroyed by the summer of 1942. No mention is made of the failure to reach Moscow or of the Soviet counter-attacks since then.

19 March General Slim arrives in Burma to take command of the British forces there.

22 March The Italian battleship *Littorio* and a significant fleet of cruisers and destroyers is sent to attack a Malta convoy which, because of the demands for warships in the Far East, is only protected by five light cruisers and seventeen destroyers.

The Italians fail to take advantage of their superior strength and only German and Italian air attacks can damage the merchant ships. The convoy finally reaches Malta but with little of its cargo intact.

Operation 'Ironclad'

23 March Because of Churchill's fear that the island of Madagascar could become something of a 'halfway house' between the Japanese in the Indian Ocean and the Axis powers in the Middle East, he mounts Operation 'Ironclad', aimed at occupying that island.

24 March The Japanese are well north of Rangoon now as Alexander and Chiang Kai-shek meet to discuss liaison between their forces.

US positions on Bataan and Corregidor come under attack.

27 March The RAF and the American volunteer aviators are forced to leave Burma.

British Commandos raid St-Nazaire

28 March The strategically important port of St-Nazaire has its dock gates damaged in a raid by British Commandos whose mission is to render the port unusable for the battleship *Tirpitz*. Most of those taking part in the mission are killed or taken prisoner, but the success of the attack is guaranteed when the old destroyer HMS *Campbeltown*, loaded with explosives, rams the gates and later explodes alongside them.

29 March RAF Bomber Command is now receiving the new Lancaster bomber and it is used on a bombing raid on Lübeck. The success of the mission will stir Hitler to order reprisals.

The presence of *Tirpitz* in Norwegian waters, together with other large German ships, will now begin to exercise the minds of the British Admiralty to a remarkable degree.

APRIL 1942

1 April The remaining American and Filipino forces on the Bataan Peninsula come under heavy attack from the Japanese. The defenders are short of food and military supplies

In Burma, the Chinese are retreating north of Toungoo, which is already in Japanese hands, and the British are struggling to hold Prome and will have to leave it within 24 hours.

3 April The Japanese bomb Mandalay north of the British/Chinese retreat through Burma.

A renewed Japanese bombardment of US defensive positions on the Bataan Peninsula causes a withdrawal.

4 April A reconnaissance flight over the Indian Ocean sights a major Japanese naval force. It includes their main carrier strength and four battleships and is far too powerful to be engaged by the meagre forces available to Admiral Somerville in Ceylon. He orders his remaining ships to disperse from the port of Colombo.

5 April Hitler issues a Directive ordering a German offensive along the southern sector of the Eastern Front. He believes that he can still capture the oilfields of the Caucasus and move on to fulfil the expressed aim of joining up with the Japanese expansion through Asia.

Unaware of the British ships' departure, the Japanese fleet deploys 130 aircraft against Colombo. Only later do their recce aircraft locate the heavy cruisers HMSS *Dorsetshire* and *Cornwall* which are hunted down and sunk. *Dorsetshire and* Other vessels escape detection for the moment. Alongside this operation, *Cornwall* sunk the Japanese are also in the Bay of Bengal where Vice-Admiral Ozawa leads his Malaya group against merchant shipping to claim 23 British vessels in just four days.

US Naval Task Force 39 arrives at Scapa Flow to support British action around home waters and in the Mediterranean.

6 April The smaller vessels which fled Colombo during the Japanese attack are gradually located by a second Japanese unit and clinically destroyed.

7 April The Japanese forces in Burma are strengthened by the arrival of their 18th Infantry Division from Singapore.

Resistance on the Bataan Peninsula finally comes to an end. Resistance on the

8 April Reuters Press Agency in Valletta report the 2,000th bombing raid Bataan Peninsula ends on Malta. This coincides with a fresh airborne offensive by the Axis air forces which have been instructed to so damage the island that it becomes ripe for invasion. While this ultimate result is not achieved, the raids do delay the vital convoy runs from the island to North Africa. Shortly, however, Rommel's demand for air support for his push to the Nile will take the aircraft away from the island raids when they are close to success. This makes Rommel's own decision a major factor in his own downfall because the Malta-based forces are able to inflict renewed damage on his forces and the convoys heading for them; it also removes the chance of the bombardment of Malta being followed by an invasion.

9 April In Ceylon the Japanese attack the east coast port of Trincomalee and the carrier HMS *Hermes* is sunk. At this point the Japanese Navy and its air element are suggesting an invincibility but this has yet to be severely tested.

Hermes sunk

A total of 75,000 men are taken prisoner with the collapse of the Bataan positions; 12,000 of them are American. The march they are now required to make, first to San Fernando some 100 miles away, will see many die of sickness or ill-treatment.

In Burma the British are anxious to begin offensive action against the Japanese, but the latter are benefiting from the faster arrival of reinforcements and the fact that the new men have had successful combat experience elsewhere.

10 April Having achieved many of their aims in the Indian Ocean, the Japanese units there begin to return to the Pacific. The British Far East Fleet withdraws to the Persian Gulf to lick its wounds.

13 April The British are forced to move to new positions in Burma and the Chinese Army is diverted west to Mandalay.

U252 is sunk by the corvette HMS *Vetch* and the sloop HMS *Stork*, marking the first success for the new 10cm type 271 radar equipment.

14 April The still retreating British begin to destroy oil installations to deny them to the Japanese.

On the Eastern Front, the commander of Soviet 33rd Army commits suicide after his and other Red Army formations are annihilated by the encircling Germans south-east of Vyazma.

The US destroyer *Roper* sinks *U85*.

16 April King George VI awards the island of Malta the George Cross to mark the fortitude and resilience of its people against the continued Axis attacks and shortage of supplies.

17 April In Burma the Japanese have reached Yenangyaung. The capture of this strategic town and its control of a major route to the north, further isolates units of 1st Burma Division to the south. Elsewhere in the country Chinese forces remain under pressure from advanced Japanese units.

18 April Action along most of the Eastern Front comes to a halt as the winter ends and the terrain reverts to spring mud. The Germans use the break to re-equip.

The Japanese clear their path towards Lashio in northern Burma after destroying the Chinese 55th Division.

Doolittle raid

Japan is bombed. Sixteen B-25 bombers, flying under the command of Colonel James Doolittle from the US carrier *Hornet*, raid Tokyo and other military and civilian sites. The immediate results of the raids are minimal, but the influence on morale and future tactics is immense. Not only do the

US pilots break new ground by flying these bomber aircraft from a carrier, and in rough seas, but they also begin the flight knowing that they will not be able to return to the ship but have to fly on to land in China. From the point where it believes in its invincibility, the Japanese nation suddenly becomes paranoid about its vulnerability and the military hierarchy over-reacts by bringing back fighter aircraft needed at the fronts to defend home positions. In doing so they severely weaken themselves for forth-coming Pacific battles where fighter cover is lacking. The B-25 mission has been risky; the take-off of bomb-laden aircraft is dangerous, and at best they will be landing in strange territory. Poor weather will mean that some crews will have to parachute; of these five will die in the attempt and eight will be captured.

21 April Improving air supply on the Eastern Front is building up German resources ready for a stronger defence of the territory gained the previous year. It will prevent troops from being cut off by the uneven advance of Soviet forces.

23 April Some British forces are building a defensive position at Meiktila in Burma, but other units are being driven back in the Irrawaddy and Sittang valleys.

British forces driven back in Burma

24 April The first of Hitler's reprisal raids for the bombing of Lübeck sees Exeter attacked.

25 April The defensive position at Meiktila is quickly abandoned on instructions from General Alexander. The Japanese sacrifice Taunggyi to the Chinese but are still driving north towards Lashio.

Further reprisal raids by German bombers hit Bath. They will return to Exeter and freshly hit York, Hull and Norwich during the coming days.

29 April In the Philippines Japanese reinforcements land on Mindanao and attacks against the Filipino garrison increase in intensity; the bombardment of Corregidor continues.

In Burma the Japanese enter Lashio, having completed their advance – across inhospitable terrain and under constant attack from the defending British and Chinese – in fourteen weeks. With the fall of Lashio, the Allies have to open their first major air bridge, from Assam to Kunming in China, so as to maintain supplies to British and Chinese troops; this is a 530-mile route across the Himalayas which becomes known as 'the Hump.'

MAY 1942

1 May Mandalay falls to the Japanese.

Mandalay falls

2 May Their policy now will be to move on from New Guinea and gain a foothold in Papua by capturing Port Moresby with a naval force from Rabaul in New Britain. But the Americans are intercepting Japanese radio messages and deciphering them, and Admiral Nimitz concentrates a stronger force than the Japanese have anticipated. The resultant confrontation will become the Battle of the Coral Sea.

4 May Aircraft from the US carrier *Yorktown* attack a Japanese seaplane base at Tulagi in the Solomons.

Madagascar invaded

5 May In Operation 'Ironclad', British forces land in Madagascar.

The Japanese bombardment of Corregidor has rendered much of the island's defences untenable, but the Japanese landing there suffer heavy losses before consolidating their positions.

Marshal Timoshenko leads the Soviet South-west Front in a major drive from its bridgehead on the river Donets in an attempt to take Kharkov.

In the Burma theatre, Japanese forces have reached the Chinese border and crossed it.

Corregidor surrenders

6 May The brave defence of Corregidor ends with the surrender of 15,000 US and Filipino troops.

Stalin sends a telegram to Churchill begging him to find enough ships to escort desperately needed supplies which are currently languishing in Iceland. He says 'some ninety steamers' are there. On 9 May he receives assurances from Churchill, but is told that the threat of *Tirpitz* and other ships based at Trondheim is the reason for caution.

Battle of the Coral Sea

7 May The Battle of the Coral Sea develops as a US naval force is sent to attack the Japanese troopships heading for Port Moresby. The Japanese fly land-based aircraft against this mission without great success, but they do locate and sink the US destroyer *Sims* and the tanker *Neosho*, which they mistakenly identify as a carrier. A later sortie of Japanese aircraft proves disastrous; they fail to find the US carriers and, in a state of remarkable confusion, lose 21 aircraft and are so lacking in informed leadership that some of the aircraft attempt to land on *Yorktown*.

Serious fighting between British and French troops in Madagascar ends with the former in control of the island. Sporadic fighting continues for some months, but the securing of the island is later referred to by Churchill as news arriving 'at a time when we sorely needed success'.

8 May A move by von Manstein's Eleventh Army aims at breaking the Soviet forces on the Crimean front.

In the Coral Sea, although the opposing battle fleets never come into visual contact, they are now well aware of each other's position thanks to aerial reconnaissance and the deciphering of coded radio messages. The opposing carriers sortie their aircraft. Japanese aircraft cripple *Lexington* and badly damage *Yorktown*; the Japanese carrier *Shokaku* is also hit hard. Japanese aircraft losses are greater and they do not have a large pool of replacement pilots. The Japanese fleet heading for Port Moresby has to abandon its plan and, still unseen by the US carriers, heads back whence it came. It is the first major reversal for the Japanese in their advance across the Pacific.

11 May A flight of élite German pilots based in Crete sinks three British destroyers in the Mediterranean.

12 May The Soviets counter-attack near Kharkov in an attempt to force the Germans into a narrow front north of the Sea of Azov.

13 May The Germans have some success in the Crimea when they force the Soviets to withdraw from the Kerch Peninsula in the east.

14 May US code-breakers are now decrypting messages between Japanese commanders that indicate a planned offensive against the island of Midway.

15 May The exhausted British troops who have retreated through Burma cross into India. They have lost two-thirds of their original forces. The Japanese have occupied Burma before the onset of the monsoon with a combination of skilled tactics, clear strategy and excellent air support.

On the Eastern Front not all the Russians escape the German capture of Kerch; 170,000 are taken prisoner; the remainder have escaped to the Taman Peninsula. German Eleventh Army can now concentrate on attacking the prime target of Sevastopol.

17 May An indication that they have taken note of the historical significance of their failure to take Moscow comes from the German hierarchy through an article by Josef Goebbels, which points out that while Napoleon's army had to contend with temperatures of minus 25°, forces of the Third Reich have had to endure temperatures of minus 50°.

Timoshenko's drive towards Kharkov is countered by First Panzer and Seventeenth Armies.

19 May The Germans counter extensive Soviet attacks near Kharkov with one of their own.

23 May On the Eastern Front the tide turns again, some Soviet units that have crossed the Donets becoming encircled by the Germans.

25 May The Japanese begin moves against the Aleutian Islands to divert the Americans from the Midway arena. But they are basing their tactics on faulty intelligence which suggests that *Yorktown* is still out of commission (in fact she has returned to Pearl Harbor and been repaired in two days) and that other carriers are too far away to have any influence.

26 May In North Africa the reinforced British positions at Gazala come under attack during a new offensive by Rommel. Not only do the Allied troops outnumber the combined German and Italian forces, but they can now boast superior firepower including the US Grant and Lee tanks which fire high-explosive shells. The Germans have good numbers of tanks but lack essential levels of infantry support; even so, they push the Allies back. The 50-mile length of the Gazala Line defences is expected to force Rommel to attack via the coastal route, but, in typical maverick fashion, he attempts an inland drive which aims to move around the south of the line.

Nagumo's fleet leaves for its Midway mission with four carriers plus battleships, cruisers and destroyers. Midway atoll is just five miles long; a tiny scrap of land for so great an effort.

27 May Japanese transports carrying 500 troops leave Guam and Saipan with the Midway invasion force.

Nazi terror chief Reinhard Heydrich is fatally wounded in an assassination attempt by Czech resistance personnel in Prague. He will die on 4 June and reprisals will be launched against the town which has harboured his killers.

Heavy losses are suffered by both sides in North Africa where a section of the Afrika Korps engages British 4th Armoured Brigade and 3rd Indian Motorised Brigade, north-east of Bir Hacheim. The Axis forces are now seriously short of fuel and water.

Convoy PQ-16 to Russia is attacked by Ju 88s and He 111s and loses seven freighters. Worse damage will be prevented by the skill of Russian pilots who drive off attackers as the ships near their destination.

28 May Rommel's forces lose cohesion when, short of supplies, some units stop to wait for replenishment while others struggle on.

The Soviet push for Kharkov ends with a German strike against the large forces seeking to liberate the city. More than 200,000 prisoners are taken.

Yamamoto's plan for Midway is a quick, fierce bombardment of its defences followed by action against the US fleet which, he believes, will be sent to defend it. He is sure that he will be best positioned and better equipped for this battle, but his entire plan is based on the initial advantage he will gain in taking the Americans by surprise. But the US fleet, of course, is well aware of his movements and Task Force 16 sets sail from Oahu with the carriers *Enterprise* and *Hornet*, followed shortly by Task Force 17 led by the patched-up *Yorktown*.

29 May Rommel regroups his forces personally but chooses to call a pause in the action, bringing his armour within an unorthodox defensive position, the 'Cauldron', east of the minefields. At this juncture he seems to be inviting the Allies to make the next move.

The Soviets lose 250,000 men to German encirclement west of the Donets. They have made brief rushes against German forces they believe to be small and poorly equipped, thereby leaving themselves open to the superior field intelligence and tactics of the opposition.

30 May The Japanese have sent four submarines to patrol the waters outside Pearl Harbor to delay US intervention at Midway, but the ships have already left.

In Harris' most dramatic stroke since assuming control of RAF Bomber Command, more than 1,000 bombers raid Cologne. Following criticism at home that the bombing war was bringing no obvious rewards, he has brought out every serviceable aircraft and uses pupils and instructors among the air crew. Only 40 aircraft are lost and the Germans' morale receives a severe blow; their most sophisticated radar warning system has a flaw – it cannot cope with massed aircraft formations.

31 May Japanese midget submarines are released from their transports off the south-east coast of Australia in order to raid Sydney Harbour. No operational naval vessel is hit; none of the midgets return. This is as far south as the Japanese Navy will get during the war.

Japanese midget submarines raid Sydney Harbour

JUNE 1942

1 June The US build-up for Midway includes the positioning of 25 submarines in the area.

The RAF follows the Cologne raid with one by 1,036 bombers on Essen.

2 June French troops perform well to delay Rommel's 90th Light and Trieste Divisions at Bir Hacheim.

The Germans add their new heavy 'super' artillery – the Karl mortar and the 80cm Dora gun – to the bombardment of Sevastopol. If they can take this city it may lead to a reversal of the trends on the Eastern Front.

The carrier attack on the Aleutians comes as no surprise to the Americans, who are not distracted by it as the Japanese intend. Their carrier groups have now joined up north-east of Midway; they bring more than 250 aircraft to the battle and so match the Japanese in the air.

3 June Reconnaissance flights from Midway locate the Japanese invasion fleet and a flight of B-17s is sent to attack it. The move is unsuccessful, but the Japanese are encouraged to believe that this could be the full level of US defence.

4 June As their submarines are still committed to the seas between Pearl Harbor and Midway in the belief that US carriers have not yet left port, the Japanese send an attack force of 108 aircraft to Midway. Defending US fighters sent to intercept are badly beaten, but the Japanese raid falls short of their own expectations and a second flight is called. The US carriers locate Nagumo's ships at dawn and send in their first strike just as the second Japanese strike force is being prepared. The Japanese commander, knowing now that US carriers are in the area, is in a quandary; his flight decks are crammed with aircraft and armaments, his fighters have been busy with an attack mounted by the US aircraft from Midway and are not yet ready to fly again, and his first strike force aircraft are still on their way back to his carriers. He decides to collect all his aircraft before sending a flight against the US ships.

At about 0900 hours 41 US torpedo-bombers reach the Japanese ships and make a poorly co-ordinated attack; most of the aircraft are lost and no hits are scored. The attack has disrupted Japanese planning, however, and a second wave of aircraft, dive-bombers this time, record fatal hits on *Soryu, Kaga* and *Akagi*. The carrier *Hiryu* survives and launches air strikes which inflict critical damage on *Yorktown*. Later, *Hiryu* is badly damaged by aircraft from *Enterprise* and *Hornet*. The Japanese lose all four of their carriers, sunk or scuttled, within 24 hours.

Battle of Midway

111

5 June Ill-chosen attacks by the British in North Africa see them lose 108 tanks when 32nd Army Tank Brigade drives into a minefield.

At Midway, Yamamoto considers closing on the US ships in an attempt to bring them to action, but finally chooses to withdraw. The action around this tiny island, halfway between Japan and Hawaii, has seen the Japanese defeated in a significant battle for the first time in almost three and a half centuries; such news is kept from the Japanese public for some time.

Japanese land on Aleutians

6 June The attack on the Aleutians, having failed to divert the Americans from Midway, proves more successful than the main mission. The Japanese land on the islands and quickly gain territory.

7 June The Soviet garrison at Sevastopol is badly under strength as the Germans continue their heavy attacks.

At Midway, a Japanese submarine claims the carrier, *Yorktown*, in a final success for the Japanese in what has been a turning-point sea battle in the Pacific. The Japanese are left with only two carriers and have been found seriously naïve with regard to the value of superior battle intelligence. Yamamoto's scheme while theoretically sound was complex, and given the other failings which afflicted his forces, it never had a chance of success and proved inflexible under pressure. Good fortune runs with the American forces, and they now have the initiative.

Massacre at Lidice

9 June In the wake of the late May attempted assassination and later death of Heydrich, the village of Lidice and its inhabitants are destroyed in reprisal attacks by the Germans who believe that those who attacked the Reichs Protector have been sheltered there.

General 'Hap' Arnold, commander of the US Army Air Force, announces that the USAAF numbers are to be increased to one million men. He adds that raids like those on Cologne and Essen 'are only the prelude' to more Allied bombing of Germany.

10 June The US Pacific Fleet is supplemented by the carrier *Wasp*, the battleship *North Carolina* and cruisers and destroyers.

11 June Rommel makes a move to bring the Battle of Gazala to an end when he drives north out of the 'Cauldron'. General Ritchie has to engage with numerically weaker forces and loses 320 tanks in a two-day battle.

Convoys 'Harpoon' and 'Vigorous'

Convoys from Gibraltar and Egypt set out for Malta. The first, Operation 'Harpoon', has six merchantmen escorted by the battleship HMS *Malaya*, the carriers HMSS *Eagle* and *Argus* plus cruisers and destroyers; the second, Operation 'Vigorous', has eleven merchantmen protected by eight cruisers and 26 destroyers.

U-boats begin minelaying operations on the US eastern seaboard.

12 June In North Africa the British lose yet more tanks in poorly directed counter-attacks and have lost their armoured numerical advantage, having now only half as many tanks as Rommel. Auchinleck is appalled by these setbacks and flies in from his Cairo headquarters; he agrees to withdraw the Allied units to a new line from El Adem to Tobruk.

13 June The British and South African units still at the Gazala Line begin to pull out.

Allied units withdraw from Gazala Line

The ships of Operation 'Vigorous' suffer their first attacks.

14 June German and Italian aircraft attacking the 'Harpoon' convoy sink one merchantman and damage a cruiser. The 'Vigorous' convoy is hit by torpedo-boats and loses a destroyer.

15 June The 'Harpoon' ships are hit again by air strikes and only two merchantmen reach Malta. 'Vigorous' is reduced to six merchantmen by further attacks and chooses to turn back when it is heard that the battle-ships *Littorio* and *Vittorio Veneto* are in the area. *Littorio* is damaged by an air strike and a British submarine sinks the heavy cruiser *Trento*. The involvement of German aircraft from North Africa has afforded Eighth Army time to reconsider its strategy.

17 June The new Allied line in North Africa is swiftly broken when El Adem is captured by German forces. A further withdrawal of Eighth Army HQ, to Sollum, is necessary. Tobruk is now isolated.

Germans capture El Adem

18 June Rommel issues orders to his tiring forces for the big attack on Tobruk; it is to take place on the 20th and he plans to use 15th, 21st Panzer and Ariete Divisions to make a sudden push in the south-east sector ahead of a drive for the harbour area. Every possible Luftwaffe bomber will be made available.

Churchill is in the USA, discussing the opening of a second front with Roosevelt. The two men agree to pool resources on atomic research and Churchill secures the prompt supply of 300 Sherman tanks and 100 self-propelled guns which are desperately needed in North Africa.

20 June The offensive against Tobruk opens with a dive-bomber attack and is followed by quick thrusts in accordance with Rommel's plan. By evening his forces have reached the harbour.

On the Eastern Front, the Germans reach another important harbour, that of Sevastopol.

21 June The garrison at Tobruk is not as galvanised under the South African General Klopper as it was when the Australians were defending the town. The surrender is not long in coming and brings the Germans 30,000 prisoners and much needed supplies. Excited by his success, Rommel proposes to Hitler that he pursue the Allies to Egypt, though he is not supported by Kesselring who wants to deal with Malta first. Hitler concurs and promotes Rommel to Field Marshal. None of the parties in this theatre, nor the critics of Churchill who table a motion of censure against him in parliament, is aware of the imminent arrival of the fire-power the British Prime Minister has secured from America during his recent visit. He has been calling for a major offensive in the desert for months and is now about to provide the weaponry it needs.

Germans take Tobruk

22 June Churchill sends a message of support to Stalin which includes the assurance that: 'We shall confound our enemies and, when the war is over, build a sure peace for all freedom-loving peoples.'

The Germans already recognise Churchill as the prime co-ordinator of Allied resistance and the focal point for the chances of success in the war. Goebbels urges the German press to castigate Churchill for every error and loss on the Allied side, to suggest that he always leaves the country during a crisis, and constantly to accuse him of a readiness to kill civilians.

Rommel enters Egypt

23 June Typically, Rommel does not delay in his push east and quickly crosses into Egypt.

25 June General Ritchie, who is judged to have under-performed in North Africa, is removed from command of Eighth Army by Auchinleck who takes the role himself.

In Washington, 51-year-old General Eisenhower is appointed to command American land forces in Europe. He has never seen action, being a tank warfare trainer during World War One; he has also served as MacArthur's Chief of Staff.

26 June The Germans continue their advance in Egypt.

The German city of Bremen is the last to be hit by a 'thousand bomber raid'.

The Soviet destroyer *Tashkent* makes the last of 40 passages between Novorossisk and Sevastopol, and takes off nearly 1,000 troops plus supplies. The Russians' only way of reaching Sevastopol now is by submarine.

27 June In North Africa the Allied forces face the advancing Germans at Mersa Matruh but are quickly made to withdraw.

Convoy PQ-17 leaves Iceland for Archangel with 56 freighters and a tanker escorted by six destroyers plus thirteen other vessels. Convoy QP-13 has 35 ships and is leaving Murmansk and Archangel on its return passage.

Germans capture
Mersa Matruh

28 June Mersa Matruh and its substantial store of supplies falls to the Germans. The Allied troops meander back to El Alamein which is Auchinleck's choice for the next big stand. At least it offers a location that is difficult to outflank, and can be quickly re-supplied; the Germans are daily moving farther from their own supply point.

Army Group South drives east from Kursk at the beginning of the German summer offensive, Operation 'Blue'.

Two battleships, HMS *Duke of York* and the USS *Washington*, the carrier *Victorious* plus cruisers and destroyers leave Scapa Flow to escort Convoy PQ-17.

30 June The evacuation of Sevastopol is ordered from Moscow, but the Black Sea Fleet is too weak to supply the necessary support.

The Afrika Korps has pursued the Allies to El Alamein and immediately tries to break their lines. The British defend stoutly and the small German units have to draw back.

The Germans track the movement of Convoy QP-13 but do not attack it.

JULY 1942

1 July In North Africa the German thrust closes on El Alamein, but fifteen miles to the south there is already heavy fighting around Ruweisat Ridge.

Sevastopol falls. Its conqueror, General von Manstein, is promoted to Field Marshal by an elated Führer. The Germans have expended more than 46,000 shells and 20,000 tons of bombs in their campaign against the city; the latter figure is only marginally less than the total dropped on the UK during 1941.

Sevastopol falls

The first heavy bomber from the US Eighth Army Air Force, a B-17 Flying Fortress, lands at Prestwick.

Convoy PQ-17 is located by a German reconnaissance aircraft which summons *U255* and *U408* to the area.

Convoy PQ-17

2 July During a parliamentary debate, concern about Churchill's workload is expressed, but he urges members to allow the *status quo* to continue and be supportive; he carries the vote decisively.

Units of Soviet Fortieth Army are put at risk of isolation by an advance of Hoth's Fourth Panzer Army.

Convoys QP-13 and PQ-17 pass each other on the same day that *Tirpitz*, *Hipper* and six destroyers leave Trondheim. So far air and U-boat attacks on PQ-17 have had little effect.

3 July The 2nd New Zealand Division smashes the Italian Ariete Division when the latter makes a ill-prepared attack near Alam Nayil Ridge, 25 miles south of El Alamein. The Axis drive to penetrate Allied lines around El Alamein has failed; Rommel has not achieved the quick breakthrough that he knows was necessary. His weakened forces and ineffectual supply lines bring his momentum to a halt at the very moment when the opposition is most vulnerable.

Rommel halted

In the Arctic the German fleet is supplemented by the departure from Narvik of *Admiral Scheer*, *Lützow* and an escort of destroyers.

4 July At Sevastopol the Germans have taken more than 90,000 prisoners, but an even greater number of Russian soldiers have lost their lives

The USAAF units in the UK begin operations when they join an RAF attack on Dutch airfields used by the Luftwaffe.

First USAAF operations in Europe

Following a more successful attack on Convoy PQ-17, the First Sea Lord, Admiral Pound, working on imprecise information as to the whereabouts of the German capital ships, orders the convoy to scatter and the escort to withdraw. He and his colleagues are of the opinion that they cannot comprehensively protect the formation now that the German heavy warships have been let loose and the merchant ships are within range of German bombers. The commanders of the convoy are not convinced that the instructions are correct but they implement them. Admiral Tovey later claims: 'Scattering the convoy was nothing more than sheer bloody murder.' It certainly contravenes the long-held belief that a convoy stood a better chance of surviving attack if it stayed together.

5 July Convoy PQ-17 loses thirteen ships but to U-boats and aircraft rather than surface vessels. In fact *Tirpitz* is only now leaving the shelter of the Norwegian fiords.

German advances increase

7 July On the Eastern Front German advances increase daily. Voronezh falls, and they continue to regain lost ground elsewhere.

PQ-17 loses another eight ships, making the episode a disaster of embarrassing proportions. Whatever the shortage of protection Pound felt he could provide, it must surely have been better than to leave each merchantman alone and easy prey to aircraft and U-boats.

8 July Although the German attacks on the Soviet lines between the Don and the Donets have enjoyed success, the defenders have mostly escaped capture and conducted an orderly retreat.

9 July As the surviving vessels from PQ-17 begin to arrive in Russian ports the full story of the débâcle unfolds. The 24 ships which have been lost were carrying a total of 3,350 vehicles, 430 tanks, more than 200 aircraft and 96,000 tons of supplies. The ships which did get through delivered just 896 vehicles, 164 tanks, 87 aircraft and 57,000 tons of other cargo. Admiral Pound has probably placed too great a significance on the threat of the German battleships rather than factual reports as to their whereabouts. By his premature order to scatter he has left a major merchant fleet defenceless against more than 200 aircraft and nine U-boats.

Minor successes for Auchinleck

10 July In North Africa the wise head of Auchinleck brings the Allies some minor successes by his deployment of small strikes against the weaker Italian units which, in turn, draws the Germans out of their preferred formations.

12 July On the Eastern Front the ten-day offensive by Model's Ninth Army against the Soviet salient west of Sychevka ends with victory and 30,000 prisoners.

13 July Another example of Hitler's choosing the wrong strategy from the safety of his headquarters is seen when he redirects Army Group B to take Stalingrad without first ensuring that it has the means and ability to do so. Meanwhile, Hoth and von Kleist's forces make rapid progress.

14 July In North Africa both sides are short of supplies whose delivery across the Mediterranean becomes frenetic; submarines and faster, smaller surface craft are now being used.

15 July The new Allied command in North Africa begins to have an influence. The more concerted and efficient use of artillery brings fresh successes; the Germans lose heavily until they adapt their tactics against this improved British performance.

Hitler sacks Field Marshal von Bock, commander of Army Group B, in another example of impatience with a field commander of proven pedigree.

17 July Hitler is again open to accusations of making ill-informed strategic decisions from his HQ when he transfers Fourth Panzer Group from Army Group B to Army Group A, which he sees as needing help to make progress across the Don. Inevitably this weakens the former Group badly and slows their momentum.

In North Africa, Rommel has acknowledged the fact that further offensives are out of the question because he is so short of resources. Both sides now prepare their defences and lay mines. Modest Allied moves against Italian X Corps bring easy success in that sector but have little bearing on the general situation.

19 July The German thrusts on the Eastern Front continue to regain the ground they had taken in their first advance but had lost to Soviet counterattacks.

Germans on Eastern Front regain lost ground

21 July Because they are able to intercept and decode his communications, the Allied commanders in North Africa are well aware that Rommel is telling German High Command that he will have to retreat unless he receives reinforcements and *matériel*. Auchinleck mounts a series of attacks against German positions, but despite some early successes fails to administer a truly telling defeat.

22 July The fighting in North Africa reaches an impasse. The Allies suffer losses when 23rd Armoured Brigade is mauled during advances south of Ruweisat Ridge, but Rommel, despite this and other small achievements, knows his units are unable to sustain either attack or defence until supplies get through. The British hold the key here because they can be reached through their main supply base on the Nile and, at the same time, use available Malta forces to disrupt the route to Rommel.

North African stalemate

Fourth Panzer Army crosses the Don east of Rostov and the German thrust on Stalingrad gathers pace. This leads Hitler to believe that the city can be taken by Sixth Army alone so he directs Fourth Panzer Army southwards. This order has to be quickly countermanded when Sixth Army is halted by Soviet resistance; Fourth Panzer is now ordered to aim for Stalingrad again, but from the south.

The Japanese have landed in New Guinea and are faced only by a small Australian force.

Allied leaders in London agree that North Africa should be the venue for the first land-based involvement of the Americans. Operation 'Torch' is born.

23 July Rostov falls to Army Group A after heavy street fighting. This formation will now move forward to attack the Caucasus.

Rostov falls

29 July Hitler transfers Fourth Panzer Army yet again, sending it back to Army Group B which he now agrees is being hampered by the loss of this asset earlier in the month. This constant movement of forces in non-combative action is foolishly wasteful and can be quoted as a contributory reason for poor performance in the coming months.

Kokoda falls

Failure to re-supply the Australian units holding off the Japanese advance in New Guinea sees Kokoda fall.

The Japanese, with their eyes still on the capture of Port Moresby, occupy islands between Timor and New Guinea.

31 July US aircraft bomb Tulagi and Guadalcanal to disrupt the building of Japanese air bases.

AUGUST 1942

I August The Soviet forces confronting Army Group A are unable to prevent further advances. Stalingrad is truly under threat and Stavropol, on the route to the Caspian Sea, is within sight.

2 August Churchill visits Eighth Army in North Africa. Auchinleck has improved the tactical use of men and available equipment, but the Prime Minister leaves with the conviction that greater resources will be needed to win the day.

The transit of US troops to UK aboard the large liners *Queen Elizabeth*, *Queen Mary* and *Nieuw Amsterdam* begins. These vessels cannot be given standard escorts because of their high speed, but the Admiralty chooses their route based on knowledge of U-boat locations via the code-breaking services.

6 August Changes in British military hierarchy see General Alexander given command of the Middle East forces and General Gott charged with enhancing the tactical capability of the Eighth Army.

First Panzer Army is making good progress towards the Maikop oilfields at the foot of the Caucasus.

General Gott killed

7 August En route from Cairo after his appointment to lead Eighth Army, General Gott is killed in an air crash. General Montgomery is chosen as his replacement.

The Americans begin landings in the Solomons. Troops gain footholds on Guadalcanal, Tulagi and Gavutu.

8 August General Eisenhower is chosen to command Operation 'Torch'.

Guadalcanal landings

On Guadalcanal, a second force of US troops lands and joins in the easy retaking of the airstrip which the Japanese have built since their May occupation; the other two islands are fully captured. At this point, Admiral Fletcher, whose carrier force has supported the raids, withdraws his ships in the face of heavy air and submarine threat; the cruisers and transport vessels stay in position.

Battle of Savo Island

9 August A Japanese cruiser squadron engages an Allied force south of Savo Island, off Guadalcanal, under cover of darkness and sinks four cruisers. But it fails to halt the off-loading of troops from landing ships at Lunga Point, near the airstrip, though these ships do leave before completing the discharge of the accompanying supplies.

A Bomber Command raid on Osnabruck goes badly wrong when, in mid-flight, the RAF pilots find their 'Gee' radar jammed. It appears that the Germans have sited jamming equipment all over Europe, including one in Paris on the Eiffel Tower, and now the British have to work fast to develop their new bombing aid 'Oboe'.

10 August A US submarine, returning from patrol around Savo Island, spots, attacks and sinks the Japanese heavy cruiser *Kako*.

11 August The Soviet 62nd Army and the new First Armoured Army are defeated by Paulus' Sixth Army in a flanking move which costs the Russians 270 tanks and more than 35,000 prisoners taken.

A major Malta Convoy, 'Pedestal', is attacked by Axis aircraft and submarines. One of the latter accounts for the carrier HMS *Eagle*, but the massive protection afforded this important shipment sees it survive the onslaught. *Eagle sunk*

12 August Churchill goes to Moscow to explain to Stalin why he has agreed with Roosevelt that British and American efforts in the coming months will focus on North Africa rather than the opening of a 'second front'.

The 'Pedestal' convoy, with its escort of battleships, carriers, cruisers and no less than 32 destroyers, is attacked throughout the day. It loses three freighters, two cruisers and a destroyer, and the carrier HMS *Indomitable* and the tanker *Ohio* are damaged.

13 August Montgomery and Alexander make an immediate impact in North Africa. The former takes command of Eighth Army during what is believed to be an introductory visit to the front, and the latter begins the handover from Auchinleck. Both are able to benefit from the decoding of radio traffic between the German command centres.

Axis attacks on 'Pedestal' account for the loss of the cruiser HMS *Manchester* and seven freighters. Four of the merchantmen eventually make Valletta harbour as does, under tow, the vital fuel cargo in *Ohio*.

14 August Soviet resistance around the Don at its nearest point to Stalingrad is finally cleared by Sixth Army though many of the defeated Russian troops escape to the east to fight again. *Soviets cleared from the Don*

15 August The British set up the Pathfinder Force under Air Commodore Don Bennett. To increase the potency of their bombing missions, the RAF assemble this team of their finest aircrews to lead the main bomber formations and mark the target with flares dropped in a complex pattern. This not only increases accuracy but cuts the time needed for deployment over the target by 50 per cent.

Fast transports get supplies through to the US forces on Guadalcanal.

17 August Rommel is ordered to take immediate action to defeat Eighth Army, move on to the Nile Delta, take Alexandria and Cairo and assume control of the Suez Canal. Even to so ambitious a battlefield genius these are impossible demands to which he is entitled to reply, 'with what?'

The first solely US-manned air raid over Europe targets Rouen. It marks the entry into the European air war by the US Eighth Army Air

119

Force which, in time, will prove mightily effective. Initially, however, aircraft are diverted to the needs of Operation 'Torch' and the crews will take time to become accustomed to different operational conditions.

18 August Hitler receives reports about the hindrance of partisan activities on the Eastern Front. The consequent directive gives almost unlimited power to SS Special Units on the ground and marks a new wave of horrendous brutality conducted quite separately from action on the battlefield.

On Guadalcanal the Japanese land 1,000 fresh troops who begin to advance on US positions. The Americans have the airstrip fully functional and already have three times the number of troops on the island that the Japanese expect.

The first Pathfinder mission is flown on a run to Flensburg docks, but radar jamming causes its failure.

Dieppe raid

19 August This day sees the disastrous raid on Dieppe, foreseen as a test of Allied forces in a coastal offensive and of German defence methods against such a move. Nearly six thousand men are involved, mostly Canadian but also including British, American and Free French. Although the landing is completed, few of the targeted installations are attacked. Fifty per cent of the Canadian troops are killed or captured on the beach. Allied equipment is knocked out by German anti-tank guns, and only a fraction of the invading force is evacuated. Some 3,350 men are killed or captured, plus 106 aircraft, a destroyer, 30 tanks and three dozen landing-craft. The Germans lose 600 men and 170 aircraft (RAF claim). The failure of the mission is substantially due to the advance warning the Germans have received via their radio intelligence service which has been intercepting British transmissions between stations along the south coast. In the event, this frightful escapade is probably a blessing in disguise in that it brings a more determined assessment of the tactics for such multi-force actions and convinces the planners that a preliminary bombardment is vital to a major amphibious landing.

21 August Army Group A is within sight of the Black Sea and Army Group B crosses the Don near Kletskaya.

The Japanese forces on Guadalcanal are destroyed when they mount several fanatical attacks on the US base.

Army Group B
reaches Volga

23 August Army Group B reaches the Volga north of Stalingrad.

The focus is very much on Guadalcanal as the combatants' fleets sail towards the island on supply missions. The US ships, under Admiral Fletcher, include the carriers *Enterprise*, *Saratoga* and *Wasp*; the Japanese have three carriers divided among their two groups of ships.

Ryujo sunk

24 August In the eastern Solomons the opposing fleets attack each other. The Japanese carrier *Ryujo* is sunk and the US carrier *Enterprise* damaged.

25 August The Duke of Kent, brother of the King and an RAF officer, is killed in an air crash in Scotland.

Japanese transports continue to approach Guadalcanal but are turned back when a destroyer and two troopships are sunk by US aircraft.

27 August The Soviet defence lines around Stalingrad contract as German forces move closer. Near Leningrad, however, the Soviets breach German Eighteenth Army positions.

The US Navy is reduced to just one aircraft carrier in the Pacific when *Saratoga* follows *Enterprise* on to the 'damaged list' after an attack by the Japanese submarine *I26*.

28 August Night supply missions by fast destroyers of Admiral Tanaka's 2nd Destroyer Flotilla, which will become known as the 'Tokyo Express', reach Guadalcanal. The US forces on the island are being resupplied via the airstrip and the new equipment includes many aircraft.

30 August Augmented by 164th Division and a parachute brigade, Rommel decides to mount an attack which he hopes will force the Allies out of Egypt. His supply situation is not much improved so his action must be short, sharp and successful if he is not to be made dangerously vulnerable to counter-moves. For this nine-day Battle of Alam Halfa, the British have recomposed the formation damaged by the early summer skirmishes and Montgomery has refined the skilled planning he has inherited from Auchinleck. Rommel's moves have been sanctioned by German High Command because of his success to date; the chance of gaining control of the Suez Canal is mistakenly allowed to take priority over the invasion of Malta.

Battle of Alam Halfa

31 August The Desert Fox, master of the Blitzkrieg battle style, has set a plan aimed at cutting a path through the Allied minefields south of Alam Nayil. But these are well guarded and more extensive than Rommel expects and his early moves under cover of darkness are slowed. He promptly decides to withdraw but is urged to allow the drive to continue by another route. He turns north-east to attack Alam Halfa Ridge but is rebuffed and is now constantly harried by ground and air bombardment.

On the Eastern Front the Germans are just sixteen miles from Stalingrad, but their momentum grinds to a halt in the face of fierce Soviet resistance. Although von Manstein's Eleventh Army is moved from the Crimea to the Leningrad theatre, the Soviets make an early push against Eighteenth Army already there with the result that the German forces preparing for the assault on Leningrad remain weak.

Germans approach Stalingrad

The Japanese land 1,200 more men on Guadalcanal.

SEPTEMBER 1942

1 September On the Eastern Front the German and Russian troops are fighting at close quarters in and around the suburbs of Stalingrad. The Soviet 62nd Army is becoming isolated.

Japanese Foreign Minister Togo resigns and Prime Minister Tojo takes over his duties. Togo has sought to retain the chances of peace and his departure leaves the militants in full control.

In North Africa Rommel is restricted to small-scale offensives, though 15th Panzer Division inflicts damage on 8th Armoured Brigade in an exchange of artillery fire.

The Pathfinder Force suffers a second failure when a flight to Saarbrucken ends with the wrong town being marked by flares. The faults are remedied in time for a raid on Frankfurt next day.

Rommel withdraws

2 September Rommel orders a withdrawal to give Montgomery the first taste of success since his appointment. The Allies have discovered his plans before they are implemented and have adjusted their defences accordingly. Montgomery is able to place his artillery in prime positions on Rommel's known route and devise plans to force the German thrusts along lines which favour his strategy. For his part, Rommel blames this setback on the lack of supplies and already believes his chance to reach Suez has been lost.

3 September In North Africa the New Zealand Division attempts to cut off Rommel's retreat but its heavyweight engagements with the German units fail to achieve their objective.

Germans five miles from centre of Stalingrad.

The German 71st Infantry Division is five miles from the centre of Stalingrad.

4 September South of Stalingrad German troops have reached the Volga. From above, the city is hammered by more than 1,000 German aircraft.

Off Guadalcanal two US destroyers, pressed into service as transports, are sunk by Japanese destroyers as more reinforcements reach the Japanese-held ports.

6 September In North Africa Rommel's forces have been pushed back to their starting-point and begin to prepare more sophisticated defence lines. With the imminent arrival of substantial Allied reinforcements, both sides are aware that the big battle is approaching; Rommel knows that his position is hopeless unless he too receives reinforcements and *matériel*.

7 September The battle of Alam Halfa has seen Rommel fail in his last attempt to break the British lines defending Egypt; it has been a fine example of Allied army-air liaison.

8 September US Marines landing on Guadalcanal attack the Japanese base at Taivu and disrupt plans to move on the principal US position.

Convoy PQ-18 is spotted by a German reconnaissance flight. Its 39 freighters and one tanker have a small escort.

9 September Hitler dismisses Field Marshal List and takes personal command of Army Group A.

General Hyakutake, commander of Seventeenth Army, arrives at Guadalcanal with supplies.

10 September In the North Atlantic a pack of thirteen U-boats sink twelve freighters and a destroyer from Convoy ON-127; each of the boats makes at least one attack.

12 September The nature of the action in and around Stalingrad suits the Russians more than it does the Germans. General Chuikov has arrived to mastermind the defence of the city and he has immediately noted the German weakness against small unit attacks in an urban environment.

At Guadalcanal the Japanese mount major attacks. The US troops are supported by new aircraft from the carrier *Wasp* operating nearby.

Japanese mount major attacks on Guadalcanal

The liner *Laconia*, carrying troops and their families and Italian prisoners, is sunk by *U156* north-east of Ascension Island. While attempting to rescue survivors and having notified the pilot of the situation, the U-boat is attacked by a US Liberator from 343 Bombardment Squadron. Dönitz forbids future rescue work of this kind.

Liner Laconia sunk

13 September In North Africa Allied action diversifies with Long Range Desert Group deployment against airfields at Barce and Benghazi and amphibious landing attempts at Tobruk.

The Germans attempt to storm Stalingrad and do take valuable high ground. Against them the Soviets have complemented their military forces with armed workers' groups, youngsters and children.

On Guadalcanal only extreme US artillery fire staves off full Japanese onslaughts.

Convoy PQ-18 suffers the inevitable air and U-boat attacks. Although it will lose thirteen ships it will fare better than its predecessor; the Germans will lose two U-boats and 20 aircraft. Churchill again suspends convoy traffic on the Arctic route.

Convoy PQ-18

14 September Stalingrad sees much street fighting at which, it is quickly seen, the Russians are very much more adept. The Germans, used to sweeping movement across open terrain, have not been trained for urban warfare and the Soviet use of small, mobile groups of armour and troops is far more suitable to this situation. The battle-proven German armour is found wanting but the accumulating losses are not so noticeable.

In New Guinea, the Australian defenders have been pushed farther back and the Japanese are only 30 miles from Port Moresby.

Australians pushed back in New Guinea

15 September With the most effective torpedo salvo of the war, the sole US carrier off Guadalcanal is lost when *Wasp* is sunk by the Japanese submarine *I.19*. Having got among a US escort fleet, Commander Narahara fires six torpedoes which, in turn, hit the battleship *North Carolina*, the destroyer *O'Brien*, a strike of three on *Wasp*, and a near miss at the carrier *Hornet*.

Wasp sunk

16 September The air superiority enjoyed by the Americans around Port Moresby brings the Japanese advance across New Guinea to a halt. US troops are landing there to support the retreating Australian units.

Hand-to-hand fighting is seen in Stalingrad as small strategic territories are constantly fought over.

18 September The US position on Guadalcanal improves with the arrival of 7th Marine Regiment which brings the US presence there to more than 23,000.

The British make further landings in Madagascar, believing that the entire island must be secured.

23 September The British occupy the capital of Madagascar.

Rommel leaves North Africa to fly to Germany for medical treatment.

Début of Tiger tank

Four Tiger tanks make their début at Leningrad but, unable to negotiate the marshlands in the area, are forced to advance in single file along narrow roads; three of them are knocked out by the Soviets, who take great pleasure in examining the new machine; one is destroyed by its crew as being irrecoverable.

The continuing arrival of US forces at Port Moresby encourages the Australians to take the offensive in New Guinea.

Zeitzler replaces Halder

24 September Hitler now sacks General Halder, one of the architects of German military strategy, and replaces him by the more subservient General Zeitzler. Halder has become too critical of Hitler's personal involvement in the Eastern Front and the two men have constantly argued. The Führer must frequently have hesitated dismiss so important an adviser, but finally would accept no more insubordination.

Commerce raider *Stier* sunk

The career of the German commerce raider *Stier* comes to a bizarre end when she attacks and sinks the Liberty ship *Stephen Hopkins*, only to be mortally damaged herself by the paltry 4-inch guns of the American ship.

25 September The city of Oslo is shaken by an RAF low-level bombing raid on the Gestapo office there. With remarkable precision Gestapo HQ is destroyed together with its records of resistance fighters in the country.

Japanese retreat in New Guinea

27 September The Japanese retreat down the line of their earlier attack as the Australians turn the tables in New Guinea.

29 September In the second and final raid of its mission, a Japanese aircraft deployed from a submarine off the coast of Oregon, flies over forests inland to drop incendiary bombs. These were the only bombing raids made on the United States.

OCTOBER 1942

1 October The Allied forces in New Guinea are now fully on the offensive. They move on Gona and Buna, and US units set up a pincer movement with the Australians aimed at cutting off the Japanese retreat.

2 October A freak accident off the coast of Ireland sees the liner *Queen Mary* collide with the cruiser HMS *Curacao* which sinks. In use as a troopship, the liner is unaccustomed to sailing in consort.

4 October Sixth Army's General Paulus is rapidly running out of ideas as to how to break through into the centre of Stalingrad but one more effort is called for. The Germans now have more skilled urban fighters in their ranks but they are still struggling to make an impact. The Soviets plan to force any German breakthrough into zones which they control, and then counter on their terms.

7 October The Tractor Factory in Stalingrad is the scene of the most fierce fighting the city has witnessed.

Fierce fighting in Stalingrad

On Guadalcanal the US 1st Marine Division breaks out from the beachhead to try to create a larger safety zone around the airstrip, Henderson Field.

9 October The type of central political influence which Adolf Hitler has forced on his field commanders during the war has often afflicted the Soviets in similar fashion when the political commissars in Moscow have sought to exert control over battlefield decision-making. The Soviets have put a stop to this and henceforward responsibility will be firmly in the hands of the commanding officers at the front.

Roumanian Third Army, previously in the Caucasus, is moved to the Stalingrad sector alongside German Sixth and Italian Eighth Armies. The Roumanians will not prove effective when the Soviets counter-attack.

US attacks on Guadalcanal are halted and their forces regroup for the anticipated Japanese onslaught on the main US beachhead.

10 October Kesselring orders an aerial offensive against Malta. For the next nine days between 200 and 270 flights of Italian or German aircraft are sortied daily. Only when 70 planes have been lost is the operation abandoned. If the German leaders had had the nerve to continue the strikes, the outcome in North Africa might have been different.

Malta heavily bombed

11 October As the combatants on Guadalcanal struggle to maintain their supply routes, the fleets charged with this responsibility clash in the waters between Savo Island and Tenaro. Both sides have a particular advantage; the Americans have radar, but use it poorly, the Japanese have better torpedoes. The confused state of the confrontation sees several examples of 'friendly fire' and both sides' troopships reach their destinations. The Americans get 3,000 men ashore; the Japanese will land artillery, tanks and other *matériel*, but lose more ships.

Struggle to maintain Guadalcanal supply routes

12 October A Coastal Command Liberator sinks *U597* in the first success by a single aircraft from this section of the Royal Air Force.

13 October The impasse continues in Stalingrad despite frenetic fighting in various parts of the city.

The Japanese call in their battleships *Kongo* and *Haruna* to bombard Henderson Field in the hope of stopping the increasingly effective sorties of bombers from there. While the Americans are distracted by this raid, Tanaka lands 4,500 more men and equipment.

14 October Once again the Tractor Factory in Stalingrad is the scene of fierce fighting as five German divisions are launched together in an attempt to take it. The Russian Guards Division has joined the fray and the Germans are unable to break through.

In New Guinea the Japanese turn to fight their pursuers on the Kokoda Trail and a three-day battle ensues.

Commerce raider *Komet* sunk

Alerted to the sailing by intercepts of German coded messages, the British motor torpedo-boat *MTB236* sinks the German commerce raider *Komet* as she makes for a home port in the English Channel.

16 October The Japanese are preparing for their big attack on Guadalcanal and US aircraft from the carrier *Hornet* attack Japanese supply bases on Santa Isabel

17 October In New Guinea the Allies have to airlift troops from Port Moresby to support their units struggling against the Japanese at Waniegela.

Soviets counter-moves at Stalingrad

18 October The Soviets have held their defences in Stalingrad and begin some counter-moves.

Admiral William 'Bull' Halsey takes command of the South Pacific Command area. The US forces in New Guinea reach Pongani.

20 October Indicative of the tensions being felt in Germany, the Reich press chief urges publications to avoid the 'winter' theme in their reports of the Eastern Front.

21 October The Germans refocus their thrusts in Stalingrad and make some gains.

The Japanese forces in Guadalcanal, now 20,000 strong, begin an attack on two lines, but they have not planned the route well and are still unaware of American strength or state of readiness.

U-boats off Gibraltar are distracted by the movements of Convoy SL-125 and allow the transports carrying the forces to North Africa for Operation 'Torch' to go unmolested. It is a poor start to the German response to this major Allied initiative.

22 October Further Japanese advances on Guadalcanal are seen off by US artillery.

One hundred Lancasters attack the port and city of Genoa. This is just one example of the regular sorties against Mediterranean convoys and their supply ports which are having a major impact on the war in North Africa.

23 October The British forces advancing through Burma make their first contact with the Japanese.

Battle of El Alamein

24 October With Rommel still on sick leave, though due to return on the 25th, Montgomery has launched the Battle of El Alamein with a ferocious 1,000-gun bombardment of the German positions and minefields, followed by a night thrust by ten divisions and seven armoured brigades. This is aimed at driving corridors through the minefields so that the Allied tanks can get through to attack the German heavy armour. General

Stumme has a mix of German and Italian troops manning the forward positions. At the outset Montgomery can boast a significant advantage in men and heavy armour and a theoretical supremacy in the air. He will use XXX Corps for this first thrust, and employ diversionary tactics to persuade 15th Panzer Division to stay south of a line from Kidney Ridge. Initial success is limited and X Corps' tanks fail to get through the mine-fields on time; the bottleneck of armoured vehicles becomes a target for the German guns. During the afternoon General Stumme has a heart attack and dies. Montgomery has more than 1,500 aircraft, mostly based in Egypt or Palestine, and hammers the Germans' deployment zone with more than 80 tons of bombs.

On Guadalcanal the Japanese mount a night attack on US positions but are thrown back after heavy losses.

Japanese heavy losses on Guadalcanal

25 October The momentum of the British forces at El Alamein increases and though they lose tanks they still have many more than the Germans. Rommel arrives in the battlezone to find that 9th Australian Division has made gains in the north.

The Japanese show that they have failed to learn the lessons of Midway when they again split a naval fleet bound for Guadalcanal and so diminish its potential. The formation of four battleships, four carriers and numerous cruisers and destroyers approaches Guadalcanal to support the offensive there and is encouraged to come close to the island after a false report that Japanese forces there had captured Henderson Field. The Americans can call on only two carriers – *Enterprise* and *Hornet* are back in action – and a battleship, and find themselves outnumbered in aircraft. The Americans locate the Japanese ships but their attacks do not bring much success; the Battle of Santa Cruz will begin in earnest next day.

26 October Montgomery calls a halt to his forward move so as to regroup and is criticised by Churchill for doing so. But the cautious general has no illusions as to the ability of the man he faces and is not surprised when Rommel, unwilling to stay on the defensive for long, begins a series of sharp counter-attacks which have to be attended to. The Desert Fox does, however, take the Australian success in the north as an indication of the route the Allies intend to take for their main attack and makes an error when he moves 15th Panzer to that location.

Montgomery regroups

Off Guadalcanal daylight sees both sides launch attacks and the Japanese draw first blood by hitting *Hornet* which retires and later sinks. The US aircraft, operating at the extremes of their range, raid the leading Japanese group randomly and damage the cruiser *Chikuma* and the carrier *Shokaku*. The second Japanese strike hits home on the carrier *Enterprise* but the firepower of *South Dakota* has a mighty effect on this and the following sortie. The Americans withdraw and the Japanese can claim a victory, but they are continuing to lose too many prized pilots which, in

Battle of Santa Cruz

turn, reduces the effectiveness of their carrier aviation superiority. They too withdraw as they have lost so many aircraft that they feel unable to mount an attack on Henderson Field.

Rommel counter-attacks

27 October Rommel's counter-attacks in the northern sector of the El Alamein battlefield do not achieve much; Montgomery is regrouping rather than committing troops to worthless small-scale fighting.

The city of Stalingrad is held by a very thin but determined Soviet line of resistance. The Germans are gaining some ground but are doing this with large numbers of troops while the Soviets are continuing to keep men in reserve. German intelligence is led into believing that Soviet casualties are greater than is the case.

Japanese withdraw on Guadalcanal

In Guadalcanal the Japanese withdraw, having lost the initiative and suffered more than 3,500 casualties. So weak a fighting strategy in such a small battlezone betrays a new failing in Japanese military ability; masters of jungle fighting and vigorous advance behind a retreating enemy, they have been found wanting when called upon to assault and capture a defended position.

28 October The Allies have been having discussions with sympathetic French leaders in North Africa so as to ensure their support for the 'Torch' landings. The organisation of supportive groups is placed in the hands of French General Mast in Algeria but does not progress well.

29 October More German troops are put in to stem the Australians' advance towards the coast at El Alamein. The deployment of 90th Light Division for this task prompts Montgomery to alter the course of his main drive and attack the poorly supported Italians close to Kidney Ridge.

Malta very short of food

Malta is once again very short of food and *matériel*. Axis intelligence strives to establish the plans for what must surely be a very large convoy attempt in the near future.

The US forces in Guadalcanal, aware of the Japanese withdrawal, plan to pursue the enemy units.

The island of Madagascar is close to falling to the Allies.

31 October Although the Australians continue to do battle against the fortified German positions at El Alamein, Montgomery refuses to augment them because he is nearly ready to launch Operation 'Supercharge', his move against the Italian positions. He is also aware that his heavy losses to date have not earned a sufficient advantage, let alone a victory.

NOVEMBER 1942

Americans advance on Guadalcanal

1 November The Americans move out of their bases on Guadalcanal to attack westwards in pursuit of the Japanese, and to the east where they believe more landings may be attempted.

2 November In North Africa Operation 'Supercharge' has begun, but early infantry efforts to clear the minefields are held up and the first

Above: Hitler with the other signatories to the Munich agreement, 30 September 1938. From left to right: The British Prime Minister Neville Chamberlain, French Prime Minister Edward Daladier, Adolf Hitler, Benito Mussolini and the Italian Foriegn Minister, Count Ciano. IWM NYP 68066

Below: British troops in forward positions during the so-called 'Phoney War', late 1939, early 1940. IWM F4213

Upper left: A German Mk III tank advances across the desert during the Afrika Korps drive on Bir Hacheim, June 1941. IWM MH 5852

Left: Australian troops occupy a front line position at Tobruk, 13 August 1941. Tobruk was besieged by German forces between April and December 1941. The port finally fell to the Axis forces five months later. IWM EA 4792

Above: A British Crusader Mk III tank crosses a wide ditch during the later stages of the North African campaign. IWM E 19315

Right: General Montgomery (left) and General Eisenhower, during the latter's visit to Montgomery's headquarters, 31 March 1943. IWM NA 1696

Above: The Supermarine Spitfire. Along with the Hawker Hurricane, this superb fighter gave the Germans their first set back by defeating the Luftwaffe during the Battle of Britain. IWM CH 1448

Below: The German U-boat U32; she was sunk by surface ships in the North Atlantic in 1940. IWM HU 1011

Right: Feldmarschall Erwin Rommel, Commander of the German Afrika Korps, with his aides during the North African campaign. IWM HU 5625

Above: The German 'pocket battleship' *Admiral Graf Spee*. She was hunted down by British naval forces and scuttled by her crew after the Battle of the River Plate. IWM HU 3285

Below: A French Char B1 knocked out during the Battle for France, 1940. IWM F4633

Top right: German 'Stormtroopers' firing a light machine-gun while covering advancing reconnaissance troops. IWM MH 1912

Lower right: The Junkers Ju 87 'Stuka' dive bomber. This aircraft played a prominent part in the German Blitzkrieg tactics during the early part of the war. IWM MH 7519

Above: The Casablanca Conference, 24 January 1943. From left to right: General Giraud, French Commissioner for North Africa, President Roosevelt, General de Gaulle and Winston Churchill. IWM NA 480

Left: The escort carrier HMS *Avenger*, with six Sea Hurricane fighters on her flight deck. It was ships such as this that played a critical role in the final defeat of the U-boat and the Luftwaffe's long range aircraft during the many convoy battles. IWM FL 1268

Top right: Soviet infantry, one armed with an anti-tank rifle, advance under the cover of a smoke screen. IWM AP 23743

Centre right: British Matilda and Valentine tanks bound for the Soviet Army are being loaded on to merchant ships at a British port, October 1941. IWM H 14786

Right: The destroyer USS *Wainwright*, which successfully broke up an air attack on the Russia-bound convoy PQ-17 on 4 July 1942. IWM A 10690

Upper left: An American Sherman tank passes a knocked-out German armoured half-track on a country road during the battle for Normandy, 25 July 1944. IWM PL 31235

Lower left: A Japanese aircraft crashes into the sea after being shot down by anti-aircraft fire from an American aircraft carrier during the raid on Kwajalein, 4 December 1943. IWM NYP 11545

Above: The Japanese aircraft carrier *Shokaku*. She was torpedoed and sunk by the US submarine *Cavalla* on 19 June 1944 during the Battle of the Philippine Sea. IWM MH 5931

Below: A US Marine uses a flamethrower to clear a Japanese-held strongpoint during the fighting for Saipan. IWM NYF 30343

Above: The youngest USAAF bomber crew in the European theatre was that of 2nd Lieutenant Joe Novicki, aged 21, of the 34th Bombardment Group, based at Mendlesham, Suffolk, England. His crew were all aged between 19 and 20. IWM EA 56560

Left: A B-17 Flying Fortress unloads its bombs on to the Szob railway bridge north of Budapest, Hungary, 10 October 1944. IWM NYF 41983

Right: GIs tend to a wounded comrade on the Normandy invasion beach, June 1944. IWM OWIL 44977

Left: Supported by a Mk IV tank a group of German infantry rest before resuming the attack during the Battle of Stalingrad. IWM HU 5148

Below: A Soviet T34 tank with supporting infantry. IWM RUS 2010

Right: British troops of the 6th Royal West Kent Regiment manning a 3-inch mortar at Cassino, 26 March 1944. IWM NA 13365

Lower right: British and Italian personnel at Brindisi after the signing of the Italian Armistice. An Italian Macchi C.202 fighter is behind them. IWM CNA 1448

Left: A pall of smoke rises as a V-1 flying bomb falls near Drury Lane, London, striking the Aldwych, 30 June 1944. IWM HU 638

Below: Stalin salutes the guard of honour provided by the Scots Guards on his arrival at the residence of Winston Churchill for a reception during the Yalta Conference, February 1945. IWM BU 9192

forward movement of heavy armour is badly hit by fire from prepared German positions. Montgomery is ready to accept these predictable setbacks because of his superior tank strength; Rommel calls up 21st Panzer but still has only 35 tanks and very little fuel. He quickly concludes that he will not be able to prevent a breakthrough and advises Hitler accordingly.

On Guadalcanal, the Japanese benefit from a series of supply runs by sea. The Americans are aware of these missions by the 'Tokyo Express' but do not have the naval power to prevent them.

The end is close in New Guinea as the Australians recapture Kokoda and can now use its airstrip to bring in supplies and reinforcements.

3 November Rommel receives Hitler's order that he and his men 'stand and die' but disregards it because both German and Italian units are already committed to withdrawal at various points. The opportunity to harass this retreat is lost to the Allied forces because their cleared paths through the minefields are too narrow and prove to be bottlenecks.

The Japanese succeed in landing 1,500 troops at Koli Point on Guadalcanal and the Americans call a halt to their pursuit in order to deploy more troops to the landing beach.

4 November In North Africa the Allied heavy armour is now in open ground and able to drive unchallenged around Axis positions behind the minefields; Italian Ariete and German 90th Light Divisions suffer heavy losses. Across the battle zone the Allies have taken 30,000 prisoners and their enemy is in disarray. At 1530 hours Rommel takes it upon himself to order a retreat towards Sollum. Although the Axis forces are still not pursued with the determination Montgomery calls for, the Alamein action has been the turning-point of the Desert War. Rommel will have to run for his Tripoli base, but the 'Torch' landings are just days away and the Axis presence in North Africa is unsustainable.

The Germans have noticed the increased shipping activity off Gibraltar and fully 40 U-boats and Italian submarines are deployed to the western Mediterranean.

US troops make significant landings on Guadalcanal but will fail to achieve one of their objectives, the building of another airstrip.

5 November Rommel continues his retreat to Fuqa and beyond, though many of his Italian troops are not able to be part of this. The Allies will come to rue their failure to re-engage Rommel; their pursuit has been lethargic and error-ridden.

General Eisenhower is now in Gibraltar where he will base himself for Operation 'Torch'.

The Vichy forces in Madagascar accept their fate and ask to discuss terms for an armistice.

6 November The remains of 21st Panzer Division, at a halt and waiting for fuel, is caught and destroyed by 7th Armoured Division. The Allied

Australians recapture Kokoda

Rommel continues his retreat

units are not much better supplied and the pace of their drive westwards continues to be slow. This does not deter General Alexander from sending a message to Churchill which opens with the words: 'Ring out the bells.'

The Italian Chief of Staff, Marshal Cavallero, is at a meeting between Göring and Kesselring during which, he later reports, the former says he is certain the Allied invasion forces will land in Corsica and Sardinia and at Derna and Tripoli. Kesselring is said to favour a North African port.

7 November General Giraud, spirited out of southern France, arrives in Gibraltar to demonstrate to any doubting French the support they should give to the 'Torch' landings. The Allies believe this high-level endorsement will free them of any trouble from French North Africans.

'Torch' landings

8 November Three main task forces land in Morocco and Algeria to mark the start of Operation 'Torch'. The Eastern Task Force lands at Algiers with 33,000 troops and 52 warships; the Central Task Force at Oran with 39,000 men and a naval force; the Western Task Force, which has sailed directly from the USA with ground troops under the command of General George Patton, lands at three points on the Moroccan coast. The Algiers landing is successful and the port is quickly taken, but Oran is only taken after fighting and with the loss of two destroyers. Only one of the Western Task Force landings, at Safi, goes well; those at Casablanca and Port Lyautey meeting resistance. The management of the operation is a masterpiece of deceptive diplomacy: the Spanish and Portuguese being assured of the British involvement in the operation so as to ensure they do nothing to affect the smooth passage of Allied shipping around their coasts; the French being shown that almost all the assault troops are Americans, ergo the USA is in charge of the affair.

The Atlantic U-boat fleet is ordered to deploy in the vicinity of the 'Torch' beachheads.

9 November General Anderson, commander of units of First Army which have landed at Algiers, has to send men in support of those who are struggling to take Oran. There is further fighting at Port Lyautey but the beachhead at Casablanca is secured. The Vichy French accept German demands to use the airfields in Tunisia and German forces arrive there within hours. Jean Darlan, head of the French Armed Forces and High Commissioner in French North Africa, is now seen as a more valuable ally than Giraud and pressure is put on him publicly to announce his support.

New Zealand Division reaches Sidi Barrani

Farther east, the New Zealand Division reaches Sidi Barrani as the German units retreat ahead of them.

Early in the day, French fighters engage aircraft from the US carrier *Ranger* over Casablanca in defence of the French warships in the harbour there. Destroyers, submarines and transports are hit.

At the entrance to Algiers harbour the destroyer HMS *Broke* is sunk by shore artillery and French bombers as she tries to enter the harbour.

10 November Darlan broadcasts an order to all his forces in North Africa to cease fighting the Allied invasion troops. While Churchill proclaims that the 'Torch' landings are 'the beginning of the end', Hitler is meeting French and Italian leaders in Munich where he forces their agreement to fight on and hold as much of North Africa as they can.

On Guadalcanal US troops disrupt the Japanese units which have landed at Koli Point, and can resume their pursuit westwards, but news of more Japanese supply convoys prompts them to hold back.

11 November The French authorities in North Africa sign an armistice and the Allied forces can occupy Casablanca and begin their trek to the east. The march would have been shorter had the Americans not vetoed the British preference for landings farther east, but now the long lines of advancing infantry suffer from lack of air cover and from an early shortage of supplies after raids by the Luftwaffe on ships still en route to this theatre.

The sanctity of Vichy France is violated by Hitler's order that it be occupied. German troops move in promptly and Italian troops enter Cannes.

Germans occupy Vichy France

Leading units of Eighth Army are now through the Halfaya Pass and enter Libya where Bardia is taken without sight of the enemy.

In Stalingrad General Paulus launches his last offensive; it will last six days, but, again, the Soviet use of small teams will prove more malleable than the concentrated formations of the Germans. Beyond the control of central command and constantly split up by Soviet sniping, the German moves will become ever more fragmented and ineffective.

Soviet air power is enjoying success on the Eastern Front. The support of the ground troops sees many daring, low-level attacks which differ from the German practice of diving from high altitudes.

The Indian minesweeper *Bengal* records a remarkable success in the Indian Ocean when she and the tanker *Ondina* are attacked by two Japanese commerce raiders. Her single 3-inch gun sinks one of the attackers and drives off the other in a true 'David and Goliath' act.

12 November Tobruk sees Allied forces again as units of 1st and 7th Armoured Divisions enter the town that has seen such vicious fighting. This time they are unopposed.

Allies retake Tobruk

Farther west, Bône and its nearby airfield are taken by 'Torch' forces and German troops land at Bizerte, which the British had wanted as one of the 'Torch' landing sites. Hitler is sending large forces to Tunisia; their armour will include a battalion of the new Tiger tanks.

Germans reinforce Tunisia

US naval units seeking to re-supply their forces on Guadalcanal are constrained to keep clear of the island because of the heavy Japanese naval presence there.

In the Caucasus, German forces come under pressure; 13th Panzer Division is encircled for a time.

Admiral Nimitz announces that many of the warships damaged at Pearl Harbor are operational, having been repaired more swiftly than expected.

13 November In North Africa British 36th Brigade has moved 200 miles on from its Algiers beachhead. The wrangle over French involvement in this theatre is resolved when an agreement is signed by Admiral Darlan and General Clark recognising the former as head of the French administration in North Africa; Giraud is to command the French armed forces.

In their most significant move on the island to date, the Japanese send 11,000 men to Guadalcanal in eleven transports escorted by destroyers. Another Japanese force of two battleships, two cruisers and fourteen destroyers is sent to bombard Henderson Field. There are also two carriers in the area. With just five cruisers and eight destroyers, US Admiral Callaghan moves to locate the ships heading for the position offshore of the airfield. When the two fleets engage the Japanese lose two cruisers and many of their other ships are damaged; the Americans lose two cruisers and four destroyers. Although the Americans should have used their superior radar to secure an even greater advantage, the Japanese transports are forced to turn away.

A US shipbuilding yard claims to have built a 10,500-ton merchant vessel within four days and fifteen hours of its being laid down. It is fully equipped and ready for service within a further two days.

A 'Liberty ship' built in less than 5 days

14 November Admiral Tanaka attempts a new approach for his troops bound for Guadalcanal. The US carrier *Enterprise* is back on duty and her aircraft join with those from Henderson Field to attack the Japanese ships. Seven transports and two warships are lost, but Tanaka sails on, now receiving protection from a new formation consisting of the battleship *Kirishima*, four cruisers and nine destroyers under the command of Admiral Kondo. The Americans have also reformed their fleet, deploying the battleships *Washington* and *South Dakota* and four destroyers. In the middle of the night the two forces clash.

15 November In Tunisia German troop reinforcements have swelled to 10,000 men with 100 aircraft able to use local airfields. The 36th Brigade continues to advance but the 'Torch' invasion forces will not be so well served from the air, its aircraft having to operate from temporary or more distant airstrips.

Kirishima sunk

The naval action off Guadalcanal sees *South Dakota* retiring damaged early on, but *Washington* sinking *Kirishima*. Tanaka manages to land 4,000 troops but the hazards of surface approach and landing will see the Japanese resorting to submarine-borne supply in future.

16 November French politics interfere with the Allied moves in North Africa. British doubts about the true allegiance of Darlan are fuelled by General de Gaulle's announcement that his Free French supporters do not accept the Admiral's authority. The Americans, still content with the arrangement they have brokered, argue for Darlan.

17 November Advanced units of Eighth Army are now at Derna and Mechili. German troops from Sicily, who continue to arrive at Tunisian ports and airfields, find themselves in a position which is being approached from east and west by an enemy that is not currently being confronted on the ground.

The march across New Guinea by Australian and US forces is threatened by a landing of 1,000 Japanese troops at Buna.

A small convoy sails from Gibraltar for Malta. It has four freighters but is escorted by three cruisers and ten destroyers; the siege of the island must be lifted if support for the Allies' efforts in North Africa is to be maintained.

18 November Pierre Laval is given extra powers within the Vichy regime as Pétain loses some of his influence and control.

19 November The British troops moving westwards in Libya take Benghazi.

British take Benghazi

The Americans attack the newly reinforced Buna in New Guinea but are easily forced back.

The Battle for Stalingrad has sucked in so many German troops and such quantities of *matériel* that, almost imperceptibly, the army's potential for any positive action elsewhere has been reduced to zero.

The Soviets' winter offensive, Operation 'Uranus', begins along the Don in fog and heavy snow, and it is now that the Soviet commanders are able to demonstrate their tactical skill in the advance. At their head is Marshal Georgi Zhukov and he can immediately call on half a million men, 900 new T34 tanks, good supplies of artillery and more than 1,000 modern attack aircraft. The battle-weary German infantry has lost many men, is struggling to care for its sick and keep its fit men up to scratch. The first to feel the fresh cutting edge of the Soviet advance will be Roumanian Third Army which has been fighting alongside the Germans. Even in the Caucasus, the German advance has ground to a halt and will now be driven back.

Soviet winter offensive begins

Churchill appoints World War One veteran, Admiral Max Horton, as CinC Western Approaches with the specific remit to improve British performance in the Battle of the Atlantic. Dönitz will write later that Horton's appointment made a substantial difference.

20 November To the south of Stalingrad the Germans resist Russian pressure but are forced back by superior numbers and equipment. Roumanian Fourth Army is soundly beaten; their horse-drawn Flak guns are no match for the modern armour of their opponents.

The critical convoy heading for Malta reaches its destination with only one of its ships suffering minor damage.

21 November The massed Soviet forces thrusting from the south of Stalingrad continue to ride roughshod over Roumanian Fourth Army. Some sweep north towards Kalach, while others drive due west and

133

south. To the north-west of Stalingrad an even broader gap is punched through Roumanian Third Army formations. Threatened by the Soviet pincers, German Sixth Army's HQ has to move, but more than 250,000 German troops with 10,000 vehicles and 1,800 guns are encircled. Hitler calmly orders Paulus to take up defensive positions and await reinforcements.

23 November Soviet forces racing south capture a crossing of the Don at Kalach and then combine with 51st Army troops to begin the encirclement of the Germans remaining in and around Stalingrad. Roumanian Third Army divisions surrender around Raspopinskaya as they too are surrounded. Rather than make a broader advance to the west, Zhukov decides to annihilate the German forces in Stalingrad.

Germans fall back to El Agheila

In Libya the retreating German forces make a stand at Agedabia but have to give way and fall back to El Agheila. The British advance of 600 miles in two weeks has been delayed by booby-traps and demolitions but it might still have been expected to prevent so many German troops escaping towards Tunisia.

24 November Field Marshal von Manstein has been ordered to take command of the new Army Group Don and bring it to Paulus' rescue. Sixth Army is trapped but Hitler has ordered Paulus to stand fast and not attempt a breakout to the west. Von Manstein has less faith than the Führer in Göring's assurance that the Luftwaffe can supply beleaguered Sixth Army from the air.

Airlift into Stalingrad begins

25 November The promised airlift of supplies into Stalingrad begins. The heavy, defenceless transport aircraft suffer enormous losses to deliver a fraction of what is required.

More Japanese reinforcements land in New Guinea.

27 November In North Africa Allied forces reach Tebourba and Bizerte.

French fleet scuttled at Toulon

In France German forces occupy the port of Toulon but not before Admiral Laborde orders the scuttling of the remaining French fleet there. More than 70 ships are disabled by their crews, including three battleships and seven cruisers.

29 November In a radio broadcast from London, Churchill warns the Italians that they must choose between the overthrow of Mussolini or an all-out Allied attack.

30 November In Burma British moves back into the Arakan region are held up by atrocious weather.

The continuing efforts of the 'Tokyo Express' to resupply the Japanese on Guadalcanal sees Tanaka make another attempt with eight destroyers. During the next 24 hours he is confronted by Admiral Wright's fleet of five heavy cruisers and seven destroyers and sinks a US cruiser and damages three others for the loss of one of his own ships. This is a remarkable achievement for this resourceful naval commander, but he is unable to complete his mission.

DECEMBER 1942

1 December In Tunisia the Axis powers are making a great effort: the Germans with men and *matériel* – they now have 15,000 men there and more on the way; the Italians with supply convoys. Rommel's troops remain poorly supplied.

Four Italian convoys set out to cross the Mediterranean but three are forced to abort because of the threat posed by a small British squadron of cruisers and destroyers. In the next four weeks only half the cargoes loaded for North Africa will arrive and 32 ships will be lost.

2 December There is a change of Allied command in New Guinea as the Japanese are forced to abandon a troop landing at Buna only to be allowed to bring them ashore further to the west.

3 December In Tunisia German counter-attacks see Djedeida and Tebourba revert to Axis hands.

German counter-attack in Tunisia

Guadalcanal. Another Tanaka-led supply mission drops 1,500 containers but barely 300 reach the beach because American PT boats puncture them with machine-gun fire.

4 December The first US bombing mission against Italy sees US Ninth Air Force attack Naples. Two Italian cruisers are sunk.

6 December In New Guinea the Japanese counter-attack the Allied force which has reached the beach at Buna.

Japanese counter-attack in New Guinea

The RAF sends 272 bombers against Mannheim, using concentrated jamming of the German interceptor defence network. Only nine aircraft are lost.

7 December At Stalingrad 11th Panzer Division suffers losses while halting a Soviet move on German-held airfields.

8 December In Tunisia German forces occupy Bizerte and capture sixteen French vessels including nine submarines.

9 December General Patch arrives at Guadalcanal with XIV Corps to replace the battle-weary 1st Marine Division.

10 December 'The Cockleshell Heroes'. A raid on shipping in Bordeaux harbour by British Commandos in canoes deployed from the submarine HMS *Tuna* damages four large freighters, but all but two of the canoes are lost.

'Cockleshell Heroes' raid

11 December In North Africa Montgomery allows Eighth Army to advance once more and an attack against German positions at Mersa-el-Brega forces a retreat.

Another Guadalcanal supply mission fails when, once again, few of the containers dropped survive fire from US attack boats.

12 December Von Manstein chooses a southerly, though longer, route for his relief march to Stalingrad. He has one Luftwaffe, four panzer and ten infantry divisions plus the remnants of some Roumanian formations and is faced by limited Soviet forces.

Algiers harbour sees a daring raid by Italian midget submarines which sinks four ships.

13 December Rommel moves back from his position at El Agheila now that the Eighth Army is on the move and has taken Mersa-el-Brega.

To the west US air raids hammer the ports of Tunis and Bizerte.

Stranded troops in Stalingrad receive airlifted supplies

14 December The stranded troops in Stalingrad receive 180 tons of airlifted supplies as von Manstein's units push forward south of the city.

The El Agheila line is attacked by 7th Armoured Division. The New Zealand Division manoeuvres around the obstacles to the south.

In New Guinea US forces attack and take Buna, but more Japanese reinforcements have landed west of Gona.

16 December Italian Eighth Army is annihilated by a sudden Soviet advance. Von Manstein's relief mission proceeds slowly.

The Germans at El Agheila have been outflanked by the New Zealanders' move to the south and have to disperse to avoid a pincer movement.

The Japanese forces in Burma withdraw before a British attack on their lines between Maungdaw and Buthidaung can be tested.

17 December The Russian winter comes to the aid of the home forces when the Volga freezes over and makes it easier to resupply the troops on the west side of Stalingrad. The bad weather almost brings an end to the German airlift; fewer than 40 per cent of the aircraft are getting back to their bases.

18 December In New Guinea the fighting sways in favour of the Australians leading the Allied attacks; they have received fresh tank support.

Paulus ordered to break out of Stalingrad

19 December Contrary to earlier orders, General Paulus is now instructed to attempt a breakout from Stalingrad but he refuses von Manstein's demand. The latter's attempt to get forces through to him is beginning to flounder.

20 December The northern wing of von Manstein's force is under threat from Soviet advances so he encourages General Zeitzler at German High Command to press Paulus to breakout. Zeitzler is reluctant to intervene but does clarify the situation for the encircled German general; although now fully aware of his parlous situation, Paulus declines to make a move, citing a shortage of fuel.

The RAF uses its 'Oboe' precision bombing system during a raid by Mosquitos on a power plant in Holland. 'Oboe' – observer bombing over enemy – replaces the Gee system which the Germans have been able to jam for some time.

22 December In Tunisia an attack by British V Corps of First Army north of Medjez el Bab leads to fierce action around Longstop Hill in atrocious weather.

In Burma General Lloyd divides his forces to track either side of the

Mayu Peninsula with another group left to move towards Rathedaung, but this strategy weakens the British troops' situation.

23 December General Hoth's forces, leading von Manstein's relief march have pushed round the south of Stalingrad but are brought to a halt, frustratingly short of their target.

24 December Hoth is now driven back and, within Stalingrad itself, the besieged German forces who have been able to hear the fighting to the south, begin to give ground. A Soviet tank offensive reaches Tazinskaya airfield, one of the departure points for the relief flights into Stalingrad, and the resulting artillery barrage destroys many aircraft which have remained on the ground because of low cloud.

In Tunisia Longstop Hill is taken by British forces but the Allied commanders decide to call a halt at this point. Admiral Darlan is assassinated in his office in Algiers. *British forces take Longstop Hill*

In New Guinea Allied forces break though Japanese positions, but suffer many casualties and are again running short of tanks.

25 December Axis forces withdraw from the Libyan coastal town of Sirte and the Germans retake Longstop Hill in Tunisia, where bad weather and weak supply chains are afflicting both sides.

26 December Von Manstein is forced into full retreat south of the Don. The Soviets close in on Kotelnikovo. The relief flights to Sixth Army in Stalingrad are severely reduced. These flights have been a bad joke from the start; needing thousands of tons *per day*, the army has been lucky to receive a few hundred tons now and then. *Von Manstein in full retreat*

27 December Following their successes outside Stalingrad, the Soviets are now moving forward in the Caucasus where von Kleist is having to withdraw.

28 December British forces in Burma try to take Rathedaung but are repelled by the Japanese who, unknown to the British, have received reinforcements. *British repelled in Burma*

30 December The battleship *Lützow*, the heavy cruiser *Admiral Hipper* and six destroyers sail from Norway in search of Convoy JW-51B. The merchantmen are escorted by three separate groups under different commanders.

31 December The decision is taken in Tokyo to evacuate Guadalcanal.

The larger German warships close on Convoy JW-51B from different directions, but destroyer smoke-screens prohibit full engagement. One destroyer is sunk and another damaged, but *Hipper* is also damaged and a destroyer sunk. Despite an overwhelming numerical superiority, the Germans withdraw. *Battle of Barents Sea*

1943

JANUARY 1943

1 January On the Eastern Front the year begins with the Germans in retreat at many points; First and Fourth Panzer Armies are among those having to retrace their steps.

2 January Two Chariot midget submarines cut through nets at the entrance to Palermo harbour and place explosives against the hulls of the Italian cruiser *Ulpio Traiano* (launched in 1942) and the 8,600-ton transporter *Viminale*. The cruiser is damaged beyond repair.

3 January In the Caucasus the Soviet offensive is gathering pace and the German forces lack supplies and are in danger of becoming isolated.

5 January In Tunisia British troops gain some ground; General Mark Clark brings his US Fifth Army to operational status.

The Japanese rearguard stand on Guadalcanal continues around Mount Austen although a withdrawal is being planned.

6 January Criticised for his lack of success against Convoy JW-51B the previous month, Admiral Raeder, CinC Kriegsmarine, resigns.

7 January Unaware of the Japanese intention to pull out, US forces in Guadalcanal firm up their positions prior to a final push.

8 January The Soviets invite Paulus to surrender. He rejects this, but his troops, though still numerically strong, remain so poorly supplied and so completely enveloped that a breakout is impossible. Prospects of relief by von Manstein are remote.

9 January In New Guinea Allied forces are still pressing the Japanese at Buna and Sanananda and Australian 17th Brigade is flown in to establish a forward base for when the breakthrough is achieved.

10 January Soviet troops go all out to capture Stalingrad. A fierce artillery bombardment is followed by a rapid attack which pushes the Germans farther back.

On Guadalcanal the final US offensive begins; the Americans outnumber the Japanese by more than three to one. Desperate attempts to resupply the Japanese by surface ships are hampered by US PT boats.

11 January Russian troops open a corridor into the heart of Stalingrad. In the Caucasus they continue to gain ground.

The Japanese hold some strong points on Guadalcanal but the US forces make gains.

12 January Soviet formations break through Hungarian, Italian and German resistance on their drive towards Kharkov; von Manstein and von Kleist, struggling to save something from the ill-fated Caucasus operation, now face a real danger of being cut off.

The US destroyer *Worden* is lost when Amchitka Island in the Aleutians is retaken by the Americans.

13 January At Stalingrad the Russians reach the river Rossoshka.

14 January Soviet troops have crossed the river Chervlennaya; Pitomnik airfield, the only one with night-flying facilities left to the Germans, is overrun.

The Japanese land a small number of troops on Guadalcanal to support their withdrawal.

The Casablanca Conference commences. Churchill and Roosevelt with their respective Chiefs of Staff will hammer out strategies for the coming months of the war, having had long debates about the present situation. Differences of opinion and mutual concerns about each others' priorities will be resolved so that a programme can be set that gives due importance to: the U-boat threat; securing the convoys to Russia; planning a landing in Europe; advancing into Sicily and Italy once North Africa has been dealt with; pressing home the advantages presently being gained by the bombing offensive on Germany. It will later become apparent that policies for some of the theatres have been prejudiced by an over-confident estimate of shipping availability.

Casablanca Conference

16 January In Libya Montgomery's forces have regrouped and are on the move again.

The Eastern Front sees von Manstein fighting to hold Rostov as von Kleist continues his testing but orderly withdrawal from the Caucasus; the Russians fighting to clear their narrow 'corridor of death' supply route into Leningrad; and Paulus defending a Stalingrad pocket of only 250 square miles.

US forces gain more ground in Guadalcanal and, with the Australians, in New Guinea.

17 January German and Italian forces are encircled west of the Don. One unit breaks through the cordon to fight its way back to the German lines at Valuyki.

German bombers make their first night raid on London since May 1941; 118 aircraft are committed to this rare mission.

First German night raid on London since May 1941

18 January The German Tiger tank makes its first appearance in Tunisia.

19 January In Libya German positions on a line between Tarhuna and the sea are outflanked by Eighth Army. The 51st Highland Division will take Homs next day.

22 January The Germans lose their last airfield at Stalingrad when Gumrak is taken. Paulus is now completely cut off; his position is hopeless as the final Soviet assault begins with massive bombardments.

Stalingrad completely cut off

In Guadalcanal, the might of the US advance, using air, land and sea power, begins to overwhelm the tough Japanese rearguard.

Papua is regained for the Allies when Japanese troops are finally cleared from there.

Papua cleared of Japanese

23 January The Allies enter Tripoli which has been vacated by the Germans. They begin to repair the harbour which has been deliberately wrecked.

Allies enter Tripoli

The Japanese stronghold at Gifu finally falls to the Americans and the Japanese continue their intended withdrawal from Guadalcanal.

Gifu falls to Americans

24 January Hitler rejects von Manstein's proposal that he order General Paulus to surrender. Von Manstein now believes that he can extricate Army Group A cavalry units from the Caucasus, but has no chance of diverting to help the besieged Sixth Army.

25 January The Soviet troops who have entered Stalingrad in two thrusts meet in the centre of the city, knowing that they have now split the remaining German units into two small pockets.

26 January The changing course of the war in North Africa has brought recriminations between Field Marshal Rommel and the Italian High Command which was supposed to have control over the Desert Fox. The German commander, who has seen his Italian allies fail to get convoys through, or halt the British routing of men and supplies, and has grounds for criticising the performance of Italian units in the fighting, launches vitriolic complaints and is advised that he will be replaced by General Messe, an Italian. He chooses to disregard this information.

First USAAF bombing mission against German target

27 January In the first USAAF mission against a German target, sixty-four B-17 and B-24 bombers attack Wilhelmshaven, which had also been the target for the first British daylight raid in 1939. Good fortune favours the mission and engenders the mistaken belief that the US bombers will be able to defend themselves more successfully than their British counterparts.

28 January As the German authorities plan greater mobilisation of civilian men and women, their forces continue to suffer on almost every sector of the Eastern Front. The majority of First Panzer Army has trekked 300 miles out of the Caucasus to reach the forces at Rostov who need their immediate help to defend their position between the Rivers Don and Mius.

Chicago sunk

29 January The US heavy cruiser *Chicago* is lost during a supply mission to Guadalcanal.

30 January As speeches are made at the German Air Ministry in Berlin to commemorate the tenth anniversary of Hitler's regime, the RAF sends Mosquitos on a daylight bombing raid. Two 2-ton aerial mines hit the radio broadcasting building. Hitler appoints Dönitz CinC Kriegsmarine,

Dönitz appointed CinC Kriegsmarine

and promotes General Paulus to Field Marshal (this in the hope that he will commit suicide, no German field marshal having ever surrendered). In Stalingrad the new Field Marshal's HQ is surrounded.

In the Caucasus, the Maykop oilfields are recaptured and First Panzer Army retreats towards Rostov which isolates Seventeenth Army in the Kuban Peninsula.

In Tunisia, inexperienced French and US units are driven back by the seasoned 21st Panzer Division at Faid.

German southern forces in Stalingrad surrender

31 January Field Marshal Paulus surrenders his southern unit in Stalingrad. General Stecker, commanding the men in the northern sector, continues to fight.

General Ambrosio takes over as Chief of the Italian General Staff upon Marshal Cavallero's dismissal. When Mussolini is deposed the latter will make a weak attempt to replace him.

During the month bad weather in the Atlantic has curtailed U-boat activity, but elsewhere they have sunk more than 200,000 tons of shipping.

FEBRUARY 1943

1 February The Japanese begin to evacuate their troops from Guadalcanal. The Americans are fooled into believing that the naval activity signals a new offensive and more than 5,000 of the enemy are taken off the island with little opposition.

2 February General Stecker surrenders his remaining men in Stalingrad. In attempting to supply or rescue the defending forces, the Germans have brought out 34,000 wounded but have lost 495 transport aircraft and upwards of 1,000 aircrew, and the Soviets will later claim to have found nearly 150,000 German bodies in the city. Of those taken prisoner, only 5,000 will return to Germany; many will die from ill-treatment. The recapture of the area has been a central core of the Soviet counter-offensive and has seen their battlefield strategy to be sound and determined, but they have had to devote 80 units to the attack and this has reduced their push against the Germans elsewhere, especially at Rostov.

Following information gleaned from a survivor of a U-boat attack the previous day, a pack of 20 U-boats attacks Convoy SC-118 from Halifax, Nova Scotia, outward bound for the UK. Thirteen ships are sunk for the loss of three U-boats. The British Admiralty urges a more offensive role on escort vessels.

3 February The German nation is told of the loss of Stalingrad and three days of national mourning declared.

4 February Eighth Army crosses into Tunisia. The German and Italian forces are now facing the 'Torch' troops approaching from the west and Montgomery's forces turning up the coast towards the Mareth Line – the prewar French-built defensive system which runs 22 miles inland from the coast.

On the Eastern Front Seventeenth Army is now cut off in the Kuban and can only be reached by sea from the Crimea. Soviet forces are only 40 miles east of Kursk and less from the Sea of Azov.

More Japanese troops are evacuated from Guadalcanal.

6 February Von Manstein flies to see Hitler to get permission to withdraw. The Führer accepts a retreat to new defensive positions behind the Mius.

8 February In Burma 77th Indian Brigade goes into action for the first time. This long-range penetration unit, which will become known as

First Chindit
operation

Wingate's Chindits, is a combined force of British, Gurkha and Burmese troops. They intend to use the same tactics as the Japanese, namely, small units making harassing and sniping attacks. The Chindits start out from Imphal and will have some success hitting Japanese supply lines. General Orde Wingate, their leader, has fought with distinction in Palestine and is seen as an early developer of special-purpose forces.

Soviets capture Kursk

On the Eastern Front the Soviets capture Kursk.

9 February A further 2,000 Japanese troops leave Guadalcanal, bringing the total to more than 12,000. The loss of the island is a major blow to Japanese morale, and they have lost nearly 10,000 men, but the strength of their fighting resistance has cost many US troops and much US strategic effort which, if repeated on every other Pacific island of this size, would prolong the war to a damaging extent.

10 February A B-24 Liberator sinks *U519* off the Azores in the first success for the new aerial offensive against U-boats in this area. U-boats returning to their bases on the French Atlantic coast are being increasingly menaced by aircraft which are having more effect than the regular bombing of the U-boat pens at Lorient and St-Nazaire.

14 February In Tunisia Rommel continues to disregard Italian demands that he accept their High Command's orders. General Arnim has been brought into the area to ease the impasse and he overrules Rommel's plan for an attack towards Tebessa, preferring a lesser action against US positions west of Faid; the Americans are badly defeated. The British propaganda film, *Desert Victory*, is sent by Churchill to Roosevelt by air so that he can see the Sherman tank in action. A copy also goes to Stalin who will later tell Churchill that it is being shown to politicians and commanders in Moscow to remove doubts held there that the British are fighting as hard as the Soviets. Such exchanges of films is commonplace; Churchill applauds the Soviet film showing the action at Stalingrad.

Soviets capture
Rostov and
Voroshilovgrad

The Soviets capture Rostov and Voroshilovgrad.

15 February In Tunisia Rommel leads part of 15th Panzer Division in the German and Italian advance which takes Gafsa. Other troops of his are now manning the Mareth Line on the coast where Montgomery is now approaching to capture Medenine.

16 February Hitler urges Hausser's II SS Panzer Corps to hold the strategic town of Kharkov 'to the death' but it falls after fierce fighting.

17 February General Von Arnim and Rommel are inflicting heavy losses on US 1st Armored Division, but the latter is annoyed by his colleague's cautious approach. The Desert Fox knows that the US troops are inexperienced and feels that the Italian and German High Commands must allow him to take advantage of this, but they are slow to back him up.

In a rare excursion to the battle zone, Hitler visits von Manstein's HQ with the intention of dismissing him, but is persuaded to back the Field Marshal's plan for a counter-attack.

18 February A U-boat attack on Convoy ON-166 is beyond the range of Coastal Command protection and fourteen ships are sunk.

20 February Rommel continues to press his case for an ambitious push against what he perceives to be weak US sectors, but the next Axis attack, while more adventurous, still has restricted aims. It will move on Le Kef from Kasserine and Sbiba, but Rommel is not given the Tiger battalion he covets. This advance has been anticipated by the Allies who are ready for a fierce confrontation.

21 February The Allies defend Sbiba and Kasserine but sacrifice the latter when the Germans bring up extra troops.

Kasserine action

In a significant failure of tactical awareness on their drive to recapture territory, Soviet forces press south-west into a self-made salient towards Pavlovograd and Krasnograd. Meanwhile, Hitler appoints Guderian to the post of Inspector General of Armoured Troops with massive theoretical control over the training and organisation of mobile forces. The tank specialist, who had been relieved of duties for some months previously, is thus finally acknowledged by the Führer as invaluable to the cause of German tank development but now his remit is as difficult as any previous demand made of him.

Guderian Inspector General of Armoured Troops

In the Pacific the Americans begin the landing of 9,000 troops on Banika and Pavuvu in the Russell Islands.

Banika and Pavuvu landings

22 February In Tunisia the Axis advance is held by determined Allied resistance despite the diversionary move by a German division towards Tebessa. Rommel, who has been leading the drive from the front, is persuaded to move back after fierce night fighting sways in favour of the Allies when US artillery units join the battle after a four-day march from Oran. A combination of more mountainous terrain than the expert German desert fighters have been used to, the split command of their forces and the quick learning curve of the well-equipped Americans has turned this close-run action the Allied way, but had Rommel been allowed to pursue his more adventurous plan he might have gained more ground before the arrival of the US reinforcements. From now on the Allied cause will be greatly aided by increased air supremacy.

Convoy ON-166 loses fourteen ships to a U-boat attack in the Atlantic.

22 February The Soviet advance has left its forward units short of fuel and ammunition. It is now prey to von Manstein's concentric counter which, though employing just a fraction of the men the Soviets have at their disposal, now attacks north and south into the salient the Russians have created.

24 February Rommel's persistence seems to have paid off when he is given command of Army Group Afrika which is to include von Arnim's

Rommel commands Army Group Afrika

Fifth Panzer Army and General Messe's Italian First Army. It solves the problem of a too complex command structure, but some German officers are beginning to press for new thinking on the part of the High Command.

26 February In Tunisia British troops at Medjez el Bab hold an attack by von Arnim spearheading 10th and 21st Panzer Divisions and this prevents Rommel from gathering sufficient forces for a strike against the limited numbers the British have brought up towards the Mareth Line.

27 February General Alexander sends a message to Churchill informing him of progress in North Africa, but adds that victory 'is not just around the corner'.

28 February On the Eastern Front von Manstein's brilliant move has created a yawning gap of 120 miles in the Soviet Front.

Norsk Hydro 'heavy water' plant raid

A team of Norwegian soldiers, trained in the UK and parachuted in by the RAF, inflicts serious damage to the 'heavy water' plant at the Norsk Hydro power station near Ryukan; this is a setback to the German atomic research programme.

MARCH 1943

1 March On the Eastern Front the German High Command orders an evacuation of the salient at Rzhev and a straightening of the German lines; this shortens them by 200 miles and frees some 20 divisions for action elsewhere.

Battle of the Bismarck Sea

2 March In the Pacific a Japanese troop convoy bound for New Guinea is attacked by aircraft of US Fifth Air Force. During the next three days all eight transports and 50 per cent of the 7,000 men aboard will be lost, as well as four destroyers and 25 aircraft. This Battle of the Bismarck Sea ruins the Japanese plans for New Guinea.

3 March von Manstein's counter-offensive has been brilliant in its execution but now faces two major problems: the ground, which will shortly thaw and hamper further progress, and manpower; he is too short of men to maintain the encirclement of strong Soviet units which his tactics have brought about.

Chindits cut Mandalay-Kyitkyina railway

In Burma the Chindits succeed in cutting the Mandalay–Kyitkyina railway line. It will be their only significant success until Wingate has greater numbers seconded to him.

4 March In Tunis the Allied forces at Medenine sight the approach of 10th and 21st Panzer Divisions, but they now have more units at this formal line of defence, including new artillery.

Von Manstein switches his line of counter-attack to Kharkov.

In the Atlantic a Wellington bomber attacking *U333* is shot down by AA fire directed at the aircraft's Leigh Light.

5 March On the Eastern Front the thaw hampers German progress; General Hoth is unable to move his Fourth Panzer Army across the Donets on which floating ice precludes any bridging.

146

An RAF Bomber Command raid on the Krupp munitions factory at Essen marks the beginning of weeks of action against the industrial heartland of Germany, the Ruhr. This first mission numbers 412 aircraft including Lancasters, Halifaxes, Stirlings and Wellingtons.

RAF begins Ruhr bombing

6 March In Tunisia German troops make two attacks on Allied positions at Medenine but are driven off. These foolhardy and lack-lustre efforts which lose the attackers one-third of their tanks were not sanctioned by Rommel who would have preferred to withdraw and regroup. Thanks to Ultra reading of the German Enigma coded signals, Montgomery is able to make adequate preparation.

Medenine action

7 March Another UK-bound convoy from Halifax, Nova Scotia, becomes partially dispersed in heavy storms and U-boats sink thirteen ships.

9 March The end of an era. Rommel leaves North Africa. He visits Mussolini in Rome before reporting back to Hitler; neither leader will tolerate a withdrawal from Africa and the Führer urges his man to rest and recuperate so as to be fit for leading a new offensive against Casablanca. Germany has many fine battlefield generals, but Rommel has proved masterly in the desert, at least in so far as his superiors and the course of the war have permitted. Had he received better supplies, or if the Italians had been up to the standard of his German troops, the Desert Fox might have seen a more successful outcome to his North African adventure.

Rommel leaves North Africa

On the Eastern Front the Germans attack Kharkov from the west and north and hard fighting is seen in the area.

Germans attack Kharkov

10 March In Tunisia the Free French units under General Leclerc stave off German attacks south-east of Mareth.

11 March In Russia, Kharkov is entered by II SS Panzer Corps after heavy fighting.

12 March In Tunisia a flanking move around the Mareth Line is begun by a mix of Allied troops.

Eighth Army attacks Mareth Line

15 March The Eastern Front battles ebb and flow with the Germans being driven back in the central sector, but the remnants of the Soviet forces being pushed out of the Kharkov area.

16 March The fast Convoy HX-229 of 40 ships from New York, and the slower Convoy SC-122 of 58 ships from Nova Scotia are attacked by 37 U-boats in three groups. Twenty-one ships are lost in return for one U-boat. These first three weeks of March signal a turning-point: from now on carrier support groups and long-range reconnaissance aircraft will take their toll of the U-boats. There will no longer be substantial gaps in Allied coverage of the Atlantic, no areas where U-boats can operate freely.

Convoy HX-229

17 March In Burma a major skirmish sees 123rd Indian Brigade forced to retreat after attacks by Japanese units north of Rathedaung.

18 March On the Eastern Front German troops attack Belgorod by land and air in the final phase of von Manstein's counter-offensive. His bril-

Germans attack Belgorod

liant operation has cost the Soviet troops (advancing elsewhere) 600 tanks and about 40,000 casualties. It has proved that the war on this front is far from over.

Patton retakes Gafsa In Tunisia, Gafsa is retaken by General Patton's US II Corps.

In Burma the Japanese are becoming conscious of Wingate's Chindits and take action to hunt them down. Elsewhere, British moves are being damaged by skilled Japanese tactics in difficult terrain.

20 March In Tunisia a night bombardment of the Mareth Line is undertaken as the New Zealand flanking moves accelerate. At this point in the North Africa campaign the Allies have more than 5,000 aircraft in the region; the Axis forces have fewer than 300.

21 March Wadi Zigzaou is crossed by a small British force during the skirmishes around the Mareth Line. It will be reinforced the following day, but attacks by 15th Panzer Division preclude further advances at this juncture. Meanwhile the New Zealanders will be held at Tebaga Gap.

23 March Montgomery, switching his main Mareth attack to the Tebaga Gap, moves General Horrocks there with 1st Armoured Division.

24 March Montgomery deploys 4th Indian Division in a small flanking move towards Beni Zelten.

Chindits disbanded In Burma the Chindits are ordered to split up. Their losses have been heavy, partly because of their *modus operandi*, but their exploits have boosted Allied morale in the region.

25 March In Tunisia, 1st Armoured Division's advance and the threat posed by US forces at Maknassy prompt von Arnim to pull his infantry away from the Mareth Line.

26 March Continuing ground bombardment of the Axis troops in the Tebaga Gap is augmented by increasingly heavy air attacks by the British and Americans. By the end of the day the German defences are so ragged that 1st Armoured Division can advance towards El Hamma.

Battle of the Bering Sea Battle of the Bering Sea. Off the Soviet Komandorski Islands a patrolling US squadron of two cruisers and four destroyers intercepts a Japanese force of one heavy and two light cruisers and eight destroyers escorting Aleutian-bound supply ships. The US cruiser *Salt Lake City* and the Japanese heavy cruiser *Nachi* are badly damaged and the Japanese head for home.

27 March In Tunisia the Italian First Army is forced away from the Mareth Line.

28 March Axis infantry from Mareth arrive at Wadi Akarit. They are badly mauled and some, especially the Italian units, seem to have lost the will to fight on.

29 March Montgomery chooses not to advance on the hastily created Axis defences around Wadi Akarit, despite the fact that General Messe has reported to Italian High Command on the unsuitability of the position. The New Zealanders have entered Gabes, on the coast above Mareth.

APRIL 1943

3 April A determined push by Patton's forces around El Guettar is held back by German counter-fire.

4 April US bombers raid the Renault plant on the outskirts of Paris and prepare for a similar mission to Antwerp the following day.

5 April In Tunis, instead of immediately pursuing the Axis forces on 29 March, Montgomery has built-up his forces again and is ready to move on. This cautious approach is much favoured by his junior officers who can feel for the front-line soldier ordered to move too far beyond the range of support and reinforcement. Montgomery will advance 4th Indian Division by night against the defences at Djebel Fatnassa. The operation starts well, but their attack at daybreak lacks co-ordination and begins to struggle when Axis reinforcements arrive.

7 April As Axis forces move back from their lines at Wadi Akarit, advance units of Eighth Army join up with scouting patrols from Patton's corps on the Gafsa road.

Hitler and Mussolini meet in Salzburg. They decide to hold on as long as possible in North Africa, though Rommel's report of the parlous situation there is not the only one that they have received.

Hitler and Mussolini meet in Salzburg

In the Pacific, the Japanese, alarmed at the solid preparations being made by the Americans, seek to distract and delay them by a massive air operation. Yamamoto plans 'Operation I' which begins with a raid by nearly 200 aircraft on US positions on Guadalcanal and Tulagi and their ships in the region. The first day sees a destroyer and some smaller vessels hit, but the Japanese carriers are very short of aircraft and trained pilots.

Japanese 'Operation I' begins with raid on Guadalcanal and Tulagi

8 April In a bid to extend their control over northern Burma, the Japanese decide to build a new railway to aid their logistic needs. They force about 60,000 Allied prisoners of war to perform this task, of whom 25 per cent will die of exhaustion, lack of food and ill-treatment.

9 April The Allies continue to advance in Tunisia. They take Mahares and are less than 150 miles from Tunis when they enter Sfax after the retreating Axis units have left.

Allies enter Sfax

10 April The Italian heavy cruiser *Trieste* is sunk at La Maddalena, Sardinia, by attacks from 84 B-24 Liberator bombers. Other Allied aircraft continue to disrupt all attempts to fly in adequate supplies to Axis forces in Tunisia.

Trieste sunk

11 April On the Eastern Front the Soviet salient to the west of Kursk is a prime target for the Germans if they are to blunt the Soviet advances. It is a massive undertaking and too great for some of the commanders, von Manstein and Guderian included. Others, such as General Zeitzler and Field Marshals Keitel and von Kluge are in favour. It would be a huge task for a German Army at the height of its Blitzkrieg successes and it is to regain some of those former glories that some officers wish to see it tried. There are plenty who would rather extend themselves with this gamble than fight ever more defensive withdrawals.

14 April It seems that the battle for North Africa must surely be drawing to a close as the Allies now occupy an arc of positions from the north coast of Tunisia west of Bizerte to the east coast north of Enfidaville. Unless large and immediate supplies arrive to fuel an Axis counter from the enveloped area, it can only be a matter of time before the Allied forces which have arrived from the east and west can close in.

USAAF bombs Bremen

17 April The US Eighth Army Air Force sends 115 B-17 bombers to raid aircraft factories at Bremen; the majority return unscathed and German aviation suffers another blow.

18 April In Tunisia the desperate need to resupply the Axis forces sees a convoy of aircraft leave Sicily. More than half are shot down by Allied fighters and such items as do arrive are well short of requirements.

Hitler agrees to Mussolini's plea for Italian II Corps to be returned from the Eastern Front. This ends Italian involvement there.

Yamamoto killed

Admiral Yamamoto is killed when his aircraft is shot down by US P-38 Lightnings over Bougainville. On 13 April the Americans had intercepted a coded message giving details of the flight. The US aircraft fly from Guadalcanal and engage Yamamoto's G4M bomber for no more than thirty seconds before sending it into the jungle below. The loss of their master strategist and national hero is a severe blow to the Japanese; there is no official announcement of his death for a month, and his state funeral is only the twelfth in Japan's long history.

19 April In Tunisia another attempt to resupply Axis forces fails when the flight is intercepted and cut down.

Warsaw Jewish ghetto uprising

In a major civilian rebellion, the inhabitants of the Jewish ghetto in Warsaw rise against the German occupation forces. Their numbers have been hugely reduced by systematic extermination.

The British believe that the Germans may be accelerating their research and testing of rockets; photo-reconnaissance of the Peenemünde site is ordered.

20 April In Tunisia Montgomery, uncharacteristically, permits a succession of small attacks against strongly defended Axis positions at Enfidaville. He suffers heavy casualties.

22 April As another 30 transport aircraft are shot down while trying to reach the Axis forces in Tunisia, Allied units target German hill positions. British V Corps raid Longstop Hill and Peter's Corner, and IX Corps moves in on locations between Goubellat and Bou Arada; US II Corps attacks Hill 609 on a planned route to Mateur.

24 April Warsaw is the scene of horrific slaughter as the occupying forces seek to suppress the uprising. Captured Jews are shot without question or taken away to the extermination camps.

26 April In Tunisia British tank superiority comes into play as the British take Longstop Hill.

New plans for US operations in the Solomon Islands see Halsey's South Pacific Area units given a route through New Georgia and Bougainville with MacArthur's South-West Pacific group required to advance along the coast of New Guinea. The two will then join in cutting off the Japanese bases at Rabaul and Kavieng from supplies.

28 April In Tunisia the Germans are fighting hard, responding to the loss of Djebel Bou Aoukaz with a counter-attack by 8th Panzer Division.

30 April The Germans retake Djebel Bou Aoukaz but lose much armour in the process. US forces, fighting for control of Hill 609, gain footholds. — Battle for Hill 609

The Allies employ deception when planning the invasion of Sicily. Off the coast of Spain a body wearing the uniform of an officer of Royal Marines is found floating. Documents on the body suggest that the man was Eisenhower's go-between with British military Chiefs General Nye, Admiral Mountbatten, Alexander and Cunningham, and refer to a planned invasion through Sardinia and a feint attack on Sicily. The papers reach the Germans and Hitler orders priority in the Mediterranean to be given to Sardinia and northern Italy.

MAY 1943

I May In Tunisia the switchback nature of the fighting at this time is shown by the Germans' recapture of Hill 609. Having regained the position they find themselves in a state of siege.

3 May The US 1st Division exits Mousetrap Valley and takes Mateur. Its advance is now held up by stronger German defensive positions.

4 May East-bound Convoy ONS-5, protected by eighteen escorts, is threat- — Convoy ONS-5
ened by 60 U-boats in four groups. During a battle which extended over three nights, thirteen merchantmen are lost and one is damaged, but the escorts sink six U-boats and badly damage four more. Another two collide and are lost. This result is achieved without the normal level of air support.

5 May In Tunisia Djebel Bou Aoukaz returns to Allied hands after a another British assault on the Axis positions.

6 May Using their full advantage of air supremacy and artillery fire power, V Corps calls in a massive bombardment to decimate 15th Panzer Division formations and break through Axis defences to move on towards Tunis. The Americans are advancing on Bizerte in the north and the French are closing on Pont du Fahs in the south-west.

7 May Tunis and Bizerte are taken by mid-afternoon and Axis forces flee — Allies take Tunis and
to the Cape Bon Peninsula. — Bizerte

8 May There they are unable to regroup because of the intervention of 6th Armoured Division which has swept north from Hammamet. Alexander tells Churchill: 'Things have gone even better than could have been hoped ... The Axis front has completely collapsed and disintegrated.'

9 May A Ju 88, fitted with the new Liechtenstein BC radar set, is secretly flown to Scotland by a British intelligence agent. The analysis of this new advanced equipment and other data about the organisation and tactics of German night-fighters is vital to the Allies.

10 May There is massed surrender on Cape Bon as the Axis forces realise their plight. Further resistance is futile, supplies have not got through and there is no chance of evacuation.

On the Eastern Front the German High Command discusses the situation around Kursk. Hitler agrees to an attack there but soon delays the start date from mid-June to early July on the assurance that a supply of Panther tanks will be available by then.

Slim to command
Fourteenth Army in
Burma

11 May In Burma the British campaign in the Arakan comes to an end when 26th Division is withdrawn from Maungdaw. Japanese casualties have been half the British total of about 3,000 and the morale of the defeated units is very low. Generals Irwin and Lloyd are removed from command and General Slim will arrive to command Fourteenth Army within the week.

Axis forces surrender
in Tunisia

12 May In Tunisia the official surrender of Axis forces is signed by General von Arnim. Alexander signals Churchill: The Tunisian campaign is over ... we are masters of the North African shore.'

Trident Conference in
Washington

This day sees the start of the Trident Conference in Washington. Top priority of the Americans is to settle a date for the invasion of Europe.

Having already obtained agreement for the move on Sicily, the British argue that the logical short-term preference must be to continue the advance from there into mainland Italy and to the troublesome Balkans thereafter, but the Americans see the spectre of unrelated European politics in this and again insist that they are under increasing pressure at home to devote more men, money and time to the Pacific.

The British remind the US of its commitment to the 'Europe First' policy and claim that the resources already sent to the Pacific have denuded the northern theatres of vital shipping, with the resultant limitation on the progress of the war there. The end result is that a date for an invasion of France is set – 1 May 1944 – and senior staff are appointed to commence the planning. Meanwhile, it is agreed to pursue any successes achieved in Sicily, and the Americans can follow their agenda for the Pacific.

The Allies successfully deploy the first air-launched torpedo fitted with an acoustic homing head which follows a submerged U-boat, drawn to it by the sound of its propellers. This first use sees *U456* damaged; the first sinking by this means is 24 hours away.

13 May The final prisoner count in Tunisia is 250,000 as the remnants of the Axis forces there are rounded up and surrendered by General Messe.

15 May In the Aleutians the Americans are struggling to make progress from their beachheads. Although they can claim numerical superiority, their air support is being held back by bad weather and they contribute to their own problems by 'friendly fire' incidents which bring casualties.

16 May The Warsaw uprising is finally crushed when the SS blow up the synagogue; their commander confirms that 14,000 have been killed and almost three times that number sent to the Treblinka extermination camp.

Warsaw uprising crushed

Pilots of RAF 617 Squadron spend the day finalising their plans for what is to become known as the Dambusters Raid. British inventor, Barnes Wallis, has been conducting experiments with a revolving depth-charge which, when dropped, spinning, from a low-level bomber passing over water will bounce towards a barrier at the end of the stretch of water, sink to the bottom and explode. The weapon has been designed for use against the dams on the rivers Mohne and Eder in Germany's industrial heartland. The successful execution of the raid results in enormous flooding, but eight of nineteen aircraft are lost and less damage has been inflicted than had been hoped for. The British maximise the morale-boosting news and the aircrews, especially their charismatic leader, Guy Gibson, VC, are accorded celebrity status. Goebbels notes in his diary that 'the raid was very successful. The Führer is extremely impatient and angry at the inadequate preparations made by the Luftwaffe.'

Dambusters Raid

17 May In Yugoslavia the Germans continue to be harassed by the efforts of Tito and his Partisans. They now mount a further offensive against these guerrilla teams, deploying a remarkable total of more than 120,000 troops, against such a small enemy.

German offensive in Yugoslavia

18 May In the Aleutians the Americans make some progress on Attu. Their dual advance links up and prepares to assault what they think to be the last Japanese strongholds near Chicago Harbour.

19 May In the Atlantic U-boats attack Convoy SC-130, but on this occasion come up against supporting B-24 Liberators deploying homing torpedoes. Since early April, fourteen of twenty-two convoys have crossed the North Atlantic without loss. No longer can the ageing U-boats cope with the advanced tactics employed by the Allies on sea and in the air. More than 30 U-boats have been sunk in the first three weeks of May.

Convoy SC-130

23 May A total of 754 RAF bombers drop more than 2,000 tons of bombs on Dortmund. Air Chief Marshal Harris sends a message to his crews advising them that 100,000 tons of bombs have now been dropped on a Germany which Göring had said in 1939 would not receive a single bomb.

Dortmund raided by RAF

24 May Dönitz, who loses his own son when *U954* is sunk on 19 May, has grown tired of receiving reports which indicate that his wolf packs are regularly sailing into virtual ambushes and calls off all U-boat attacks in the North Atlantic. The Allies' combination of constantly improving radar technology, increased code-breaking skill and the arrival of more and better aircraft has effectively put an end to the Battle of the Atlantic. The Germans are now losing more boats than are being built, and have failed to modernised their designs. The vessels are redeployed to safer areas of the Atlantic but this is an admission of failure and an acceptance that they will serve a lesser purpose. The Germans have lost the U-boat war.

27 May Winston Churchill goes to North Africa with US General Marshall to discuss the forthcoming campaign in Italy with the battlefield commanders there. Churchill wants Italy removed from the war; Marshall is more concerned to limit the scope of the mission so as not to detract from the plans for D-Day.

In Yugoslavia the situation becomes more complex when SOE agents, active in the area for some time, report that General Mihailovic and his Cetnik rebels seem to be siding with the Germans after failing to resolve their power struggle with Tito and his forces. The Partisans are facing complete encirclement by the latest German moves against them.

In France the Resistance is becoming more formalised with Jean Moulin, an aide of de Gaulle's, pulling the disparate factions together.

29 May In the Aleutians vigorous fighting is seen when the Japanese make a last stand against the advancing Americans. Opposition will last just another 24 hours before the Japanese concede. US losses total 600 dead and 1,200 wounded in a drive which has meant very little in the context of the Pacific War.

31 May Three Bf 110 night-fighters attack a DC-3 over the Bay of Biscay believing that Churchill is a board. This erroneous information has been fed to them through a German agent in Lisbon who reported only that he had seen someone who looked like the British Prime Minister join the flight.

U-boats *U440* and *U563* are sunk by Coastal Command aircraft, Dönitz having instructed their commanders to engage aircraft with their guns.

JUNE 1943

3 June The divisions among the Free French are healed by an agreement between de Gaulle and General Giraud and the formation of a

Committee of National Liberation under their joint control. This marks the summit of Giraud's success; he will be gradually eased out by his colleague. Resistance workers combine with SOE agents to sabotage the Michelin works in Clermont-Ferrand in one of the larger Resistance missions.

In Russia the Germans begin a series of air raids against the Molotov factories in Gorki. By 8 June the works will have been brought to a standstill.

4 June The Island of Pantelleria, equidistant between Tunisia and Sicily, has been bombarded by air and sea and will continue to be so for some days.

10 June This day sees the first of the combined bombing offensives agreed at the Casablanca Conference whereby the US deploy their aircraft on daylight precision raids while the British stay with their night deployments.

Allied combined bombing offensives begin

11 June The garrison on Pantelleria has been shelled into submission and surrenders before an Allied assault force has a chance to land. Other islands in the area, Lampedusa, Linosa and Lampione, will follow suit in the coming days.

Pantelleria surrenders to Allies

12 June Düsseldorf suffers its heaviest air raid of the war. A Pathfinder force has led 693 bombers to their target where close to 2,000 tons of bombs have been dropped inside 45 minutes. German fighters have pursued the attackers home and shot down twenty-seven.

Düsseldorf bombed

14 June After their evaluation of the Lichtenstein BC radar set obtained on 9 May, Dr R. V. Jones and his specialists have replicated it and, under the code-name 'Serrate', it enters service with British night-fighters. The German aircraft carrying their version of the device can now be identified and so the hunters become the hunted.

16 June Allied convoys in support of the invasion of Sicily sail from USA and Scotland.

In the Pacific the Japanese attempt an air strike against US vessels assembling for the action on New Georgia. US fighters take off from Guadalcanal to intercept and claim to have destroyed more than 90 aircraft.

18 June Churchill's ruthlessness against commanders who do not fulfil his expectations is seen when he appoints Wavell Viceroy of India and Auchinleck CinC India, so removing them from duty in important battle zones. Both men have been fine battlefield commanders who have suffered from being asked to undertake difficult tasks with inadequate resources. How they would have handled the larger actions of the latter part of the war will never be known.

Wavell Viceroy of India and Auchinleck CinC India

20 June In the Pacific US Sixth Army establishes its HQ at Milne Bay on the eastern tip of Papua, and in the coming days there are US landings on Woodlark Island, 100 miles to the east.

US Sixth Army begins Papua operations

22 June The early assumption of greater power over Free French affairs by de Gaulle is seen when it is announced that General Giraud will retain command of forces in North Africa with de Gaulle overseeing all other areas.

23 June British aerial reconnaissance has now secured photographs of the Peenemünde research base showing rockets available for firing.

Peenemünde rocket site discovered by Allies

28 June Heinrich Himmler visits Peenemünde to witness the first take-off of the A-4 rocket. It crash lands nearby and destroys three aircraft, but a later firing is successful, this second rocket travelling 142 miles into the Baltic Sea.

Cologne bombed

A British raid of more than 500 aircraft inflicts great damage on Cologne. It completes six months of intense bombing activity. Great damage has been done to the German urban landscape, but the armaments industry has not suffered as much as might have been expected; ammunition and aircraft production remain remarkably high.

30 June On the Eastern Front the spring thaw has given way to harder ground and the combatants begin their next moves.

New Guinea landings

In the Pacific a US amphibious force lands at Nassau Bay on the east coast of New Guinea and establishes a bridgehead after heavy fighting.

After landings on the southern tip of New Georgia earlier in the month, US forces move on to other islands in the group. The landings are undertaken during the monsoon period.

JULY 1943

1 July Discord in the Axis camp. Marshal Antonescu meets Mussolini and urges him to join Hungary and Roumania in pulling out of the alliance. The Italian leader is certainly tired of the reversals his country has suffered and nervous about the possibility of an invasion but, as ever, he is subservient to Hitler and declines to raise the issue.

2 July In New Guinea the Australian forces advancing from Wau have linked up with US troops.

Zanana, New Georgia, landings

US forces land unopposed at Zanana in New Georgia.

3 July A force of nearly 600 British aircraft en route to attack Cologne are intercepted by an experimental flight of Fw 190 and Bf 109 day fighters. Despite the danger posed by their own anti-aircraft fire, they account for a dozen of the bombers.

Sikorski killed

4 July General Sikorski, the Polish leader, is killed in an air crash near Gibraltar. His replacements, Mikolajczyk as prime minister and Kukiel as CinC, are of lesser calibre and not involved so much by the Allies.

Battle of Kursk

On the Eastern Front the greatest tank battle in history is about to commence. The Germans plan a basic severing movement against the Kursk salient thereby punching a gap through the Soviet lines. There is dissension in the German camp; Guderian says: 'It is a matter of profound indifference to the world whether we hold Kursk or not ... Why do we want to attack in the east at all this year?' He is all for rebuilding tank strength and regrouping for greater offensives in 1944. On the Soviet side Zhukov takes the view that the best Soviet policy is to defend the current position and so retain the large land area they already occupy. The combatants bring to the arena about two million men and 6,000 tanks; these forces will both enjoy substantial air support. The Soviet T-34, modern but battle-proven, will face the Panther tank for whose arrival the battle has been delayed. The Germans can also deploy the highly regarded Tiger, but the untried Panther and the new giant Elefant tanks are suffering teething problems, not surprisingly given the speed at which their production has rushed through. On this first day the Soviets open a bombardment against the German positions before the latter can make their move.

5 July A significant air battle takes place in the Kursk area as German aircraft acting in support of the ground offensive attack and damage an incoming flight of Soviet aircraft seeking to raid German-held airfields. At the end of the day the Germans have lost 26 aircraft to the 400 plus of the Soviet side. Stalin's opinion regarding the ability of his fighter pilots takes a knock .

In the Solomons more Americans land in the north of New Georgia; the Japanese attempt to bring in a further 3,000 troops by destroyer but lose two ships.

6 July General Model leads the German attacks to the north of Kursk and makes modest headway, but finds himself short of small arms to defend infantry moves. In the south, under General Hoth, more ground is made but heavy rain prohibits faster movement.

7 July Model remains restricted in his advance and will now struggle to make more than a mile a day. Hoth is close to a breakthrough in the south before Soviet reinforcements arrive to hold him back.

8 July The German commanders at Kursk are finding the confused battle-field conditions, with non-stop exchanges of heavy artillery and limited chances to make tactical manoeuvres, not to their liking. They begin to take heavy losses and are unable to keep supplies moving at the same pace as their opponents.

A U-boat is sunk by an acoustic homing torpedo for the first time when *U514* is attacked by a B-24 Liberator.

9 July Operation 'Husky', the Allied landing on Sicily, is in its final stages of preparation, the troops involved now gathering in Malta. The island will be defended by a 240,000-strong mix of Italians and German Sixth Army troops under General Guzzoni. The huge Allied landing force has at its disposal 200 warships, 300 transports and 2,000 landing-craft. Of the Allied troops eventually involved, there will be 250,000 British and 230,000 Americans under the command of Eisenhower and Alexander. The latter will control 15th Army Group which includes Patton's Seventh and Montgomery's Eighth Armies. In comparison with the Axis forces, who are dispirited by their withdrawal from North Africa, the Allied troops include battle-hardened men whose morale is high in the wake of recent successes.

Allied landing on Sicily

By deception and diversionary tactics the Allies have convinced Hitler that an operation will be mounted through Sardinia and he has sent an airborne corps to the South of France for that reason. This is one occasion when Mussolini is more aware than the Führer – he is certain that Sicily is to be the target, but, again, is unwilling to challenge the German High Command.

The invasion begins after dark with airborne landings which are affected by high winds and faulty execution; gliders are released too early and many fall into the sea. But enough troops get ashore to start the process of disrupting the defences of the island.

At Kursk, additional Soviet tank power arrives to bring setbacks to the Germans who have already committed most of their armour. They are spending much energy and ammunition in numerous attempts to break small pockets of resistance for little or no gain.

Syracuse taken by Allies

10 July In Sicily the seaborne landings are under way and meet light resistance from the poorly equipped coastal defences. By the end of the day US and British forces between them have taken Gela, Licata, Vittoria and Syracuse.

At Kursk Model is at a standstill in the north, but German units in the south are again close to breaking through. Once more the Soviets receive late help to stave off further assaults.

In New Guinea more US and Australian units link-up.

11 July The Allied advance through Sicily continues almost unchecked, although the US contingent, having suffered a more troublesome landing, have to call on naval gunfire support when counter-attacked by the Hermann Göring Panzer Division.

At Kursk German troops in the south are delayed; their range-finding equipment is hindered by dust and smoke from the battlefield.

12 July In Sicily US troops are engaged by German troops brought across the island from the west, and British reinforcements have to be called in. Lentini is captured by the British.

End of German Kursk offensive

At Kursk the German forces engaging the northern perimeter of the salient are counter-attacked and pushed back towards Orel. Hitler calls a halt to the battle because he is losing ground, tanks, and aircraft at a time when, rather than commit the extra resources necessary, he would prefer to be transferring troops from the Eastern Front to Italy. He expressly forbids withdrawal, but the damage has been done; Kursk, the greatest ever tank battle, marks the point at which the Germans will slide to defeat on the Eastern Front.

In the Solomons off Kolombagara a Japanese formation of one cruiser and nine destroyers inflicts damage on a US task force of three cruisers and ten destroyers, but then has its cruiser crippled by radar-directed fire from the US ships.

13 July On Sicily the British capture Augusta and make a push from Lentini towards Catania which is not completed because an advance unit of paratroops suffer heavy casualties.

On the Eastern Front the Soviets push on to Orel, but the Germans continue to fight small actions in the south.

15 July On Sicily the defenders of Catania are forced back.

South of Kursk the Germans begin to fall back to the positions whence they started their ill-fated advance.

16 July Churchill and Roosevelt call on the Italians to surrender and urge rebellion against Mussolini. The Allied advance has almost reached Catania.

18 July Only on the east coast of Sicily do the Allied forces meet significant opposition.

The US troops have a new battlefield weapon, a portable anti-tank rocket, which quickly assumes the name of 'bazooka'.

19 July Hitler and Mussolini meet at Feltre, near Verona, in northern Italy. The Führer complains about the performance of Italian troops and insists that they fight harder; Il Duce promises to do what he can but knows that his people have no desire to fight on. The two leaders agree to mount a fighting withdrawal in Italy while a fortified defensive position – the Gustav Line – is formed across the 72 miles from the mouth of the Garigliano to the river Sangro south of Ortona. Montgomery continues his push on the east coast of Sicily but, with the Germans defending well here, he also sends units to advance by an inland route.

Hitler and Mussolini meet at Feltre

A total of 270 B-17 Flying Fortresses and B-24 Liberators raids Rome for the first time, concentrating on rail and air targets.

USAAF raids Rome

22 July Patton's US Seventh Army enters Palermo, thereby cutting off many Italian troops.

Palermo taken by Allies

24 July Mussolini and his remaining supporters are outvoted after a debate at the Fascist Grand Council.

Operation 'Gomorrah', the first of four major Allied air raids on Hamburg designed to destroy the city. On this and the next four nights 3,015 RAF bombers use 'Window' for the first time. This consists of strips of aluminium foil dropped from the aircraft to produce false echoes on the radar and confuse the defences. Eighty-seven of the aircraft fail to return. The US Army Air Force makes two daylight raids with 281 aircraft, losing twenty-one of them. Hamburg is devastated and 40,000 inhabitants are killed, largely from the firestorm that has been created. Hitler's Armaments Minister, Albert Speer, warns him that a few more raids of this kind will end the war.

Hamburg bombing begins

25 July Marshal Badoglio is asked to form a new government after King Victor Emmanuel III relieves Mussolini of his office. The ambitious dictator, who has lacked any organisational or leadership attributes is arrested as he leaves the meeting.

Fall of Mussolini

On Sicily the US drive is now being resisted strongly, but more troops are landing from North Africa all the time.

In response to first Hamburg raid Hitler re-activates the rocket programme and calls for the production of 900 weapons per month.

US bombers fly against targets in Norway for the first time when they

USAAF raids targets in Norway

US offensive in New Georgia

attack the Heruya aluminium factory and the U-boat berths at Trondheim.

In the Pacific the Americans launch their offensive in New Georgia.

26 July Badoglio expresses his backing for the Axis aims, but, behind the scenes, he has begun to plan Italy's exit from the war.

The German commanders order their forces to evacuate the Kursk salient.

27 July For the next few days the Allies have good success against U-boats in the Bay of Biscay; ten are sunk in four days. Dönitz reports: 'The endeavours of the enemy to block our exit routes seem to have reached their zenith.'

29 July As Britain commits its entire population of fit men to the war, the government announces that all women below the age of 50 must register for work.

In his diary entry for this day, Goebbels writes of the raids on Hamburg. Knowing that only a few of the bombers have been shot down, he concedes 'we cannot claim that the assailants paid for what they did'. His note indicates that he has seen the reports which speak of 'a catastrophe of hitherto inconceivable proportions'.

Adolf Hitler declines to visit Hamburg, despite requests to do so. He also refuses to meet delegations from the city.

AUGUST 1943

I August De Gaulle takes further control of the Free French movement by assuming the Presidency of the National Liberation Committee for the bulk of its business; Giraud will only occupy the post when military topics are being considered.

In Burma, Ba Maw, the head of Japan's puppet regime, signs an agreement with his masters. They announce that Burma is now independent and has declared war on Great Britain and the USA.

The captain of a Swedish ship sunk in Hamburg harbour describes the air raids: 'Dante's *Inferno* is as nothing compared to this hell.' During the Hamburg raids the Blohm & Voss yards have been hit and U-boats nearing completion destroyed including *U996*, *U1011* and *U1012* .

USAAF raids Ploesti oilfields

A US Ninth Army Air Force group of 163 B-24 Liberator aircraft fly from Benghazi in Libya to attack the Roumanian oilfields at Ploesti. The long-distance mission requires each aircraft to carry nine tons of fuel. An accident en route sees the chief navigator for the mission lost when his aircraft crashes into the sea and, then, his deputy become separated from the main force as his aircraft searches for survivors. The oilfields are very heavily defended because it is known that an attack is imminent. At the end of a tortuous flight the aircraft arrive over the target in a very confused state, differing hugely from the set plan and having to concentrate on avoiding collision rather than the heavy defensive fire. The raid is quickly over. Of the aircraft that started the mission, only eleven get back to Benghazi, 54 are shot down and 532 aircrew lost. Forty per cent of the refining capacity is destroyed, but the Americans decline to mount follow-up raids and the industry recovers.

2 August In the Solomons, the Japanese prepare to sacrifice their position in New Georgia and move all resources to Kolombangara.

Dönitz orders his U-boats to stay in their bases rather than risk the run to and from open waters through the Bay of Biscay.

3 August The German news bureau reports that the Ploesti raid appears to have been a disaster for the attackers with heavy losses and several forced landings because of damage on their return.

4 August On Sicily the British begin their attacks on Catania.

The Soviets take Orel to the north of Kursk and prepare to move on Belgorod in the south as the tide of war on the Eastern Front continues against the Germans.

Soviets take Orel

5 August The Soviets race into Belgorod and move on. The attack has hit a weak position in the German lines, between Fourth Panzer Army and Eighth Army. Around Orel Second Panzer Army has been decimated; its stragglers are placed with Ninth Army. Stalin orders a victory salute to be fired in Moscow.

Soviets take Belgorod

6 August On Sicily after a bitter fight, the Americans take Troina to continue the Allied advance on all lines.

The effects of the Hamburg raids rumble on. Goebbels announces that residents of Berlin will be evacuated unless they are actively working in the city.

Japanese destroyers conveying troops from New Georgia to Kolombangara are attacked by six US destroyers. Three of the Japanese ships are sunk.

8 August On Sicily a small amphibious operation sees US forces push the Germans out of Sant' Agata. Cesarò also falls and the British take Brönte and Acireale.

10 August Another US amphibious landing on the north coast of Sicily sees the Germans fall back.

12 August Having cut rail communications between the German garrisons of Kharkov and Poltava, the Soviets now threaten the latter town. If it falls many German forces in Kharkov and further south will be isolated.

13 August The Quebec Conference of Allied military leaders is joined by Roosevelt and Churchill to assess the evolving plans for the invasion of France. It is now that Churchill agrees to the Supreme Commander of the operation being American as well as confirming that the US can continue to control operations in the Pacific. For their part, the Americans accept that the expected defeat of Italy can be used to make political and military moves which feature on Britain's agenda.

Quebec Conference

161

The Soviets occupy towns on their way to Kharkov and are mounting new drives west of Moscow, heading for Smolensk.

USAAF raids Balikpapan, Borneo

US aircraft take off from Darwin in northern Australia to attack the oil refineries at Balikpapan in Borneo. The 17-hour flight is the longest strategic aerial mission of the war.

15 August The Allied advance in Sicily continues apace. British and US units link up when Randazzo falls and British troops enter Taormina. Continued north coast amphibious landings force the Germans to retreat and save the Allied forces from having to trek across the island.

Allies occupy Vella Lavella and Kiska

In the Solomons US troops occupy Vella Lavella and 34,000 US and Canadian troops are landed on Kiska in the Aleutians

Allies take Messina

16 August On Sicily advanced US units reach Messina.

The armies of Soviet Southern Front uprate their offensive against German Sixth Army and press on towards Stalino.

US bombs Wewak

Many Japanese aircraft are destroyed in US Fifth Army Air Force raids on airfields at Wewak in New Guinea.

Allies take Messina

17 August On Sicily the Allies converge on Messina and enter it to complete the occupation of the island. The ease with which they have completed the task is partly explained by the wholesale evacuation of German and Italian troops which they have been unable to prevent. Why greater efforts, by way of aerial and naval bombardment, have not been used to reduce, delay or cancel the exodus is difficult to fathom. Admittedly 100,000 Italian troops have been captured, but the same number of Germans and Italians have made it to the mainland with tanks and guns. The Allies have lost 7,000 killed and twice as many wounded; Axis losses have been greater.

Peenemünde bombed

British aircraft attack the German rocket research facility at Peenemünde and delay work there by several weeks. The deployment of 'Window' strips causes confusion for the Luftwaffe; their aircraft are lured into flying to Berlin and, while there, are fired on by their own air defences.

Schweinfurt and Regensburg raids by USAAF

Operation 'Double Strike'. A disastrous attack by 376 bombers of US Eighth Army Air Force in a dual raid on Schweinfurt and Regensburg sees the Americans attempting a daylight raid without fighter escort and losing 60 aircraft with twice that number damaged.

19 August In Lisbon there are secret negotiations between the Italians, represented by General Castellano, and the Allies to discuss the logistics of an Italian surrender.

Jeschonnek suicide

After being accused of lethargy and incompetence following recent air raids, such as the one on Peenemünde, the Chief of Staff of the Luftwaffe, Hans Jeschonnek, commits suicide.

22 August The Germans begin to pull out of Kharkov as surrounding towns fall to the Soviets. Von Manstein can only see a repeat of Stalingrad if he chooses to stay and fight.

162

23 August The Soviet government, which had vacated Moscow in the autumn of 1941, returns to work in the capital. Kharkov is liberated after hectic street fighting.

Soviet government returns to Moscow

Kharkov taken

Some 57 out of 719 RAF bombers fail to return from a night raid on Berlin.

25 August New Georgia is taken by the Americans, though many Japanese have completed the evacuation to Kolombangara.

US take New Georgia

The first use by the Germans of glide bombs against Allied naval targets in the Atlantic is unsuccessful. The device carries a 1,100-pound explosive charge and, after being dropped from an aircraft, is remotely guided to its target by an observer operating a radio-controlled joystick. Operator error continues to afflict the performance of this novel weapon, though it does have some successes.

28 August Following sporadic Resistance activity in Denmark and the government refusing to allow anyone charged with such acts to be tried in Germany, the Danish government resigns and the German commander in the country declares martial law. Some small Danish vessels are commandeered by the Germans but most are scuttled.

30 August On the Eastern Front the Soviets are going from strength to strength, capturing more towns around Kharkov and closing in on Smolensk.

SEPTEMBER 1943

2 September Following the capture of Sicily, the Allies subject Italian mainland coastal targets to aerial bombardment. The battleships HMSS *Valiant* and *Warspite* bombard Reggio.

3 September On Sicily General Castellano signs the Italian surrender, but this is kept secret while discussions are held as to how to prevent Germany taking over political and military control of the country.

The Allies set foot in Europe when XIII Corps of Montgomery's Eighth Army lands just north of Reggio. They meet minimal resistance from 29th Panzer Grenadier Division and quickly occupy other towns. The retreating German forces leave a network of makeshift obstacles and booby-traps in their wake.

Reggio landings

6 September On the Eastern Front continuing advances by the Soviets see Konotop fall, giving them even greater control of the railway network. It is in this central southern region that the momentum, in the direction of Kiev, is strongest. German Seventeenth Army begins its evacuation from the Kuban Peninsula to the Crimea.

Soviets take Konotop

The battleship *Tirpitz* and the battlecruiser *Scharnhorst* with nine destroyers sail from Altafiord to attack the Allied bases on Spitsbergen.

Spitsbergen raided by German naval forces

8 September Eighth Army makes another landing, at Pizzo, as the build-up to the main landing at Salerno continues. The Italian surrender is

Pizzo landings

announced by Eisenhower and Badoglio. Italian naval vessels sail from Genoa and La Spezia to surrender to the Allies in Malta, but will suffer German air strikes en route. Tito's Partisans capture Italian Second Army's equipment in Dalmatia.

The German ships reach Spitsbergen and the radio and meteorological stations there are blown up.

9 September The Allies land Eighth Army's 1st Airborne Division at Taranto and the port is seized without fighting. At Salerno the landings on a 20-mile front are more troublesome; General Clark's US Fifth Army meets heavy opposition. The left flank of the operation sees US Rangers and British Commandos make good progress at Maiori and Vietri. British X Corps lands south of Salerno in the teeth of resistance. Units of US VI Corps land around Paestum without a preliminary bombardment and encounter some opposition.

The Italian battleship *Roma* en route to surrender at Malta is sunk by German FX1400 3,000-pound glide bombs; other vessels are damaged. Remarkably, neither Hitler nor Göring ever get to hear the full story behind the sinking. The principal reason for this is that Adolf Galland, commander of the Luftwaffe's fighter arm, was fearful that much needed finance for fighter production would be diverted to produce the new weapon.

10 September At Salerno British forces moving inland face German counter-attacks and by the end of the day have had to withdraw in some places. Farther south, Montgomery encounters little opposition as German forces are withdrawn to concentrate on the Salerno beachhead.

The Germans begin to evacuate Sardinia. They will move to Corsica and then to the Italian mainland and will come under some pressure from Allied air and submarine attack.

On the Eastern Front the Soviets take Mariupol on the Sea of Azov and land forces near Novorossisk in the Kuban to pressurise German Seventeenth Army.

In the Solomons, the Americans have to send more troops to Arundel Island where their landing has not yet secured control.

The Italian fleet arrives at Malta to surrender.

11 September Progress from the Salerno beachhead is blunted by German reinforcements arriving to reclaim occupied ground. There is a battle for air supremacy over the beachhead. The Allied troops who landed at Taranto occupy Brindisi.

Six submarines, each towing a midget, sail from their base in northern Scotland on a daring mission to attack *Tirpitz* and other naval vessels moored in Altafiord.

12 September The Hermann Göring Panzer Division is deployed at Salerno. Five German divisions now seal the bridgehead and attempt to split it by a thrust through Battipaglia towards the coast.

Margin notes:

Salerno and Taranto landings

Roma sunk by glide bomb

Germans evacuate Sardinia

Soviets take Mariupol

Italian fleet surrenders at Malta

Brindisi taken

Hitler, reacting to the Italian surrender and nervous about the fate of Mussolini who is being held by Badoglio's men at the Campo Imperatore ski lodge in the Abruzzi mountains, sends Otto Skorzeny and a team of élite paratroops to kidnap him and bring him to Germany. This daring mission is undertaken with great expertise by this creator of German special forces.

Skorzeny rescues Mussolini

The massive withdrawal of German Seventeenth Army from the Kuban begins. It will involve more than 250,000 troops plus civilians and supplies.

Germans evacuate Kuban

13 September The attempted German wedge at Salerno is held close to the beach by accurate naval gunfire when Admiral Cunningham makes the crucial decision to bring HMSS *Warspite* and *Valiant* close inshore. The prospect of evacuation looms and it is believed that only speedy reinforcement will prevent it. Troops from the US 82nd Airborne Division are dropped on the beaches in the evening.

In Greece, the Italian Acqui Division engages German units on Cephalonia but surrenders after losing 1,500 men. The Germans then kill many more and send the rest to labour camps.

14 September In Italy, the Allied troops who landed in the south have reached Bari on the east and Belvedere on the west coasts. At Salerno continued naval bombardments curtail German ambitions.

In the Kuban Peninsula there is fierce fighting as the Soviets harry the German withdrawal. The Germans are also planning a retreat from Bryansk.

In the Solomons US reinforcements have to be sent to Vella Lavella where Japanese attacks are stretching the Australian and US contingents there.

15 September *Valiant* and *Warspite* join the ships off Salerno as General Alexander visits the beachhead to scotch any rumours of withdrawal. While the German have mustered their four divisions, the British and US commanders have more armour and seven divisions. Eighth Army continues its drive from the south and advance units are closing on General Clark's US Fifth Army.

Mussolini, now under Hitler's wing in Germany, declares that he is still leader of Italy.

Hitler awards the Knight's Cross of the Iron Cross to Otto Skorzeny.

16 September Fresh German attacks on Allied positions around the Salerno beachhead are driven off and Kesselring accepts the need to withdraw given the news of Eighth Army's imminent arrival; he is unaware that it is only the forward units that are close, the majority still having much ground to make up. The German withdrawal signals the end of the battle for Salerno and acknowledges a major Allied presence in Italy. Off the coast at Salerno *Warspite* is badly damaged by two glide bombs; she is towed to Malta and is out of action for six months.

End of the battle for Salerno

British forces begin to occupy islands in the Aegean.

The Soviet advance towards Kiev expands as more towns are taken from the retreating Germans and Novorossisk, in the Kuban, is taken after a hard struggle.

On New Guinea, Lae falls to Australian attacks but many of the Japanese defenders escape into the jungle to fight again. More air raids on Wewak destroy many Japanese aircraft.

17 September In Italy in the wake of Kesselring's withdrawal, US Fifth Army is able to move out from the beachhead.

Churchill sends Brigadier Fitzroy Maclean to visit Tito. He seeks to establish Tito's loyalty to the Allied cause and quantify his resources.

In the Pacific the island of Tarawa is attacked by B-24 Liberator bombers.

18 September The US carriers *Lexington*, *Princeton* and *Belleau Wood* deploy their aircraft in the raids on Tarawa.

20 September In the North Atlantic, U-boats' new acoustic homing torpedoes account for six ships and three escort vessels from Convoys ON-202 and ONS-18.

21 September In Italy the Allies' advance north gathers pace and will meet little opposition except en route to Naples.

In the Solomons, Japanese evacuations of Arundel and Sagekarassa leave them clear for the Americans.

22 September British X Corps is given the task of clearing the way into Naples. British 78th and 8th Indian Divisions land at Bari and Brindisi to join the advance.

More than 650 RAF bombers drop more than 2,300 tons of bombs on Hanover.

In Altafiord the midget submarines *X6* and *X7* penetrate the torpedo nets around *Tirpitz* and attach mines to her hull. The resultant explosion cripples the ship for six months.

23 September Vigorous German defence stops X Corps' progress to Naples. The British have superior numbers but the Germans have prepared well-sited positions in difficult terrain.

Mussolini announces the formation of the Italian Social Republic which immediately concedes huge sectors of northern Italy to German administration.

24 September The Soviets are just east of Kiev. Their forward push has seen them move close to Smolensk in the north and towards the western shore of the Sea of Azov in the south.

25 September The Soviets take Smolensk and Roslavl. Hitler has ordered the German forces to make a stand at the Dnieper, but the hurried nature of their retreat, as opposed to the more orderly one which von Manstein had urged, has not given them time to prepare a worthwhile counter. In most instances they have no time to build any defences before having to withdraw again.

In the Solomons the Japanese find the holding of Kolombangara of little value and so leave yet another island in the New Georgia group.

26 September In Italy the Germans withdraw ahead of X Corps which is approching Naples. The delay has enabled regrouping elsewhere and they leave the usual trail of demolished bridges and booby-traps.

27 September The Allies capture thirteen airfields at Foggia to the east and this puts US bombers within range of industrial sites in southern Germany.

The Germans defeat the Italian garrison and take charge of Corfu.

There is another huge raid on Hanover. One of the targets for this and other raids on the city is the Continental tyre works, but these and other war-related industrial sites remain almost intact.

Hanover bombed

28 September While residents of Naples begin suicidal attacks on the Germans there, British X Corps is approaching the city. US VI Corps makes slower progress up the central spine of the country and has taken Teora.

29 September The Americans attack Avellino and X Corps gets to Pompeii.

On the Eastern Front the Soviets take Kremenchug after a fierce struggle against the German rearguard.

Soviets take Kremenchug

30 September The British are at the outskirts of Naples. The Germans stop skirmishing with the locals.

OCTOBER 1943

1 October Naples falls. The Allies do not delay but advance again, with Rome as their obvious objective. Hitler, having seen the pace of the Allied moves already slowed by Kesselring's demolitions and occasional stands, orders his man to establish a strong defensive line south of the capital city.

Allies take Naples

The Soviets cross the Dnieper in various places, quickly constructing bridges and other forms of crossing.

3 October German troops land on the Greek island of Kos and gain control within 24 hours, taking 4,500 British and Italian prisoners.

4 October Free French forces liberate the island of Corsica

Corsica liberated

The Japanese complete the evacuation of Kolombangara; the US forces fail to prevent 9,000 men being taken off the island.

Japanese evacuate Kolombangara

At the British Admiralty Cunningham becomes First Sea Lord after Dudley Pound's resignation because of ill-health. The latter, so determined to be a capable, 'hands-on' leader, had taken on too great a work load and his decision-making, such as that concerning Convoy PQ-17, suffered accordingly. Admiral Cunningham, so successful in the Mediterranean is a popular choice, though Admiral Fraser has first declined the post.

Cunningham First Sea Lord

5 October Wake Island, in the central Pacific, is attacked by US ships and aircraft.

Wake Island attacked

6 October In Italy US Fifth Army takes Caserta and Capua and the British continue to advance up the east coast of Italy.

Allies take Caserta and Capua

7 October The German retreat continues and the Allies progress with little opposition.

A German convoy en route for the island of Kos is attacked by a British naval quartet of cruisers and destroyers. Seven transports and an escort are sunk.

Allies reach Volturno

8 October In Italy US Fifth Army has reached the Volturno.

Allies land in Azores

In the Atlantic, after lengthy negotiations with the Portuguese, British forces begin landing in the Azores, equidistant from Europe and the US east coast. The base will close the 'Atlantic Gap', shortening air routes and increasing air cover.

9 October On the Eastern Front the Soviets are able to complete their occupation of the Kuban, German Seventeenth Army having been sent north to defend threatened positions; but the plan for Seventeenth Army will flounder when the Soviets advance at Melitopol.

Rabaul bombed

12 October In the Pacific Rabaul, the Japanese main base in New Britain, is shaken by a huge bombing raid by US Fifth Army Air Force; vessels in the harbour and land installations are destroyed, as are many aircraft sent up to defend the base.

Volturno offensive

13 October In Italy US Fifth Army has begun its push on the German positions at the Volturno. Some attacks are held, others – at Capua – stopped completely, but some get through. The river, running high because of recent rains, forms a natural barrier. The few roads have been demolished by the Germans and bottlenecks will become a problem on the small number that are still open.

Italy declares war on Germany

Badoglio declares war on Germany from his government's temporary base in Brindisi. It is a statement aimed at showing support for the Allied moves in Italy and giving Italian civilians a clear understanding of their position as the war flows around them.

14 October British 56th Division gets across the Volturno, and US VI Corps advances.

On the Eastern Front the Soviets attack Melitopol and cut the rail links to the south. Farther north they have captured Zaporozhye.

Schweinfurt bombed again; end of US unescorted daylight raids

This day becomes known as 'Black Thursday' to US forces when, on another Eighth Army Air Force raid on the German ball-bearing works at Schweinfurt, 291 B-17s inflict much damage but lose one in five of their aircraft. These and other recent losses cause the abandonment of unescorted daylight flights which the Americans had been so sure they could carry out successfully. Their belief that modern bomber aircraft could protect themselves has been disproved.

Volturno line breached

15 October In Italy the Allies have breached the German line on the Volturno and the Germans make a fighting withdrawal to two short-term defensive lines – the Barbara Line and the Bernhard Line – while creating more substantial defences on the Gustav Line behind the rivers Garigliano, Rapido and Sangro.

16 October In the Persian Gulf *U533* is sunk by patrolling aircraft from RAF 244 Squadron.

17 October On the Eastern Front the German lines around Kremenchug and Loyev are penetrated by the Soviets.

In the Pacific the German raider *Michel*, the last of these vessels to see action, is sunk by the US submarine *Tarpon* off the Japanese coast.

18 October The Japanese air base at Buin on Bougainville comes under heavy air attack.

19 October On the Eastern Front Kiev is threatened as von Manstein brings up reinforcements to fill the numerous gaps in his lines.

22 October An RAF raid by 486 bombers is made on the Fieseler aircraft factory at Kassel which, according to British intelligence sources, is working on Peenemünde's rocket programme. Diversionary raids send the Luftwaffe to Frankfurt and Cologne, leaving the main force to drop 1,800 tons of bombs on the city. The factory is damaged and construction of the V-1 flying bomb delayed for some months. *Kassel bombed*

23 October On the Eastern Front Melitopol is rid of Germans after ten days of fighting, but the Soviets' rapid advance towards Krivoy Rog from Kremenchug is slowed by von Manstein's extra forces. *Soviets take Melitopol*

In the English Channel the cruiser HMS *Charybdis* and the destroyer HMS *Limbourne* are lost; attempting to stop a blockade runner, they are attacked by its protecting squadron.

In the Pacific Rabaul is attacked again and ships sunk at anchor include a destroyer and five freighters. *Rabaul bombed*

27 October In a desperate effort to avoid the Crimea being cut off, the Germans make minor counter-attacks south of Nikopol.

29 October One of the few German generals to prove himself capable of sound defensive tactics, Gotthard Heinrici, wins his spurs by resisting all Russian attempts to break his lines between Orsha and Vitebsk. He rotates his sparse formations to keep them fresh and beats off the attacks. He will later be demoted when questioning Hitler's demand that he stand his ground.

30 October In Italy the Barbara Line is broken near Mondragone, but elsewhere Allied progress is slowed by difficult terrain and stern German defence. *Barbara Line breached*

31 October The Soviets cut the final rail link with the Crimea when they capture Chaplinka.

NOVEMBER 1943

1 November On the Eastern Front the Crimea is finally cut off when Perekop is taken and the Soviets land units of 56th Army. Von Manstein mounts a series of counter-attacks at Krivoy Rog and holds the Soviets there. *Soviets take Perekop*

In the Pacific the Americans land at Empress Augusta Bay in Bougainville and meet little resistance. The Japanese have 40,000 soldiers and 20,000 naval *US landings on Bougainville* personnel in the south of the island. On this first day 14,000 men get ashore; in support offshore are four cruisers and eight destroyers plus, further to the west, the carriers *Saratoga* and *Lexington* whose aircraft will shortly raid the island's airfields. Japanese aircraft sent against the landing have little effect. A Japanese force of cruisers and destroyers is then called from Rabaul.

2 November This force from Rabaul is detected and engaged by the US ships off Bougainville in a night action which sees most of the Japanese vessels damaged and a cruiser and destroyer lost. The Japanese withdraw their ships but send more attacking aircraft. These fail to stop the expansion of the US beachhead.

Rabaul is attacked by land-based aircraft of US Fifth Army Air Force. Three ships are sunk in the harbour, but US and Japanese aircraft are lost in combat above the port.

4 November In Italy US VI Corps is approaching the Bernhard Line as it takes Venafro. British X Corps has taken Monte Massico and Monte Santa Croce and is attacking Monte Camino. Montgomery's Eighth Army is moving forward as the Germans retreat to the Sangro.

On the Eastern Front Kiev comes under greater threat as German defence lines weaken after heavy fighting and the constant switching of units to plug holes in the formations.

More Japanese ships arrive in Rabaul but they have been detected and the US carriers off Bougainville are ordered to attack.

5 November In Italy, on difficult terrain and deploying XIV Panzer Corps skilfully, the Germans defend the central sector of the Bernhard Line in bad weather against concerted attacks by British 56th Division and US 3rd Division.

Kiev encircled

The Soviets cut rail links around Kiev and press on to encircle the city. In the south they have control of the area south of the Dneiper and threaten Kherson.

French Resistance fighters cause long-term damage to the Peugeot factory and then sabotage delivery of new equipment.

In the Pacific more than 100 aircraft from the two US carriers attack the Japanese ships off Rabaul. Eight are damaged and then hit again by a second raid by land-based B-24 Liberators.

The Japanese mount their first significant attack on the Bougainville invasion force; it is beaten off. The Japanese leaders are unable to decide whether the US landings are mere routine or a diversionary tactic to cover action elsewhere.

Soviets take Kiev

6 November Kiev is back in Soviet hands. Many of the German defenders have eluded capture, but the recovery of this major city is still a cause for rejoicing throughout the USSR.

7 November The Japanese land troops north of the US forces on Bougainville and immediately attack. This has more effect than their pre-landing bombardment by 100 aircraft which is inaccurate.

9 November As more US troops land on Bougainville, those who have moved forward from the bridgehead encounter major Japanese resistance and fierce jungle fighting.

In the Azores, aircraft operating from the new bases achieve their first success when a B-17 bomber sinks *U707* east of the islands.

11 November In Bougainville US Marines repel Japanese attacks.

12 November The Germans are about to lose their last cross-country railway line as their position at Zhitomir is threatened.

The Germans land on the Greek island of Leros. Some 9,000 British and Italian troops surrender.

Germans take Leros

In Italy the Germans are holding their positions on the Bernhard Line.

In Rabaul, having lost two-thirds of their aircraft in recent actions, the Japanese withdraw the remainder from the island.

13 November The Soviets capture Zhitomir, 80 miles west of Kiev.

More US landings on Bougainville are completed despite Japanese attacks.

US aircraft begin daily bombing of Tawara in the Gilbert Islands in preparation for a landing there.

14 November In Italy General Alexander's HQ acknowledges that General Clark and his troops have faced 'savage resistance' by German troops in the Mignano area and reports that US Fifth Army has neared Cassino and 'is now trying to dislodge the enemy from the last mountain positions he occupies that bar the way to Cassino'. It will be six months before Cassino falls.

Beginning of Battle for Monte Cassino

A German counter-attack is mounted south of Zhitomir.

German Zhitomir counter-offensive

15 November General Clark has told General Alexander that he must call a halt to the Allied advance in Italy. Losses have been considerable and there is no sign of a lessening in German resolve to hold their strongly defended lines in terrain which gives advantage to the occupier.

16 November On the Eastern Front von Manstein's clever strategy of counter-attacking south of Zhitomir causes the Soviets to consider the wisdom of pursuing extra territory at this point. Although the German attacks are across a broad front they are being undertaken by very few men.

18 November The Soviets make gains north-west of Kiev and take Korosten, but General Hasso von Manteuffel's 7th Panzer Division is still following von Manstein's orders to the south-west and enjoying some success.

A secret SS report on German internal affairs admits that women are becoming concerned about their men at the front, their own living conditions and the likely effect of the war on their marriages.

More than 400 RAF bombers drop 1,600 tons of bombs on Berlin.

Berlin bombed

19 November In Italy Eighth Army has secured ground north of the Sangro but will need to regroup for a major offensive.

The Soviets have to retreat from Zhitomir as the German counter there has proved too strong.

US naval aviation is again active in raids on Tarawa and other islands in the area. Four carrier groups are being assembled for the landings.

20 November The Americans begin landings in the Gilbert Islands. Three battleships, four cruisers and four escort carriers with aircraft support 2nd Marine Division as its lands 18,600 men on Tarawa. The Japanese have 4,800 men with some artillery and a handful of light tanks. Landings elsewhere encounter severe problems, including on the tiny island of Betio which has been strongly fortified; a shallow reef prevents landing-craft from reaching the beaches. The landings on Makin and Butaritari succeed in the face of fierce defence.

The British evacuate the Greek island of Samos to bring to an end a disastrous episode in the area which has used too few men and shown less than thorough planning.

21 November On the Eastern Front the German counter-attack moves on Korosten.

The Americans send further troops to Betio. A change of tide enables more men to get ashore

Off the coast of Portugal the 66-ship double Convoy SL-139 and MKS-30 is sighted by German air reconnaissance and 34 U-boats are positioned on its course. The convoy escort is increased in time to ward off the attacks and only one of the freighters is lost – to air attack. Three U-boats are sunk.

22 November At a meeting with Chiang Kai-shek in Cairo, Churchill and Roosevelt find the Chinese leader unwilling to side with them in their plans to take a concerted line with Stalin at the Tehran Conference. Discussions on the Burma and Chinese war theatres are equally inconclusive.

In Italy British forces north of the Sangro have gained territory, but will have trouble with supplies if they move on by this route.

Another large bombing raid on Berlin devastates the city centre and the Moabit district.

The Japanese continue to defend Tarawa stoutly, even attempting suicidal counter-attacks at times. US forces dominate Makin and Butaritari and a landing is made on Abimama.

23 November The bloody battle for Tarawa has been won. Only a handful of Japanese are taken prisoner, the rest having died in defence of the island. The Americans have lost more than 1,000 men killed and twice that number wounded. The ratio of losses is repeated elsewhere and important lessons have been learnt.

Hitler attends a demonstration of the Me 262 jet aircraft. It has been envisaged chiefly as a superfast fighter, but he presses for its development as a light bomber; he needs whatever can cause the most damage. Consequently the aircraft does not become operational until June 1944 and never maximises its tremendous potential.

24 November In his diary Goebbels reflects that his accounts of the bombing of Berlin make very sad reading. He wonders how the British are able to destroy so much of the capital in one air raid.

25 November Three of five destroyers carrying Japanese reinforcements to Buka, north of Bougainville, are sunk when intercepted by five US ships.

The Chinese Fourteenth Air Force flies against sites on Formosa and destroys 42 aircraft on the ground there. *Formosa bombed*

26 November On the Eastern Front the strategically important town of Gomel is finally taken by the Soviets. *Soviets take Gomel*

Berlin is bombed again when a series of diversionary raids removes some of the fighter cover from the city. *Berlin bombed*

In the Mediterranean a glide bomb accounts for a British troopship off Bougie with the loss of 1,000 men.

In the North Atlantic *U764* shoots down a B-17 aircraft of Coastal Command.

28 November In Italy, having managed to get a tank brigade across the Sangro, Eighth Army feels confident to continue its advance behind a substantial air and artillery bombardment. The move is defended inadequately by 65th Division but there are more capable reserves behind them.

An RAF photo-reconnaissance aircraft diverted by low cloud over Berlin, flies over Peenemünde; interpreters studying the film notice that constructions there match constructions in northern France which they have been unable to explain. This confirms that the UK is to be targeted by new weapons.

28 November The Tehran Conference begins and for the first time Stalin will join top-level Allied strategic discussions. The date for invasion of France is confirmed and a plan to supplement it with a landing in the South of France is also agreed. The Soviet leader confirms his willingness to move against Japan once Germany has been beaten. The event comes to be considered as something of a coup for the Soviets who skilfully work the other Allies towards concessions. *Tehran Conference*

30 November The Soviets withdraw from Korosten just twelve days after taking it.

DECEMBER 1943

3 December In Italy British X Corps closes on the summit of Monte Camino as Monte Maggiore falls to II Corps.

The port of Bari is attacked by German aircraft and an ammunition ship explodes sinking eighteen adjacent transports and destroying huge *Bari bombed* quantities of *matériel*. This is one of the most successful air raids of the war in respect of the return from a single, short mission.

4 December In the Pacific six US carriers and nine cruisers attack Kwajalein in the Marshall Islands. Six Japanese transports are sunk and other vessels damaged, and 55 Japanese aircraft are shot down.

The US submarine *Sailfish* sinks the Japanese carrier *Chuyo* off the Japanese mainland.

5 December Allied aircraft mount raids on the V-1 sites in northern France. All news releases about the mission describe the targets as military installations so as to avoid public panic.

6 December In some of the fiercest fighting of the Italian campaign to date, British troops take Monte Camino.

7 December As Eighth Army moves on to attack Orsogna, US Fifth Army begins its big offensive with US II and VI Corps pushing northwards on a broad front.

8 December Some British troops are pulled out of Italy to begin preparation for Operation 'Overlord', the invasion of France. French and Italian units join the Allied ranks in Italy. Eighth Army deploys its Canadian units on the push across the river Moro.

10 December Eighth Army now makes good progress across the Moro, but US Fifth Army is held up by attritional fighting to the west and gaining little ground; but the Germans will begin to withdraw. Italian troops now fighting the Germans for their homeland are told by Badoglio: 'You represent the true Italy. It is your destiny to liberate our country and drive the aggressor from our homeland.'

15 December Fresh Fifth Army pushes improve its situation.

In the Pacific the Americans make a small landing on Awawe, off the south coast of New Britain, as a precursor to the main mission set for Boxing Day. Japanese aircraft are kept busy by air attacks on their base at Cape Gloucester.

18 December In Italy, US Fifth Army captures Monte Lungo and, as San Pietro is pressurised, the Germans are forced to mount fierce counter-attacks.

20 December Approximately 1,000 Allied aircraft drop 2,000 tons of bombs on Frankfurt, Mannheim and other industrial cities in southern Germany. There are more raids on the V-1 ramps in France.

22 December The Italian campaign sees urban combat as the Allies force their way into Ortona. The 2nd Canadian Brigade has to capture the town a block at a time from the defending German 1st Paratroop Division.

23 December Ortona is taken and, inland, Arielli also falls to Eighth Army units.

24 December On the Eastern Front General Vatutin leads a reconstituted 1st Ukraine Front to regain ground lost to recent German counter-attacks. Vatutin is proving to be one of the most active Russian commanders, and one of the most successful. He thrusts into the weakened German lines and sees the prospect of a major advance.

In the Pacific a US bombardment of the Buka Island and Buin bases on Bougainville is intended to divert Japanese attention from the imminent attack on New Britain.

25 December At sea, *Scharnhorst*, the sole operational German battle-cruiser, sails from the northern coast of Norway with a screen of destroyers in pursuit of Convoy JW-55B, unaware that the battleship HMS *Duke of York* has been alerted and is shadowing from a distance.

26 December The Battle of North Cape. The British cruiser squadron detect *Scharnhorst* on radar, close and open fire, scoring two hits before the German ship moves away. Spotting her again some hours later, they again open fire and again she moves off. Admiral Sir Bruce Fraser, CinC, Home Fleet, in HMS *Duke of York*, had been steaming east to cut off *Scharnhorst* from Altenfiord. He spots her and after a three-hour bombardment sinks her; there are only 36 survivors Admiral Bey, Flag Officer, Destroyers, is among the 1,803 men lost. It is the end of the German High Seas Fleet.

Battle of North Cape

In the Pacific US forces who have landed on New Britain are into diffi-cult terrain around Cape Gloucester but encounter little resistance.

27 December The preparatory planning for 'Overlord' is complete and the command structure is established. Eisenhower is to be Supreme Allied Commander with Air Marshal Tedder as his deputy. The British will head the air and sea components: Air Chief Marshal Leigh-Mallory, CinC Air, Admiral Sir Bertram Ramsay, CinC, Navy. Field Marshal Montgomery will lead the British ground forces, General Leese taking over Eighth Army.

British aircraft sink the German blockade-runner *Alsterufer* in the Bay of Biscay; eleven destroyers and torpedo-boats sent to escort her on her arrival are intercepted by the cruisers HMSS *Enterprise* and *Glasgow*. Three German ships are sunk and the others withdraw despite their numerical superiority.

28 December On the Eastern Front General Vatutin's troops are retrieving territory recently taken by the Germans.

The US Marines who have landed on New Britain close on a nearby Japanese airfield.

29 December On the Eastern Front the Soviets retake Korosten and Chernakov and will occupy Zhitomir before the year's end. In the north, Vitebsk is encircled.

In the last raid of the year on Berlin, a further 2,300 tons of bombs rains down on the city. The last six weeks have seen the city hit by more than 14,000 tons, a fact which should not be overlooked when studying the German prosecution of the war in other theatres during this time.

Berlin bombed

30 December In New Britain the airfield at Cape Gloucester is occupied by US Marines.

1944

JANUARY 1944

2 January Russian troops are just a few miles from the Soviet border of 1939 when they capture Radovel, west of Korosten.

In New Guinea 2,400 more Allied troops land at Saidor and quickly gain control of the airfield and harbour.

3 January Millions of counterfeit food coupons have been dropped over Germany during recent RAF Bomber Command raids. Proffered for redemption, these superbly produced fakes cause confusion and consternation among shoppers and the authorities.

Allies attack Gustav Line

4 January In Italy the southern end of the Gustav Line is attacked by US Fifth Army along a 10-mile front.

1st Ukranian Front forces push von Manstein's Army Group South back beyond the pre-war Polish border at Sarny.

The last German blockade-runner, *Rio Grande*, is sunk by the US destroyer *Jouett* and cruiser *Omaha* en route to the Far East. Next day *Burgenland*, sailing the reverse route, is scuttled before the two ships can open fire.

6 January Soviet forces cross the former Polish border to take Rakitino.

US forces extend their bridgehead at Cape Gloucester in New Britain.

7 January The deployment of the German flying bomb is hampered by a series of Allied air raids on launch sites which have been located by reconnaissance flights. A Mosquito is brought down by German air defences and its Oboe navigational aid is captured intact and counter-measures quickly devised.

Soviets take Kirovograd

8 January The Soviets take Kirovograd in another important gain for Ukranian Front.

The Italian Socialist Republic mounts a trial in Verona which prosecutes those of the Fascist Grand Council deemed to be responsible for overthrowing Mussolini. Ciano and de Bono are found guilty and executed, but most of the other verdicts concern people who are absent and now fighting in the Allied cause.

P-51 Mustang first long-range escort missions over Germany

11 January US P-38 Lightning and P-47 Thunderbolt long-range fighters flying over Germany are joined for the first time by the P-51 Mustang, but heavy losses are suffered as the Luftwaffe use rocket-firing fighters in new tactical formations against the incoming flights of bombers and escort fighters. The experience prompts the Allies to strengthen fighter escorts on such missions. Luftwaffe leaders cite evidence of the fresh successes of their fighter units to urge an increase in production, but Hitler, concentrating on the broader programme of retaliation, orders more bombers.

12 January In Italy US 34th Division takes Cervaro and moves on towards Cassino.

Soviet Leningrad offensive

14 January The Soviets go on the offensive around Leningrad, breaking the lines of German Army Group North.

US troops in New Britain are held by fierce Japanese rearguard action.

15 January In Italy US II Corps troops capture Monte Trocchio and are now clear to advance on the last German defences in the Rapido valley, and Cassino. The continued attacks on the Gustav Line by other Allied units serve a secondary purpose of diverting attention from the forthcoming Anzio landing.

Fresh efforts are made by the Soviets to recapture the beleaguered Leningrad.

16 January In New Britain US troops have still been unable to get very far from Cape Gloucester and now face stern Japanese counter-attacks.

17 January In Italy on the Garigliano three divisions of British X Corps launch a major attack. On the left flank the river is crossed, but the right flank thrust is held by strong German defence.

18 January The Germans call for reinforcements from the Anzio area as British 5th and 56th Divisions establish themselves on the north bank of the Garigliano.

On the Eastern Front Third Panzer Army fights a successful defence of Vitebsk which sees excessive Soviet losses of men and equipment.

20 January US II Corps attacks across the Rapido and closes in on Cassino, but faces strong German defences.

The Soviets take Novgorod in a hard-hitting attack which lowers the morale of the defending Germans.

21 January The Anzio landing force sails from Naples.

The first of Hitler's retaliatory raids on London and southern England sees 270 German aircraft attack in two waves. The mission is a failure; only 96 aircraft reach their targets and some of these are brought down. These large-scale raids immediately reduce to a series of nuisance flights which only succeed in taking valuable German aircraft from other battle zones. By contrast, nearly 700 RAF bombers have made successful raids on Berlin and Kiel and, for the first time, Magdeburg.

22 January The Allies land at Anzio and Nettuno. The assault troops   Anzio landing
include US 3rd Division and British 1st Division plus British Commando and US Ranger units. Kesselring, having been persuaded to reinforce the Gustav Line with men from the Anzio area, calls in reserves from wherever he can find them, but they will be too late to affect the landing which is almost unopposed and captures the port of Anzio very quickly.

The Luftwaffe deploys He 177 bombers against the landings, but the effectiveness of their guided bombs is reduced by the jamming techniques of the US destroyers supporting the operation.

On the Eastern Front Field Marshal Model replaces General von Kuechler as commander of Army Group North.

23 January The 50,000 Allied troops already ashore at Anzio advance cautiously, but as yet there is little opposition. Reserves being brought from northern Italy, the Balkans and France are sufficient, Kesselring maintains, to hold the Gustav Line and the Anzio region, and he will have eight more divisions to call on within the week. It will prove regrettable that the Allies secure so little ground inland from Anzio before these reserves arrive. The destroyer HMS *Jervis* is hit by a glide bomb while at anchor off Anzio but is able to reach Naples under her own power.

24 January While the push towards Leningrad continues, Soviet forces in the Ukraine move to surround First Panzer Army near Korsun-Sevchenovsky.

25 January The Soviets progress further in their envelopment of German Sixth Army; and on the Leningrad front close on Krasnogvardeisk.

Leningrad blockade broken

27 January The commander of Leningrad Front, General Govorov, announces the freeing of the blockade of Leningrad.

More ill-treatment of prisoners of war by the Japanese comes to light. Great Britain, Australia and the USA each formally protest and promise investigative tribunals.

Nearly 500 RAF bombers raid Berlin in very bad weather; the worst casualties to aircrews are brought about by collisions in heavy cloud; no German aircraft sortie and anti-aircraft fire is nugatory.

28 January Soviet forces advance west from Leningrad; von Manstein is building up resources to relieve the German units surrounded at Korsun.

29 January The Allies now have nearly 70,000 men ashore at Anzio with 237 tanks and more than 500 guns. Now grouped for his advance from the beachhead, the cautious commander, General Lucas, faces the German reinforcements which have been flown in. The cruiser HMS *Spartan* is sunk by a guided bomb.

Gustav Line breached

30 January In Italy British 5th Division breaks through the southern end of the Gustav Line and US 34th Division holds its position on the west bank of the Rapido despite German attacks. British and American units take heavy losses as they push forward from Anzio, and will continue to do so for some days.

Kwajalein landings

31 January In the Pacific Admiral Spruance leads US landings on Kwajalein Atoll in the Marshall Islands. The landing on the Roi islet progresses well, but the Japanese resist on Namur. Construction of a US base on Majuro Atoll is begun.

FEBRUARY 1944

1 February On the Eastern Front the Soviets have reached the Estonian border.

In the Pacific action continues on Kwajalein Atoll but only Namur and Kwajalein itself present much in the way of opposition.

2 February Impasse at Anzio. The Allied troops are unable to advance because they are sustaining heavy losses; the Germans are not strong enough to mount a full counter-attack.

180

On the Eastern Front General Hollidt's Sixth Army pocket comes under increasing pressure around Nikopol.

In the Marshall Islands only Kwajalein remains to be taken. The Japanese have lost more than 3,500 men.

3 February At Anzio the Germans attack a salient held by British 1st Division. The New Zealand Corps joins the ranks of US Fifth Army as numbers are built up for the assault on Cassino.

Hitler forbids the encircled Sixth Army to attempt to retreat. Its complete envelopment is announced in Moscow as von Manstein continues to gather troops for a rescue effort.

4 February In Italy British 1st Division is forced to yield ground at Anzio, but inland US 34th Division gains ground north of Cassino.

On the Eastern Front Hitler intervenes again to scupper von Manstein's chances of getting through to the Sixth Army pocket; the Führer sends 24th Panzer back towards Nikopol, away from von Manstein, although it is already too late for it to have any effect on the fighting in that sector.

In western Burma Japanese Fifteenth Army begins an offensive to envelop British forces at Imphal and Kohima before moving into eastern India. The Allied commanders send Chinese divisions from Ledo to Myitkyina to engage Japanese 18th Division.

Kwajalein Atoll is taken. The Japanese have lost more than 8,500 men, the Americans just 370.

Kwajalein falls

5 February Despite Soviet attempts to stop them, the Germans continue to fly supplies into the Korsun pocket.

7 February Hitler agrees to allow the troops in the Korsun pocket to attempt a breakout.

At Anzio British 1st Division is again attacked by the Germans who have the village of Aprilla and 'The Factory' as their objectives.

8 February The Soviets take Nikopol only to find that the Germans have fled. Supplies are still getting through to the Korsun pocket and wounded are being evacuated.

9 February At Anzio the British are driven back from Aprilla but hold on to 'The Factory'.

In New Guinea Australian and US forces have occupied most of the Huon Peninsula.

11 February 'The Factory' finally falls to the Germans after changing hands several times. At Cassino, US 34th Division makes an unsuccessful attempt to reach the monastery from the north.

As the Germans prepare to break out from the Korsun pocket, the Soviets close in.

Soviet aircraft bomb *Tirpitz* at anchor in Altafiord; only four of fifteen aircraft get through to the target and little damage is caused.

12 February Opposite Cassino US II Corps is relieved by the New Zealand Corps.

181

Fighting rages in the Korsun pocket.

13 February Aircraft from US Fourteenth Army Air Force, under Major General Chennault, raid a Japanese air base at Hong Kong.

15 February The monastery at the summit of Monte Cassino is bombed. Although initially the summit was not occupied by German troops, the commanders of New Zealand Corps, now charged with clearing the hill, are not convinced of this. The Germans do not move in until after the bombing and take advantage of the excellent cover provided by the crypt, cellars and damaged walls .

The Green Islands, north of Bougainville, see an amphibious landing by New Zealanders supported by US ships. The Japanese are defeated within the week.

16 February In a major effort by General von Mackensen to break the Allied beachhead at Anzio, the Luftwaffe combines with ground attacks. Although an ammunition ship is hit and explodes, no ground is conceded, but only a massive Allied air and artillery effort prevents a breakthrough. At Cassino the situation is similar though here it is the New Zealand Corps that can make no progress.

Berlin bombed

Another bombing raid on Berlin involves 800 aircraft and, in his post-raid report, Goebbels will employ the unusual tactic of playing up the amount of damage caused in the hope that the Allies will think that the city is no longer an important target.

17 February Most of the German troops who have broken out from Korsun manage to reach their own lines but are unfit for further action with von Manstein's other units. Their commander, General Stemmermann, has been killed during the breakout.

Eniwetok landing

The Americans land on Eniwetok Atoll in the Marshalls. They are faced by a 3,400-strong Japanese garrison.

18 February More German forces are committed to the effort to break the Anzio beachhead. At the end of hours of hard fighting General Clark is close to calling for an evacuation, but after a final unsuccessful counter-attack Kesselring concludes that the attempt is hopeless. The failure of this German attack, which has employed tactics they will use to combat such an invasion in France, causes much dispute within German High Command which will serve them ill on D-Day. The cruiser HMS *Penelope* is sunk off the coast after her second hit in 24 hours. At Cassino the strong German defence continues to blunt all Allied attempts to take the monastery hill and other strongholds.

Amiens air raid

A daring raid is mounted by Mosquito aircraft to liberate some 700 members of the French Resistance from a prison near Amiens. The precision bombing attack brings the temporary release of 285 of them, but 87 are killed.

London bombed

In an air raid on London, 187 Luftwaffe aircraft drop incendiary bombs
19 February RAF bomber Command loses 78 aircraft from 730 when a

182

raid on Leipzig is intercepted by night-fighters and heavy anti-aircraft fire. The targeted Messerschmitt plant survives the raid but is hammered the following day by US carpet bombing. The Americans spend some days flying against multiple targets which reduces German chances of interception, their resources being over stretched.

20 February Norwegian Resistance fighters sink a ferry carrying heavy water for the German atomic research programme.

The Americans gain the advantage on Eniwetok.

The US Air Force begins a series of raids on German aircraft manufacturing plants.

22 February Rather than risk another major encirclement by the advancing Soviet units, the Germans pull out of Krivoy Rog.

23 February General Lucas, whose timidity after the Anzio landings has been criticised, is replaced by his deputy, General Truscott. *Truscott replaces Lucas at Anzio*

US forces have landed on Parry, an islet in the Eniwetok Atoll, and overcome Japanese resistance to gain control of the area.

US naval forces attack Saipan, Tinian and Rota in the Marianas and sink some Japanese ships.

24 February US B-17 aircraft with fighter escorts raid the Schweinfurt ball-bearing factories again. *Schweinfurt bombed*

28 February In Italy four German divisions begin yet another offensive against Allied troops at Anzio; they fail to breakthrough. Further efforts next day will be foiled by bad weather.

US forces land in the Admiralty Islands and decide to complete the occupation. Japanese resistance is beaten off. *Admiralty Islands landings*

MARCH 1944

2 March In the Pacific a second landing in the Admiralty Islands sees 1,000 men of US 5th Cavalry Regiment arrive at Los Negros, while the previous group move on to take the airfield at Momote.

3 March In Italy Units of German Fourteenth Army attack US 3rd Division near Anzio, but are repelled and take up a defensive line.

5 March On the Eastern Front 1st Ukraine Front, now under the command of Marshal Zhukov, is on the move again along a 110-mile front; its first thrusts are searing attacks around Tarnopol. The pace of their advance cuts von Manstein's thin defensive line and is soon supplemented by the arrival of Konev's Second Ukrainian Front which drives against the junction of Eighth and First Panzer Armies west of Uman.

More US forces land in New Guinea, west of Saidor, and another 1,400 US troops land on Los Negros.

In Burma, 77th Long Range Penetration Brigade is flown in to the landing strip, 'Broadway', to the south of Myitkyina. Other Chindit units have been marching south towards the 'Aberdeen' site for more than a *Chindit operations in Burma* month. The operation sees much inventive flying from minuscule airstrips in dense jungle and mountainous terrain; the Dakota aircraft, in particular, proves a master of this theatre with its diverse capability, including the towing of glider transports.

First large-scale daylight bombing of Berlin

6 March US Eighth Army Air Force bombers make their first large-scale daylight raids on Berlin. They lose one in ten of their aircraft, but their escorting fighters get the better of the Luftwaffe.

Third Ukranian Front joins the Soviet offensive and von Kleist's Army Group A feels the pressure of this push.

8 March In the Pacific a regrouped and enlarged Japanese force prepares to attack the US bridgehead in Bougainville; the US aircraft have to be flown to safety elsewhere.

Battle of Imphal and Kohima begins

In northern Burma the Japanese begin their moves against the British forces in the areas around Imphal and Kohima. Operation 'U-Go' aims to destroy these units, push on through to Dimapur, cut off the Chinese and US forces, and open a route into India. The well-organised and supplied British IV Corps meets the first Japanese attacks; they know what the Japanese are planning, but are surprised by the scale of the Japanese commitment.

Berlin bombed

US Eighth Army Air Force sends some 1,800 bombers escorted by 1,100 fighters on raids to Berlin. In desperation the Germans resort to the deployment of training aircraft in their endeavours to counter this armada.

10 March In Burma the scale and pace of Japanese 33rd Division's advance causes alarm as 17th Indian Division's positions are threatened. At Witok further Japanese moves are contained, and Chindit operations farther south see Japanese communication lines hit.

Soviets reach Bug

12 March Soviet forces reach the river Bug on their advance through Poland.

In the Pacific the Japanese assault in Bougainville which has had some success, begins to peter out; US counter-attacks with tanks and air support will push the Japanese back.

In Burma Allied air support has seen more than 9,000 men plus animals and equipment dropped into the 'Broadway' stronghold in just six nights. Spitfires are now operating from the airstrip at 'Broadway' and other flights continue to complement the resourcefulness of the ground troops; the first helicopters in the history of warfare are used to evacuate wounded.

13 March Indian 17th and 20th Indian Divisions withdraw to Imphal and General Slim asks for 5th Division to be brought up from the Arakan to reinforce the northern sector. The Japanese begin air attacks against 'Broadway' airfield from which the Chindits have been directing many of their operations.

14 March Although the withdrawal of 20th Division in northern Burma proceeds efficiently, 17th Division has delayed its move for 24 hours which has given the Japanese time to block the retreat.

On the Eastern Front in the southern sector the Soviets have cut off some German units north of Kherson and move in to capture some 4,000 troops.

15 March In Italy a huge Allied bombardment of Cassino sees 1,400 tons of bombs and 190,000 shells directed against the town itself, after which the New Zealand Division attacks immediately; 4th Indian Division is earmarked for an advance on the monastery. Progress is hampered by vigorous German defence and the mountains of rubble produced by the preliminary bombardment, but gains are made in both attacks.

On the Eastern Front German Eighth Army's northern sector is overrun. The Soviets cross the Bug and cut the Odessa–Zhmerinka railway line, an important conduit for German supplies.

In Burma Japanese 15th and 31st Divisions cross the Chindwin.

16 March In the Pacific the Americans have landed on Manus in the Admiralty Islands and have encountered Japanese resistance. Their advances through Los Negros continue and, once they have cleared the Japanese out of their way they will soon capture the airfield on Manus.

17 March In Italy the German 1st Paratroop Division is defending the monastery hill at Monte Cassino with great resolve, though Allied gains at the foot of the hill are not retaken by counter-attacks.

18 March The Regent of Hungary, Mikos Horthy, is summoned by Hitler and arrested on his arrival.

Horthy arrested

The Japanese base on Wewak comes under bombardment by American destroyers.

19 March On the Eastern Front Marshal Konev, a World War One veteran and now again proving himself a master of the battlefield, has pushed forward with his 2nd Ukranian Front and now crosses the Dniester. Konev and Vatutin's momentum has produced such a broad front that the German defensive line has become wafer thin and unsustainable.

Soviets cross Dniester

With Horthy in their hands, the Germans move into Hungary to set up a corridor for the retreat of their forces and a route to oil supplies.

Germans occupy Hungary

20 March At Cassino the Germans are in a better position to bring up reinforcements than are the Allies, and General Alexander decides that his losses are proving too great. Decisive gains must be achieved within the next few days or the assault must be abandoned for the time being.

21 March In Burma, where 17th Indian Division is having to make a fighting withdrawal, 20th Division has completed its move and is holding strong positions in the Shenan Hills.

22 March The Germans announce the formation of a new Hungarian government under Field Marshal Szotjay.

At Cassino New Zealand Corps makes a final assault but to no avail. A selective withdrawal takes place, with the most valuable of recent gains being kept and consolidated.

185

23 March On the Eastern Front an acceleration of the Soviet advance, this time south of Tarnopol, threatens to break through German First and Fourth Armies.

24 March The charismatic leader of the Chindits, General Orde Wingate, is killed in an air crash in the Bishanpur mountains. Without his determined voice this unique section of the British Army in Burma will not enjoy the same recognition or dynamic deployment.

In the Pacific the main Japanese resistance on Bougainville comes to an end. Their efforts have seen them lose about 8,000 men.

25 March As the Soviets continue to threaten an encirclement of German forces after the capture of Proskurov, von Manstein orders General Hube to mount a preventive attack to the west but this is not carried out.

Japanese opposition on Manus and Los Negros fizzles out.

26 March In Italy the Allies regroup. New Zealand Corps is to be withdrawn after weeks of heroic action and replaced by units of Eighth Army. It is intended that no further major offensives will be undertaken during the weeks needed to complete this transition.

A segment of First Panzer Army is now cut off around Kamenets-Podolski by Soviet advances.

27 March In Burma British XXXIII Corps is pulled together at Dimapur ahead of an advance on Kohima. Reinforcements from the south have now arrived.

29 March Japanese 31st Division cuts the Imphal–Kohima road at Maram. The Imphal garrison now can only be supplied by air.

Advance units of 1st Ukraine Front have crossed the Roumania border and taken Kolomya.

30 March Hitler vents his anger at the situation on the Eastern Front by dismissing von Manstein and von Kleist; they are replaced by Model and General Schörner. The major railway centre of Chernovtsy is taken by the Soviets.

The Royal Air Force suffers its worst losses of the war in a raid on Nuremberg. A combination of muddled planning, no diversionary raids, weather different from what had been predicted so that the 250-mile penultimate leg of the journey is flown in a dead straight line in clear sky result in 96 aircraft being shot down by the night-fighters from a total of 795. Cloud over the city meant that only a small proportion of the force hit the target with 2,500 tons of bombs.

In the Pacific US naval forces attack Japanese shipping around Palau Island in the Carolines.

31 March The Japanese CinC Combined Fleets, Admiral Koga, is killed in an air crash on Mindanao. Less dynamic than his predecessor, Yamamoto, at the time of his death he has been planning one more mighty confrontation with the US Navy.

186

APRIL 1944

I April Advance units of the 1st and 2nd Ukraine Fronts are threatening another German encirclement near Skala.

In the Pacific US naval forces continue to sink much Japanese shipping in the Carolines and make further gains in the Admiralty Islands.

2 April In Burma, while 17th Indian Division continues its troublesome withdrawal to Imphal, the Japanese cut the Kohima road.

On the Eastern Front, Soviet forces cross the river Prut to enter Roumania.

The first B-29 Superfortress reaches India after a flight from the USA via the UK and North Africa. This heavy bomber is scheduled to enter the war against Japan.

3 April Aircraft from the carriers HMSS *Victorious* and *Furious* bomb *Tirpitz* and cause sufficient damage with 14 hits to extend the vessel's inactivity by another three months. The attack kills 122 of the crew and wounds 316. Dönitz agrees to have his mighty warship repaired, but forbids her use against convoys again, thereby reducing her role to potential threat rather than high seas weapon.

Tirpitz bombed

4 April In Burma Japanese 31st Division, itself short of supplies, moves against the British supply centre of Kohima. The road links to the north are severed. Meanwhile the last unit of 14th Brigade lands at the 'Aberdeen' stronghold, completing 463 Dakota flights which have brought in 3,756 men plus animals and equipment.

In Europe General Giraud is relegated from positions of importance in the Committee of National Liberation. De Gaulle increases his influence.

The US 20th Army Air Force is created with the intention of using the B-29 in raids against Japan. Its aircraft are based in India and China at this stage.

US 20th Army Air Force established

5 April On the Eastern Front the Soviets cut the rail link from Odessa at Razdelnaya and continue their advance on the Black Sea port itself. These recent moves have cut off Army Group A units which are destroyed during the next few days.

US bombers fly from Foggia in southern Italy to attack the Roumanian oilfields at Ploesti again.

Ploesti bombed

7 April The narrow land bridge to the Crimean Peninsula, held by German Seventeenth Army, is attacked by Soviet forces. First Panzer Army, which has been surrounded at Kamenets-Podolsk, completes its masterly breakout with few casualties while destroying considerable quantities of Soviet equipment while doing so. General Hube's men are ready for battle again within days, having retained most of their weapons and ammunition.

In Burma the Japanese block the main route west from Kohima and encircle units from General Stopford's XXXIII Corps near Jotsoma.

British midget submarines raid Narvik harbour and sink two merchantmen and damage the floating dock.

8 April The Germans begin a programme of remarkable long-distance cargo flights between Polish airfields and Manchuria during which Ju 290 A-9 aircraft, with sufficient fuel for a 5,500-mile journey, fly at altitudes of up to 38,000 feet to cross the Soviet Union without detection.

10 April In Burma a new offensive-based strategy is begun by General Slim. It requires General Stopford to break through to Kohima, the Imphal garrison to make attacking sorties into the Japanese-held areas surrounding them, and air supplies to these men to be maintained.

Soviets take Odessa

On the Eastern Front a concerted Soviet drive sees them take Odessa after heavy fighting. The Germans have evacuated men and supplies. In the Crimea the German defensive lines are attacked; the Soviet advance through Roumania continues and 2nd Ukraine Front take Radauti.

12 April Facing defeat in the Crimea, the Germans begin wholesale evacuation which will eventually see 67,000 escape without much threat from Soviet air or naval forces. The retreat towards Sevastopol is proving chaotic but the Germans will still be there at the end of the month.

14 April In Burma the Allied offensive bears fruit as the Japanese road-block to the west of Kohima is broken and the encircled unit at Jotsoma is relieved. In some of the fiercest fighting of the war, where tiny plots of land are fought over for several days, the Battle of Kohima proves a morale-boosting Allied victory despite heavy casualties.

16 April The German rearguard around Tarnopol is finally broken and the town is taken. Sevastopol is cut off as the Soviets occupy Yalta and make their final moves to take Balaclava.

18 April Although they have lost Tarnopol, the Germans make counter-attacks 50 miles south, at Buchach, in an effort to create a corridor through to trapped forces farther east.

More than 2,000 Allied bombers fly missions over Germany, dropping more than 4,000 tons of bombs, the largest quantity dropped in one day since the beginning of the war.

London bombed

In the last of the Operation 'Steinbeck' raids, more than 100 bombers of Luftflotte 9 attack London. From now on they will fly only minor bombing missions against southern ports.

21 April In the Pacific an American Task Force attacks Hollandia in New Guinea ahead of the planned landing there.

Hollandia, New Guinea, landings

22 April General Eichelberger with 84,000 men of US I Corps land at Hollandia and nearby locations. General Adachi's 11,000 defenders are ill-prepared and the US foothold is easily gained against modest harassing attacks; early moves are made inland.

American B-17 and B-24 aircraft raid the rail installations at Hamm plus other rail junctions and ground fortifications.

23 April Hollandia falls without much fighting and the invading forces meet no fierce resistance until they are well inland.

24 April An RAF Bomber Command raid on Munich reaches its target by approaching over Swiss air space thereby side-tracking the German air warning system. The raid causes much structural damage.

Munich bombed

26 April A US raid on Brunswick returns home without any aircraft losses or sight of enemy aircraft. Overcast conditions are considered to be part of the reason for the Germans not flying, but poor radar intelligence and a lack of serviceable aircraft and trained pilots also contributes.

Brunswick bombed

27 April A training exercise for the D-Day landings goes disastrously wrong off the south coast of England when 749 American troops are lost when their poorly escorted convoy to the Devon beaches is attacked by German E-boats. Limited and misleading details of the event will be released.

28 April In the Pacific the Japanese belatedly begin to resist the US troops coming inland from Hollandia in New Guinea; reinforcements have been sent from Wewak.

29 April The Japanese air base at Truk in the Carolines suffers heavy US strikes which destroy most of the aircraft.

Truk bombed

30 April In Burma the dour fighting around Imphal sees the British forces hold the Japanese attacks and, though the supplies position is dire for both sides, the tide seems to be turning as a result of Slim's offensive programme.

MAY 1944

6 May On the Eastern Front the Soviets begin their final assault on Sevastopol with a heavy bombardment. They have failed to prevent the Germans from sustaining a convoy route into the port and evacuating more than 40,000 men. Elsewhere the Soviets have advanced hundreds of miles through the Ukraine and are now at the Carpathians, having driven a massive wedge through the German Front.

Soviets assault Sevastopol

The British Home Fleet begins a series of operations off the Norwegian coast as part of the deception plan to mislead the Germans as to the intended location of the Allied landings in Europe.

8 May Hitler revises his earlier refusal to allow a full withdrawal from the Crimea. His agreement will now see a further 45,000 men leave from various ports although some 8,000 will be lost when their ships are hit by Soviet aircraft and submarines. Within 24 hours the Soviets walk into Sevastopol.

Fall of Sevastopol

11 May The Italian campaign has seen a lull while both sides bring in fresh troops and supplies. Now British, American, French and Polish units are deployed in twelve divisions plus reserves to advance against the

German lines which are manned by just six divisions, not all of which are close to the front lines.

Allied air forces send a series of attacks against airfields and coastal installations in Normandy and other sites in northern France. Calais is especially hard hit as part of the deception plan.

In the Pacific the Japanese have realised for some time that the Marianas will be invaded and have been assembling most of their capital ships at Tawitawi in the Sulu Sea. They are planning Operation 'A-Go', the destruction of the US carrier force.

12 May In Italy the Allies achieve some good early results in their latest advances. General Juin and his French forces quickly take Monte Falto and British units establish small bridgeheads across the Rapido. Cassino remains a stumbling-block, the Poles still unable to dislodge the tough German paratroop defence there.

Allied air forces bomb synthetic fuel plants at four locations in Germany. The resulting destruction has immediate effects, causing Armaments Minister Albert Speer to record: 'The technological war was decided. It meant the end of German armaments production.'

13 May The Crimean adventure is over for the Germans. They have evacuated more than 150,000 men by air and sea in recent weeks, but the campaign has seen more than 78,000 killed or captured.

A US escort destroyer sinks the Japanese submarine *RO501* (ex-*U1224*) off the Azores. She had been presented to the Japanese by the Kriegsmarine.

14 May In Italy French forces advance into the Ausente valley and then the Aurunci mountains, the Germans failing to defend adequately against this move. US troops are left with an easier push against German 94th Division.

In a German E-boat attack against Allied landing-craft lying off the coast near the Isle of Wight, the French destroyer *La Combattante* sinks *S141* in which Dönitz's second son Klaus is serving. The young German is lost with the rest of the crew.

15 May In Italy the Gustav Line is broken in several places and, of the Allied forces, only the Poles are meeting tough resistance at Cassino.

16 May In the Pacific the Americans move on from Hollandia towards Wakde Island. This phase of the New Guinea campaign has been hugely successful.

17 May In Italy Kesselring has brought in three more divisions to oppose the Allied advance, but quickly sees that this is insufficient to turn the tide. Even the stand at Cassino is weakening as the Poles capture Colle Sant' Angelo. He decides to conduct a general retreat.

In Burma Myitkyina airfield falls to Stilwell's Chinese forces fighting alongside Merrill's Marauders.

18 May Europe. In preparation for the imminent Allied invasion, Hitler announces that Field Marshal von Rundstedt will be CinC West, with General Blaskowitz and Field Marshal Rommel in subordinate positions. Rommel is quickly seen to differ in strategic thinking from von Rundstedt and this divergence of opinion, and the compromise allowed by Hitler, will prove damaging as the Germans seek to counter the imminent Allied invasion.

In Italy Allied forces walk into the remains of the Benedictine abbey on Monte Cassino from which the Germans have recently withdrawn. Farther forward, Canadian units have reached the Senger Line while the French on their left and the Americans on the coast are meeting stronger fighting withdrawals.

The campaign in the Admiralty Islands comes to an end. The Japanese have lost almost 4,000 men, the Americans a third of that number.

20 May In a coup for the Polish Resistance movement, a German V-2 rocket on a test firing lands 80 miles east of Warsaw, is seized, dismantled and sent to London for analysis. It arrives there seven weeks before the first of the rockets hits the city.

The US Eighth Army Air Force HQ reports that more than 4,000 aircraft are taking part in daylight operations over France and The Netherlands. They are targeting coastal defences, transport columns, river traffic and Luftwaffe bases, all aimed at softening up the German-occupied hinterland behind the beaches of northern France.

The small Japanese force on Wadke is overrun, giving the Americans the airfield facility there.

21 May More heavy air raids target northern France and include low-level fighter attacks on supply convoys.

22 May The US uses a destroyer force to bombard Wake Island and will follow it with air bombing within 24 hours.

23 May Allied forces at the Anzio beachhead launch an attack on Cisterna and make some gains despite heavy German counters. The Canadians break through the Dora Line and the French are close to following suit.

24 May The Germans manage to hold Cisterna, but Allied units at Anzio do reach the coastal highway near Latina, causing Hitler to agree to a withdrawal to the Caesar Line.

25 May US forces breaking out of the Anzio beachhead manage to take Cisterna and other towns. Although the plan had been to drive east to Valmontone, thereby cutting off the retreat of German Tenth Army, General Clark is tempted to divert many of his forces to the drive on Rome, and, with Kesselring bringing the Hermann Göring Division to reinforce this area, he leaves his men vulnerable. The Germans are able to get most of their men back to the Caesar Line and Tenth Army withdraws intact.

The Germans mount a remarkable paratroop mission against Marshal Tito and his Partisans at their headquarters at Drvar in Bosnia. In a complicated mix of bombardment and airborne landings, the Germans occupy the surrounding area while Tito radios for Allied help and escapes to his cave hideaway. Now the Partisans use their local knowledge to surround the Germans and the whole episode becomes a disaster for the attackers as they lose 1,100 dead and wounded and Tito remains free.

26 May US 1st Armored Division is now proving to be too weak to mount a fast advance towards Velletri. US 3rd Division takes Artena but is prevented from pushing on to Valmontone.

27 May The Germans counter-attack at Artena but the town remains in Allied hands.

Biak landings

In the Pacific, the Americans land on Biak Island, New Guinea, after bombarding Japanese positions there. There is a substantial Japanese garrison but the landing passes without much opposition; this will come when the Americans seek to move inland to their strategic targets.

28 May As the US troops make for Mokmer airfield on Biak, they meet fierce Japanese resistance and take heavy losses. General MacArthur sees these as minor setbacks and announces that the strategic aims of the New Guinea campaign have been achieved.

29 May On the Eastern Front the Soviets have been regrouping for a major advance against German Army Group Centre. Field Marshal Busch presents evidence of this build-up to Hitler but is simply ordered to improve the defensive fortifications at Vitebsk, Polotsk, Rosh, Mogilev and Bobruisk and to defend the area at all costs.

The American positions on Biak and at Arare on the New Guinea mainland come under Japanese pressure with tanks being used by the defenders on Biak.

400 US bombers attack German synthetic fuel works and oil refineries at Polits and other locations and severely set back aircraft fuel production.

30 May In Italy units of Eighth Army take Arce after tough German resistance, and US forces close in on Velletri.

The lull on the Eastern Front comes to an end when the Germans strike against Konev's forces just inside Roumania at Jassy.

31 May The Caesar Line will be broken as Velletri comes close to falling to the Allied moves in Italy.

The US destroyer *England* sinks Japanese submarine *RO105* in the Bismarck Sea, north-west of New Ireland, the sixth successful attack on submarines by this vessel in twelve days.

JUNE 1944

1 June The first coded message announcing the D-Day landings is broadcast to the French resistance by the BBC in the form of poetry. The Germans track the information given and alert some of their units in northern France.

In Italy the Americans put much effort into the drive for the Italian capital. They breach the Caesar Line as they attack through the Alban Hills and Kesselring is forced to order a fighting withdrawal to the north of Rome.

The German Army's military intelligence unit, the *Abwehr*, is removed from the control of the Wermacht by Hitler. Its chief, Admiral Canaris, is dismissed and all secret service activities are placed in the hands of Heinrich Himmler, the SS leader. Canaris has been clandestinely conspiring against Hitler.

On the Eastern Front the Soviets block German moves around Jassy

In the Pacific the Americans are deploying tanks against the Japanese on Biak.

2 June The Germans' withdrawal in Italy speeds the Allied advance.

The French National Liberation Committee re-forms as the Provisional Government of the French Republic.

In Burma the final siege of Myitkyina begins; the course of the war there is beginning to change.

In Italy US 15th Army Air Force fly their first 'shuttle' mission from Foggia against road and rail targets in Hungary before flying on to land at Ukrainian airfields.

3 June Frascati and Albano fall to the Allies advancing on Rome which has been all but deserted by German forces. The Allies will be welcomed in the capital but will not delay themselves with a triumphal entry; Alexander has already decreed that troops will only enter the city to use its roads as thoroughfares on their continued march north against the retreating Germans.

The Americans advance on Biak as Japanese attempts to bring in reinforcements fail.

4 June On the day that sees the first US units enter Rome, the invasion convoys sail from southern England for the French coast but are called back when bad weather is forecast. The strategy of the landings calls for a dawn start, at the lowest tide, all preceded by the best of moonlit nights. If the operation does not go ahead now it will have to be postponed until July. Eisenhower decides that the landings will take place on the 6th; he is unaware that the current inclement weather has relaxed the German troops in northern France, many of whose commanders are absent from their posts.

British and US aircraft continue to fly against targets in northern France, many of which are in the Calais and Boulogne area, thus maintaining the idea that the invasion will take place there.

The Germans mount an airborne attack against positions held by Tito's Partisans in Yugoslavia

5 June The second half of the coded signal is broadcast to the French Resistance and again the Germans note it but fail to react correctly; even

Seventh Army in Normandy is not told of it. In the middle of the night airborne troops fly from airfields in southern England; the convoy transporting the ground troops is already at sea. Allied bombers wreck ten of the most important coastal fortifications between Cherbourg and Le Havre.

The Allies move through Rome and press on.

Japanese losses in New Guinea and on the island of Biak mount daily as they stoutly defend their positions.

In the Far East the first operational mission by US 20th Army Air Force B-29s sees them fly from a base near Calcutta to bomb rail installations at Bangkok.

D-Day, the
Normandy landings

6 June The largest combined operation of the war gets under way. General Eisenhower is in overall command and has nearly three million men at his disposal plus a huge quantity of equipment including submersible tanks and other machines created especially for the landing. Ships of the invasion fleet will tow purpose-built concrete jetties (the 'Mulberry' harbours) which will enable vehicles to disembark. The Germans are ill-prepared for the landing of troops on five Normandy beaches between Caen and Valognes with airborne troops dropping on the flanks. Von Rundstedt had wanted to concentrate his defensive forces inland so that the invaders could be pushed back into the sea after they had landed; Rommel wanted the beaches themselves to be the point of strongest defence and the chosen battleground. The Hitler compromise left the worst of both worlds, and a dispirited command. There are just 59 German divisions in France and Holland, only a dozen more than are defending Italy and one hundred less than are deployed on the Eastern Front. The landing of the British and Canadian forces on 'Gold', 'Juno' and 'Sword' Beaches goes well, late landings and traffic jams of armour on the shoreline being the worst worries.

The US landing on 'Utah' Beach is a great success, 23,250 troops getting ashore with the loss of 200, but 'Omaha' Beach presents a less satisfactory story with poor air support, early deployment of amphibious tanks too far from shore and weak rocket and artillery fire all contributing to a greater loss of life. One thousand die on this beach alone. Some 34,250 men do get ashore but are unable to get far for the time being.

The end of the day sees almost 150,000 men on dry land and Allied aircraft already hampering German attempts to push them back or to bring up substantial reserves. Among German reports of the day are comments about the enemy dropping uniformed dolls packed with explosives which blow up when touched. Allied pilots flying in the invasion zone report no sightings of German aircraft; the British Air Ministry later suggests that the ratio of aircraft in the region is close to 200:1. The day has seen massive bombing raids on coastal installations, fighters strafing inland road and rail convoys, and constant patrols to ward off the few Luftwaffe attempts to attack the ships or the beaches.

7 June The forces which landed on 'Gold' and 'Juno' the previous day have already linked up; it is a priority for the other units to do likewise so that the move inland can be substantial and swift and the coast left clear for further landings. The British advance towards Caen keeps German reserves occupied and away from the beaches and frees the 'Omaha' contingent to expand from its perilous position; they break out as far as the inland coast road at Formigny. The 'Utah' forces move towards Carentan and Montebourg in concert with some of the paratroop units. Renewed attempts by 3rd Canadian Division to take Caen are foiled by newly arrived 12th SS Panzer Division (Hitler Youth).

Stalin, who for so long has been urging the Allies to open this second front so that German resources will be pulled out of Russia, is told by Churchill of the successful start to 'Overlord'.

The Americans on Biak capture Mokmer airfield.

8 June More Allied troops land on the D-Day beaches and more adventurous advances are under way. US 4th Division moves in the direction of Cherbourg and the Cotentin Peninsula, and Azeville becomes the scene of heavy fighting. Advance V Corps units take Isigny at the mouth of the Vire, but they have not yet linked with troops from the 'Utah' landing. British Marine Commandos take Port-en-Bessin to close the coastal gap between 'Gold' and 'Omaha' Beaches.

Fighting continues on Biak as Japanese attempts to reinforce are intercepted.

9 June Marshal Badoglio is forced to resign as Prime Minister of Italy and is replaced by Ivanoe Bonomi, a consistent opponent of the Fascist movement.

Bonomi replaces Badoglio

In France the Germans lose Azeville as VII Corps close in on Cherbourg and Carentan. Resistance by German reserves on the eastern flank of the landing area is delaying the British and Canadian advance, but the Allies have now established landing strips in the area; runways measuring 3,000 feet in length and 150 feet wide have been constructed in fifteen hours.

Some of the US forces in Italy are withdrawn to prepare for the Allied landings in southern France.

10 June Field Marshal Montgomery lands in France, where 7th Armoured Division is embroiled in fierce combat with Panzerlehr Division. Elsewhere, troops from 'Utah' and 'Omaha' finally link up and US 101st Airborne is closing in on Carentan.

In Italy Pescara and Chieti on the Adriatic coast fall as the Allies advance on all fronts, their progress delayed only by sporadic German fighting withdrawals and the demolitions they leave behind them.

Allied fighter-bombers attack Panzer Group West's HQ in the château at Thury-Harcourt on the river Orne, and destroy the German armoured communications network for the area, a massive blow to German battle zone efficiency.

SOE agents in Belgium alert London to the fact that rail transporters are taking truckloads of flying bombs to coastal launch sites.

On the Eastern Front the Soviets begin a series of actions against Finnish positions on the Karelian isthmus.

In the Pacific the carrier HMS *Illustrious* and escort carrier HMS *Atheling* are involved in diversionary raids on Sabang ahead of US attacks on the Marianas.

11 June In France Carentan and Lison fall to the Allies after bitter fighting, but German formations are holding the Allied drive in other areas.

From Italy US Fifteenth Army Air Force aircraft raid the Roumanian airfield at Foscani before flying on to a safe landing in Russia, the first occasion of such co-operation.

In the Pacific US Task Force 58 with fifteen carriers and close battleship support deploys aircraft against Saipan, Tinian and other islands in the Marianas group. Japanese aircraft, naval and merchant shipping are severely hit; 36 Japanese aircraft are shot down.

12 June In France US units strike west and south-west from their D-Day positions. Other moves are made towards the important town of St-Lô. More Allied troops have been landed and now there are more than 320,000 men in the area with 100,000 tons of supplies and 54,000 vehicles. The German air and naval arms have failed to prevent these continued landings and the German ground troops have been occupied with the Allied advances from the beachheads. Allied air forces have flown 49,000 sorties in seven days, dropping 42,000 tons of bombs and paralysing much of the rail and road hinterland behind the Normandy beaches.

In the Marianas, Tinian, Saipan and Guam suffer more attacks. The Japanese fleets held at Tawitawi and Batjan now set sail, but are outnumbered and quickly targeted by the US ships. Admirals Ozawa and Kurita have built into their strategy for this action the support of land-based aircraft from their Marianas airfields and are not yet aware of the damage caused to these squadrons by US bombing.

13 June In France British 7th Armoured Division makes rapid progress on a new line to Villers-Bocage only to meet fierce German defence there. At Carentan 17th Panzer Division nearly retakes the town in a series of determined counter-attacks.

The first salvo of ten V-1 flying bombs is launched at the UK from the Pas-de-Calais, but only four make it across the English Channel. One hits the village of Swanscombe, 20 miles from its London target, another lands in the Sussex town of Cuckfield and the third reaches the London suburb of Bethnal Green, killing six people. The German spotter plane sent to report on the raid is shot down.

14 June A third US Army Corps joins the Normandy battle.

An RAF Mosquito records the first successful chase and shooting down of a flying bomb over the English Channel.

In the Pacific there are further heavy US bombardments of Saipan and Tinian, in preparation for the imminent landings there.

The remaining German naval strength in the English Channel is decimated by a raid on the port of Le Havre by 325 RAF Lancasters. More than thirty small ships are sunk.

Le Havre bombed

15 June Residents of southern England begin to experience the fire curtain sent up by anti-aircraft defences against the increasing arrival of flying bombs. Although eight fighter squadrons are deployed to intercept the new missiles, it is ground fire that will prove the most effective deterrent in these first weeks.

From their base in China sixty-seven B-29 Superfortresses set out to bomb the Javata steelworks in Japan, but seventeen of the aircraft are lost or damaged and the mission is abandoned.

In the Pacific US forces on Biak are still facing heavy Japanese counterattacks.

The US landing force for the Marianas operation is approximately 67,500 strong; its advanced units meet fierce opposition from the Japanese defenders who have less than half the US manpower. The landing-craft come under heavy artillery fire and the beachheads prove too far apart to be easily linked; the Marines do get ashore, however, and see off the first wave of Japanese counters. The islands of Iwo Jima, Chichi Jima and Haha Jima are bombarded.

Marianas landings

16 June RAF Bomber Command raids Boulogne and destroys fourteen warships and other vessels.

Boulogne air raid

US battleships shell Guam, and in continued fighting on Saipan US forces link up and begin their advance inland.

17 June In France US forces reach the west coast of the Cotentin Peninsula and cut off German forces farther north. In an acrimonious meeting with von Rundstedt and Rommel, Hitler accuses the German troops in northern France of weakness and lack of bravery; he refuses to agree to a withdrawal to strategic defensive positions. He claims that if his Army cannot win the war his secret weapons will.

French 9th Colonial Division lands on Elba and completes the occupation within 48 hours.

Elba liberated

More US units land on Saipan.

18 June In France US VII Corps reaches the west coast of the Cotentin Peninsula at Barneville.

In Italy Eighth Army takes Assisi and moves on towards Perugia.

Soviet forces break the main Finnish positions on the Mannerheim Line and move on Viipuri.

Mannerheim Line breached

In the Pacific US naval forces rendezvous west of the Marianas as the Japanese fleets approach. Scouts locate the US ships and the Japanese decide to send aircraft against them the following day. The second part of their scheme, which sees their aircraft fly on to Guam for refuelling, is suspect in view of the damage caused to the airfields there by American attacks.

19 June A 4-day period of freak weather in the English Channel impedes the arrival of supplies; both 'Mulberry' harbours are damaged by the storms.

In Italy, the Allies are approaching the next main German defensive position, the Albert Line.

On the Eastern Front, in a massive, co-ordinated sabotage operation, 100,000 Soviet partisan guerrillas detonate more than 10,000 explosions to the rear of German Army Group Centre positions. Supply and communications are inoperable for days.

Battle of the Philippine Sea. The Japanese aircraft fly more than 370 sorties against the US fleet off the Marianas, but are met by fighters from the carriers and heavy anti-aircraft fire. In a short time the Japanese lose close to 300 aircraft to less than thirty by the Americans. Furthermore, a US dawn raid on Guam has further damaged the facilities there so when the Japanese aircraft arrive at that haven they find inadequate defences to protect them and are destroyed on the ground. The sad story worsens for the Japanese as US submarines sink their prize carriers *Taiho* and *Shokaku*. The battle can hardly be called a battle at all; inferior numbers, ill-advised tactics and a failure to communicate the true state of play on Guam make the event a one-sided affair. Individual Japanese show great resolve, including one pilot who, shortly after take-off, sees a torpedo heading for his carrier and dives into the sea on to the weapon to save the ship.

20 June In France the Germans begin their stand at Cherbourg as US troops close in. The defenders have been refused permission to attempt a breakout. On their way through the Cotentin Peninsula US forces have captured several flying bomb launch sites.

In Italy British 6th Armoured Division takes the important city of Perugia.

The Soviets capture the Finnish town of Viipuri and will continue their attacks over the coming days.

The clearing of Japanese resistance on Saipan continues.

The Japanese continue to suffer from lack of intelligence information at the end of the Philippine Sea confrontation. They withdraw their ships for refuelling in the belief that aircraft are still serviceable on Guam and can return to the battle. The US vessels harry the retreating Japanese and send their aircraft to attack and sink the carrier *Hiyo* and inflict damage on battleships and a cruiser. The remaining Japanese give up the fight and withdraw completely.

21 June In the UK RAF fighters are beginning to have more success against the flying bombs and bombing has knocked out some of the

Battle of the Philippine Sea

Perugia liberated

Soviets take Viipuri

launching ramps in France. The fighter pilots locate, chase and destroy the rockets in mid-flight; the target can only fly in a straight line so presents an easy, if fast, target.

More than 1,000 US bombers with a similar number of fighter escorts, raid Berlin and its environs. They encounter heavy anti-aircraft fire and fighter interceptors before they fly on to bases in the Soviet Union. The raid evokes a response; in one of the last German air raids of the war, General Meister, commanding Luftflotte 4, sends 200 bombers against the Soviet bases and destroys more than 60 US aircraft. **Berlin bombed**

In Italy an Anglo-Italian underwater group deploys off Spezia harbour and sinks the Italian heavy cruisers *Bolzano* and *Gorizia*, both wearing the German flag. **Bolzano and Gorizia sunk**

22 June In France the battle for Cherbourg begins with a heavy air raid. It will take five days for the Americans to take the city. A unit of German frogmen is brought into Caen with the intention of blowing up two bridges over the Orne and the Orne Canal which have been used by the Allies since the first hours of the invasion. In a daring mission the team avoids detection and does indeed blow up two bridges, but in daylight it is found that they have blown the wrong ones. **Battle for Cherbourg**

In Burma the siege of Imphal ends when 2nd and 5th Indian Divisions link at Milestone 107 on the Imphal–Kohima road. Japanese resolve is being weakened by continuing supply problems. **Siege of Imphal ends**

In New Guinea the Americans are still facing Japanese attacks at Aitape and Sarmi and on Biak.

The US Marines clearing Saipan make several gains.

23 June On the Eastern Front Marshal Zhukov begins the Soviet summer offensive with fresh heavy artillery. On a front stretching from Vitebsk, through Mogilev to the river Pripet, the Russians advance against German Army Group Centre behind a withering artillery bombardment and gain ten miles in several places on this first day. Many Luftwaffe units have been transferred to the west so Soviet aircraft have the skies almost to themselves. Stalin has given Churchill early notification of the new moves and sees them as a 'double hit' against the Germans, coming so soon after the Normandy invasion. He has deployed fourteen armies with 6,000 tanks and other heavy armour, 7,000 aircraft and 45,000 guns and mortars, plus five air armies. **Soviet summer offensive**

24 June In France the Allied invasion fleet encounters a new weapon off the coast as *Mistel*, the pilotless Ju 88, is deployed. The weapon is fitted beneath a fighter aircraft, in 'piggyback' fashion, then detached and 'flown' at enemy shipping. The first targets turn out to be rusting hulks being used as breakwaters. **First use of Mistel**

On the Eastern Front the towns which Hitler had ordered his troops to fortify are already surrounded. The Orsha–Vitebsk railway line is cut as the Soviets continue to make significant gains.

In the Pacific the southern half of Saipan is now fully cleared by the US Marines who can now join their colleagues fighting in the north.

The islands of Iwo Jima and Chichi Jima are attacked again, this time by aircraft from four US carriers.

25 June In France Allied naval bombardment supplements the ground attack on Cherbourg, which is very close to collapse despite garrison chief General von Schlieben's refusal to surrender.

Soviet advances in Belorussia gather pace and five German divisions are trapped near Vitebsk.

26 June In France General von Schlieben and his naval opposite number, Admiral Hennecke, are captured in Cherbourg as all but the docks area falls to the Allies. The battleship HMS *Rodney* is standing offshore to lend heavy gun support to the British forces struggling to take Caen, twelve miles inland.

Soviets take Vitebsk

On the Eastern Front the Soviets take Vitebsk and other valuable towns along the front. Third Panzer Army has lost 35,000 men in trying to avoid encirclement at Vitebsk.

Cherbourg liberated

27 June In France Cherbourg is now entirely in Allied hands which gives them access to a major port. Work begins immediately to rid the area of booby-traps and roadblocks and prepare the harbour for use.

In Finland Field Marshal Keitel arrives to offer support to the locals in their defence against the Soviet attacks.

Busch replaced by Model

28 June Hitler sacks Field Marshal Busch as commander of Army Group Centre and replaces him by Field Marshal Model. Ernst Busch has been one of the Führer's more subservient commanders but this has not saved him; he will be moved to Norway.

The first week of the Soviet offensive has seen the defeat of Ninth and Third Panzer Armies and the envelopment of Fourth Army.

US B-17s fly from Soviet bases to bomb Polish oil refineries being used by the Germans; they then fly on to Italy. No aircraft are lost on this mission which is one of a growing number deploying British and US aircraft from Soviet airfields.

In the Pacific Japanese resistance on Biak has been all but defeated and the Americans begin their final mopping-up operations.

29 June On the Eastern Front German Ninth Army loses 70,000 men in the futile battle for Bobruisk, but 30,000 men evade capture and escape westwards.

30 June In France the remaining German forces in the Cotentin Peninsula surrender, but further east Caen and St-Lô remain to be taken by the Allies. Of the 850,000 Allied troops brought to France since the D-Day landings on 6 June, upwards of 60,000 have now been killed or wounded.

In Italy the Germans have formed a new defensive line south of Siena and Arezzo.

200

JULY 1944

1 July In France the Allies' armoured divisions are now operating in *bocage* country and are unable to advance on a broad front. Orchards, and narrow roads with high hedges, and overgrown embankments slow them down and make them very vulnerable.

In Italy the Allied advance continues apace. On the west coast Cecina falls to US Fifth Army, and the Germans retreat before British X and XIII Corps rather than engage. Siena will fall in the next few days as will Rosinano on the Tyrrhenian coast.

In the Pacific the Allies land on Numfoor Island off New Guinea with 7,000 men from US and Australian units.

3 July In poor weather US forces move south out of the Cotentin Peninsula to join the push towards St-Lô. Field Marshal von Rundstedt is destined to be replaced as CinC West by von Kluge after replying to Field Marshal Keitel's question about his conclusions from the Normandy situation: 'We should make peace, you fools! What else?'

In Burma General Slim's Fourteenth Army captures the Japanese stronghold of Ukhrul on the Indian–Burmese frontier.

Ukhrul taken

On the Eastern Front the Soviets take Minsk. The German forces are at their lowest ebb. Army Group Centre is barely capable of offensive action; its command structure is in tatters. Fourth Army is cut off and awesome casualties are being reported daily. From a point where both combatants had had some weeks to regroup and focus on new objectives, only the Soviets have advanced their cause. The Soviet Information Bureau is sufficiently confident to report the collapse of Army Group Centre, stating that Soviet forces are by-passing German-held positions at Minsk and Polotsk in order to move towards the Baltic States.

Soviets take Minsk

4 July RAF 617 Squadron flies bombing missions against caves 30 miles north-west of Paris which are being used to store flying bombs. The limestone caves survive the attack.

On the Eastern Front Army Group North now faces attacks by 1st Baltic Front on its flank and rear. Its commander, General Lindemann, has been replaced by General Friessner.

In the Pacific Numfoor Island's airfield is captured by the Americans.

Further carrier group attacks are mounted against Guam, Iwo Jima and Chichi Jima.

5 July In Normandy La-Haye-du-Puits falls to the Americans in Normandy and the Canadians have taken Carpiquet to the west of Caen. During this time, German manned torpedoes are particularly active out of Villers-sur-Mer, a Normandy seaside town. In the coming weeks they will score hits on various Allied vessels in the Orne estuary including the Polish cruiser *Dragon*, the destroyer HMS *Isis* and some minesweepers.

In the Pacific the Allied forces on Numfoor repel Japanese counter-attacks and move on.

6 July Churchill reports to parliament that 3,745 V-1 flying bombs have been fired at England causing the deaths of 2,752 civilians. The comment is aimed at placing the effects of the 'terror weapon' in the context of the war elsewhere.

Kluge replaces Rundstedt

Field Marshal von Kluge has replaced von Rundstedt as CinC West. He has been convalescing after a car accident and will not stay long in this new post.

In Italy the Germans continue to fall back. The next substantial natural barrier they can defend will be the river Arno.

In the Pacific US troops are advancing across Saipan and have taken the Namber airstrip on Numfoor. On Saipan Admiral Nagumo and General Saito commit suicide, leaving their junior officers to plan a last futile attack.

7 July In Normandy the Allies are facing fierce opposition and call in additional bombardments from HMS *Rodney* offshore. Caen and St-Lô are the principal objectives. Allied daylight bombing raids against Germany are now combated by storm-fighter tactics from the Luftwaffe which entail armoured Fw 190 aircraft flying as close as possible to the bombers in a tight formation. The German pilots are offered the option of ramming their aircraft into the bombers to bring them down. In an action over Leipzig the Germans bring down 30 Liberators and four fighters, their best count for a German day-fighter group throughout the war.

On Saipan an attack by 3,000 demented Japanese is beaten off after vicious close-quarter fighting. The episode hastens the end of the conflict there.

8 July In Normandy British and Canadian forces attack Caen after a bombardment by 450 British aircraft, and break into the outskirts of the town. Farther west, the Americans are reinforced by newly arrived divisions.

On the Eastern Front the important rail centre of Baranovichi falls to the Soviets.

Fall of Caen

9 July Allied forces enter Caen and occupy the sector north of the river. Carpiquet airfield, three miles to the west, is also taken.

On the Eastern Front Soviet forces reach Vilna.

Saipan liberated

In the Marianas the battle for Saipan is over. The Japanese have lost up to 27,000 men, the Americans more than 3,000 and four times that number injured.

10 July In yet another example of Hitler overruling sensible requests from skilled battlefield commanders at the front, Model is refused assistance from Army Group North to strengthen his stand against the Soviet drive to the Baltic.

11 July Naval gunfire again assists the British fighting for full control of Caen and its environs. Further west US 9th Division's advance is being held by Panzer Lehr Division.

US forces on New Guinea are forced to pull back in the Aitape sector by Japanese attacks along the line of the river Driniumor.

12 July In Normandy the Americans have reached St-Lô.

The RAF deploys the Gloster Meteor, the sole jet aircraft to be used by the Allies during the war.

13 July A secret report on public morale by the German security service confirms dismay at the heavy fighting on all fronts and the desire that the V-2 rocket will have the promised impact on Germany's fortunes.

Facing stubborn German resistance at St-Lô, the Allies pause to plan a stronger attack on the town.

Crewed by trainees who had completed only 100 hours of flying, a Ju 88 G-1 lands in error at Woodbridge in East Anglia. It is fitted with the Lichtenstein SN-2 wide-angle radar which has so benefited German night-fighter techniques for many months. Its capture robs the German night-fighters of their last chance to defend the country against Allied raids because British experts quickly issue instructions which nullify its value.

In Italy the Allies are just 20 miles south of Florence.

On the Eastern Front after hard fighting a German surrender is sought at Vilna, but its rejection brings an artillery bombardment which finally brings the capitulation; Pinsk is captured by 1st Belorussian Front.

Soviets take Pinsk

15 July In Italy Eighth Army divisions attack German positions at Arezzo and, to the west, US and French units push forward, to Livorno and Castellina respectively.

16 July The Soviets open a 300-mile front with the capture of Lvov as their target.

Japanese initiative around Aitape is losing impetus.

17 July In Normandy US forces enter St-Lô on the day that Erwin Rommel, on an inspection trip, suffers a fractured skull when his car is strafed by an Allied aircraft. No replacement is appointed; von Kluge takes over Rommel's duties while remaining CinC West. Hitler still shows reluctance to bring more troops from the Calais area, remaining convinced that the deceptive manoeuvres being undertaken by the Allies, known as Operation 'Bodyguard', could still signal an invasion there.

Rommel injured

In Normandy US aircraft drop napalm for the first time in raids against German fuel dumps.

In Norway three Allied carriers and a battleship attack *Tirpitz* anchored in Kaafiord, but make little impact because of a dense smoke-screen.

Tirpitz attacked

Concern about the parlous progress of the war is being expressed among Japan's leaders who seek an equitable solution. Several role changes, including a new navy minister and a change in chief of staff, added to a reduced standing for General Tojo, indicate their nervousness but the Allies fail to react.

18 July In Normandy St-Lô is all but occupied by US XIX Corps, and British and Canadian troops begin the push south and east of Caen after calling in a huge aerial bombardment from 1,000 aircraft. The bombing certainly disorganises the German defence for a time, but traffic logistics hamper the pace of advance and soon both sides become confused and inefficient.

In Italy the Allied advance benefits from the securing of Livorno and Ancona as these ports, on opposite sides of the country, will ease the supply situation.

19 July The Allies make cautious advances south of Caen but are constantly delayed by the better tank tactics of the Germans who choose favourable positions; the Allied tank commanders are struggling to make their numerical strength tell.

In the UK anti-aircraft batteries on the south-east coast are using proximity-fused shells which explode when a nearby target is sensed. This new projectile reduces the effort and ammunition needed to bring down the V-1s.

The Soviets are now in Latvia and their advance on Lvov gathers pace.

Attempted assassination of Hitler

20 July Hitler assassination plot. During a conference at Hitler's headquarters at Rastenburg in East Prussia, Colonel Count von Stauffenberg, a hero of the fighting in Poland, France and the Western Desert – a record which saw him lose an eye and much of his right arm – is able to leave a suitcase bomb in the room where Hitler is holding the meeting. The building is a temporary one, however, and the explosion is dissipated. The Führer is shaken though not seriously injured, but the conspirators, believing that no one could have survived the explosion, spread the news of Hitler's death and thereby incriminate themselves. Stauffenberg flies to Berlin to assure his fellow plotters of the success of the mission, but failing to get confirmation of this from Rastenburg, the group, which includes Colonel General Olbricht, General Hoepner, and long-standing anti-Hitlerlite General Beck, hesitate to take control as they had planned. Before the end of the day Hitler loyalists arrive to arrest the conspirators who are either shot on the spot or subjected to show trials a few months later and hanged with piano wire. Hitler had the barbarous executions filmed.

Others who knew of the plot but have avoided direct connivance include Rommel, Halder, Witzleben and von Kluge, and Canaris, former Head of the Abwehr. Although Hitler enjoys the temporary glory of surviving the attempt on his life, the event increases his pathological distrust of all but his inner circle of sycophants and, with his declining health, excessive medication and knowledge of a diminishing support base, his ability to conduct the war reduces daily. The German news bureau reports the incident and advises that the Führer is unhurt, except for slight burns and bruises.

21 July General Zeitzler resigns as Chief of Staff at German High Command and is replaced by General Guderian.

Guderian replaces Zeitzler

In the Pacific the Americans land on Guam. Facing them are nearly 20,000 Japanese but the landings are almost unopposed and eventually 55,000 US troops will go ashore.

Guam landings

23 July In Italy the Americans have reached the outskirts of Pisa.

On the Eastern Front the last German forces on Soviet soil are pushed out of the country when the town of Pskov is taken. Stalin writes to Churchill about the situation in Poland, stating that he has found it necessary to liaise with the Polish Committee of National Liberation in Warsaw rather than the Polish government in exile in London which, he claims, has little influence in their country.

The invasion of Guam proceeds after some heavy fighting.

24 July Lublin falls to 1st Ukraine Front which also liberates the Majdenek concentration camp.

Soviets take Lublin

In the Pacific US forces land on Tinian and face a Japanese garrison of about 6,000 men. Early skirmishes are seen off but with considerable losses. Napalm is used for the first time in the Pacific theatre.

Tinian landings

25 July In Normandy the US attack on St-Lô is initially hampered by inaccurate aerial bombardment which causes some examples of 'friendly fire' casualties. Good progress is made later in the day. The British and Canadians' drive on Falaise further to the east has drawn off some of the German defenders.

The Soviets capture Lvov.

Soviets take Lvov
Sabang attacked

Off the northern tip of Sumatra, the British Eastern Fleet attacks Sabang with aircraft from HMSS *Victorious* and *Illustrious* targeting the airfield and other vessels shelling the harbour and oil depots.

26 July In the USA a meeting between Roosevelt, MacArthur and Nimitz sees heated debate as the next priorities are set for the Pacific. MacArthur wants to attack the Philippines – after all, he has vowed 'I shall return' – but the contrary argument is to continue by-passing islands and so cut them off from re-supply thereby eliminating them as a threat. The Navy wants to target Formosa.

27 July In France US forces continue to advance, having taken Marigny, St-Gilles, Lessay and Périers.

The Soviet advance in the east sees their forces barely 50 miles from Riga in the north and closing on Kaunas a little further south. Central drives have moved them close to Warsaw and in the south they are not far from the Czech and Hungarian borders.

28 July The first objective of Operation 'Cobra', the Allied assault on German forces at the western end of the Normandy invasion area, is achieved when US 4th Armored Division takes Coutances.

'Cobra' offensive

The Germans sortie their Me 163B rocket-propelled fighter for the first time.

Biak liberated The long battle on Biak, off New Guinea, is finally won when the Americans wipe out the last pocket of resistance.

Tiger II **29 July** On the Eastern Front the new German King Tiger tank is deployed against a Soviet bridgehead west of the Vistula at Baranov.

Avranches liberated **30 July** In France US troops secure Avranches with its strategically important bridges while the British make good ground at Caumont farther to the east.

The Soviets capture an Enigma M4 enciphering machine from *U250*, which they sink in the Gulf of Finland and then recover.

31 July Soviet forces move ever closer to Warsaw, taking Siedlice and Otwock, just twelve miles from the city. Farther to the north, Kaunas also falls.

AUGUST 1944

1 August In France the Allied forces that will punch their way across the country consist of General Bradley's US 12th Army Group: Hodges' US First Army and Patton's US Third Army; Field Marshal Montgomery's British 21st Army Group: General Dempsey's British Second Army and General Crerar's Canadian First Army. Montgomery has overall charge of the ground forces. Patton plans to clear the Germans out of Brittany and thrust towards Le Mans; Hodges will push for Mortain. The British and Canadians will advance south-eastwards from their positions between Caumont and Caen.

Linsen assault boats The Kriegsmarine deploys radio-controlled *Linsen* assault boats against Allied shipping. These small vessels are packed with 600lb of explosives and account for the early loss of the destroyer HMS *Quorn* and various other vessels.

Warsaw uprising On the Eastern Front the Soviets' close proximity to Warsaw encourages the local Home Army units to begin action with a view to having a measure of administrative control in place before the Soviets, with whom they are not closely allied, arrive. In fact the Soviets do not intend to enter the city but by-pass it on their way to other objectives. Radio Moscow announces the defeat of German Army Group Centre; German sources acknowledge it to be their most costly defeat.

Tinian liberated In the Pacific fighting ends on Tinian in the Marianas; the Japanese have lost more than 6,000 men, the Americans 390.

2 August US Third Army reaches Dinan and the perimeter of Rennes; US First Army takes Villedieu.

The Germans launch 316 V-1 bombs on London, the highest daily total yet. More than 100 reach the capital and cause great damage to armament factories on the outskirts; Tower Bridge is also hit.

3 August In France Mortain falls to US forces and in Brittany the Germans are being pushed back towards the major ports, leaving little chance of a breakout to the south. Farther east, Villers-Bocage is close to being taken.

On the Eastern Front German counter-attacks south of Riga re-open communications with other units farther south. Konev's 1st Ukranian Front troops are across the Vistula north of Miele.

In Burma the siege of Myitkyina ends when the town is taken by the Chinese and Americans, though they find most of the Japanese garrison has escaped.

Allies take Myitkyina

US warships shell areas of Guam where the Japanese are preparing defensive positions.

4 August In Italy the Allies enter Florence and occupy the section of the city south of the river.

5 August Patton's troops move into Vannes and close on St-Malo and Brest.

On the Eastern Front General Petrov's 4th Ukranian Front joins the Soviet forward lines in the south Poland/north Hungary sector.

6 August In France US forces are close to Lorient in Brittany and Le Mans farther east. Vire falls to US First Army units.

On the Eastern Front the Germans evacuate Drogobych, an important oil production town, as the Soviet forces close in.

7 August In France 2nd and 116th Panzer Divisions break the Allied hold on Mortain, but Allied air superiority prevents them from taking advantage of this. Substantial RAF bombing assists a Canadian advance southwest of Caen.

In the Pacific heavy resistance on Guam prevents the Americans gaining much ground.

8 August In France although the German counter at Mortain still demands Allied attention, this is a modest achievement considering that Le Mans is taken, the Brittany ports are under attack and the Allies are moving on Nantes and Angers. Allied tank formations are still struggling to adopt effective tactics on unfavourable terrain.

Much of Warsaw is in the hands of the AK local militia which have captured German equipment to use against the expected counter-attack by SS and police units. Several German commanders, including Guderian, will complain about the use of such personnel and most are withdrawn.

9 August In France German efforts at Mortain are neutralised as the Allies, screened by intensive bombing, move towards Falaise.

10 August The German counter-attacks at Mortain end as they withdraw to protect their rear flanks.

In the Pacific only small teams of survivors remain on Guam. Few of the 10,000-strong Japanese garrison have survived to be taken prisoner, but the Americans have lost upwards of 1,300 dead and five times as many wounded.

11 August In France as the Allies cross the Loire well to the south, Hitler forbids von Kluge to retreat from Mortain. Elsewhere US XV Corps close on Argentan where German 116th Division lies in wait.

On the Eastern Front the German lines are broken south of Lake Peipus and the Soviets move on apace.

13 August In France Argentan is occupied by XV Corps as units from XII and XX Corps advance on Orléans and Chartres.

Falaise gap

14 August Increased Allied bombing precedes a Canadian push towards Falaise.

15 August Divisions of German Seventh Army and units from Panzer Group Eberbach and Fifth Panzer Army are caught between advances by US VII and V Corps between Tinchebray and Argentan and attempt a hurried retreat to the east. The pace of the Allies' ground moves and their air superiority is preventing von Kluge and his fellow commanders from making a full assessment of the situation.

Allies land in the South of France

Operation 'Dragoon', the Allied landing in the South of France, begins when troops from General Patch's US Seventh Army move ashore between Toulon and Cannes. French Commandos are also among the first ashore, and II French Corps soon joins the Americans. Naval bombardment supports the beachheads and carrier aircraft outnumber the Luftwaffe 25:1. The action is watched from a distance by Winston Churchill and he sees little German opposition to the attack; General Weise has only seven infantry divisions and 11th Panzer Division to protect the entire south and south-east of France.

16 August When the Allies reach the ruins of Falaise they encounter the fiercest resistance yet. Farther south, Chartres falls and to the east the Allies have crossed the River Dives in the direction of the Seine.

The French troops landed on their southern coast move inland through the US forces holding the beachhead. German forces that had been stationed close to the Spanish border withdraw to the north-east. German High Command reports that Allied landings in the south of France have been repelled but concedes that footholds have been gained at several points.

The Soviets are just a few miles from Warsaw but facing strong German defences.

17 August The Canadians take what is left of Falaise as the Germans pull back. The Americans are at Dreux and Orléans. On the northern coast the final surrender of St-Malo is achieved.

In southern France there is little opposition to the French advance: Fréjus and St-Tropez are among the towns taken.

Inland from the Baltic the Germans make counter moves to prevent their forces being cut off in Riga.

In New Guinea, the Americans make gains around Aitape. On Numfoor the remnant of Japanese resistance is defeated.

18 August The single way out for the German forces south of the Normandy battlefield – the Falaise gap – is closed by the Allies, leaving many trapped to the north and west. The drive on Paris has been very fast and US Third Army is on the outskirts, at Versailles.

Falaise gap closed

In southern France French and US forces encounter sporadic opposition but are already close to Toulon and Marseilles.

The Kriegsmarine begins to scuttle its U-boats in French ports now under threat from the Allies. *U123* and *U129* are sacrificed at Lorient and *U78* and *U188* at Bordeaux.

19 August Allied advances between Falaise and Argentan continue to encounter opposition, but the German troops are fighting in order to survive. Far to the east Allied forces are so close to Paris that Resistance teams are confident enough to begin sniping attacks against the nervous German forces within the city.

20 August Marshal Pétain is taken into custody by the Germans because he has refused to evacuate Vichy.

Pétain arrested by Germans

In France units of Fifth Panzer and Seventh Armies evade capture at Falaise by outflanking their own formations to link up with other retreating forces. South-east of Paris XX Corps takes Fontainebleau, and the capital is further threatened by the securing of a crossing over the Seine at Mantes Grassicourt to the north-west.

On the Eastern Front German Army Group South Ukraine is subjected to heavy attacks around Jassy and Tirasopol. The battle around Riga is joined by naval bombardment from the German heavy cruiser *Prinz Eugen*; the heavy surface vessels of the Kriegsmarine will give intensive support to their ground forces during the coming weeks.

The long Japanese resistance on Biak has come to an end. They have lost 4,700 men and a few diehards will remain undetected on the island for many years.

21 August With Paris encircled by Allied forces, and by-passed by others, many retreating German units forego all attempts at a fighting withdrawal as they scurry north-eastwards towards the Belgian border. This enables the invasion timetable, behind schedule because of German resistance to date, to be brought back on course and most Allied units are ordered to pursue the fleeing Germans.

Senior diplomats from the Allied nations meet at Dumbarton Oaks in Washington to discuss post-war world order. From these early discussions will grow the United Nations.

Dumbarton Oaks conference

22 August On the Eastern Front German Naval Group Command South orders the evacuation of the Black Sea port of Constanta. With Roumania about to declare war on Germany, Dönitz accepts that the sea war there is over and allows German ships in this theatre to be scuttled.

23 August In Paris, such has been the skill and bravery of Resistance teams that the German forces there have virtually retreated from the fight. To the north-west US units have taken Evreux and others are advancing towards the Seine.

On the Eastern Front much of German Sixth Army is cut off south of Husi by the advancing of the 2nd and 3rd Ukraine Fronts. The Roumanians, who have fought bravely for the Germans in this theatre, are now deserting to join the Soviets in large numbers as their national leaders accept armistice terms; within the next two days the new Roumanian prime minister, General Senatescu, will declare war on Germany.

In the Pacific the Americans complete their battle for Numfoor Island off New Guinea and quickly transfer most of their troops there to other battle zones.

24 August As General Leclerc leads French 4th Armoured Division to the perimeter of Paris, the Germans make a final stand.

In southern France the Allies reach Grenoble and Arles.

German forces are now reeling from Roumanian defections and the pace of the Soviet advance. Army Group South Ukraine is decimated and Sixth Army is wiped out as had been its predecessor at Stalingrad.

The British Eastern Fleet is now under command of Admiral Fraser. The carriers HMSS *Victorious* and *Indomitable* are deployed in an attack on Padang in south-west Sumatra.

Paris liberated

25 August Leclerc leads his forces into Paris after the German commander General von Choltitz ignores the order to stay and fight. His surrender saves the city from the damage a futile defensive action would have caused, though an air raid later in the day, ordered by a furious Hitler, does bring some loss of life and damages more than 500 buildings. The Allies have crossed the Seine in several places, but far to the west, on the Atlantic coast, the German garrison at Brest is still resisting so strongly that HMS *Warspite* has to be called up to shell the town.

In southern France, although the Germans are still fighting in Toulon and Marseilles, the Allied advance north is continuing in the wake of a fast retreating German Nineteenth Army, and Avignon is taken.

In Estonia the Germans lose their important base at Tartu.

26 August General de Gaulle returns to Paris to join the triumphant parade through the city as Allied units stream across the Seine in many places.

In Italy Eighth Army has crossed the river Metauro.

27 August In its first large-scale daylight bombing raid on Germany since the first months of the war, RAF Bomber Command hits the oil plant at

Homberg–Meerbeck bombing

Homberg–Meerbeck putting it out of action for two months. The action demonstrates Allied air supremacy and the parlous state of the Luftwaffe.

28 August The Allied drive across France continues apace. The Marne is crossed at Meaux, and Reims and Amiens are within reach. In the South,

Toulon and Marseilles fall and some German units in the Rhone valley are cut off by the pace of the Allied advance.

Of 97 V-1 flying bombs launched at the UK on this day, only seven get through. Most are brought down by AA shells with proximity fuses. The launch sites for these flying bombs are rapidly being captured by the advancing Allied troops in northern France; the Germans will soon resort to using He-111s as flying launch ramps.

29 August In France Reims and Châlons-sur-Marne fall.

In Italy the advancing Allies are nearing the German Gothic Line.

In Warsaw the fighting between the German occupiers and the Polish Home Army units continues to be brutal and unyielding. The Soviet and Polish authorities disclose that they have evidence that 1,500,000 people have been murdered at the Majdanek concentration camp.

30 August In Italy Allied forces begin the attack on the Gothic Line.

The Soviet occupation of Ploesti denies the Roumanian oilfields to the Germans whose supplies have already been severely reduced by Allied bombing.

31 August The Roumanian capital Bucharest falls to 2nd Ukraine Front.

SEPTEMBER 1944

1 September The Allied advance across France is continuing at such pace that tactical differences of opinion split the command structure. As Canadian troops liberate Dieppe, British troops take Arras and US troops close on Cambrai and Verdun, Eisenhower declares his wish for a broad front approach with all units advancing in unison. Montgomery wants to head up a more narrow push through Belgium to the Ruhr, but this would hold back many US units whose pace of advance has been so devastating. The supply line required for either plan, though especially for the sharper, faster advance, cannot be at its most efficient until a large Channel port is in Allied hands; the commanders look to Antwerp as a short-term solution. The French ports are mostly still in Germans hands and are too small to meet the supply demands of a major offensive. Eisenhower's diplomatic touch will calm the opposing views in the Allied camp.

2 September British troops reach the Belgian border as supply problems begin to hamper the Allied advance in the north; in southern France the Allies are approaching Lyons and now have 190,000 troops ashore.

In Italy although German reserves are fed in to the Gothic Line, it is ruptured by the Allies at several points. Polish forces finally get the upper hand in the fighting for Pesaro on the east coast.

3 September The British Guards Division enters Brussels, and Tournai and Abbeville are also occupied. In the south, Lyons is taken.

In the Pacific US naval forces bombard Japanese positions on Wake Island.

4 September In France the Allies capture Lille, Louvain and Etaples, but are unable to complete their occupation of Antwerp which the Germans have realised is vital.

Russian-Finnish
armistice

The Finns and Russians sign an armistice and a ceasefire comes into force immediately. The remaining German units in Finland evacuate as quickly as they can, to Norway or via the Baltic ports.

Rundstedt CinC West
again

5 September Hitler re-appoints von Rundstedt as CinC West, though there are now many fewer troops there than when he was removed from the post a few weeks earlier. The Americans occupy Namur and Charleroi.

In Italy strong German defensive positions bring a temporary halt to the Allied advance.

6 September Calais and Boulogne are cut off by a Canadian push which reaches the English Channel to the north of these ports. The Meuse is crossed in several places and Ghent and Armentières fall to 21st Army Group.

The Soviet push through Roumania reaches the Yugoslav border at Turnu on the Danube, and at the other end of the Front advance units are only 25 miles from the boundary with East Prussia.

The satisfactory progress of the war in Europe enables the authorities in the UK to announce a relaxation in blackout rules, and an end to training for Home Guard units.

Palau attacked

In the Pacific US Task Force 38, which includes sixteen aircraft carriers, attacks Palau in the Carolines.

7 September The Allies close on Antwerp as the Albert Canal is secured east of the city.

First V-2 rocket hits
London

8 September Launched from Wassenaar, a suburb of The Hague still in German hands, the first V-2 rocket to land in England reaches Chiswick in west London. At this point the threat from the V-1 has been chiefly removed by the capture of the launch sites in France, but now the new projectile, fired from mobile launchers, poses a new problem. Its 192-mile flight is completed in five minutes and brings devastation to six houses in Staveley Road, much additional damage, and three people killed and ten injured. This was not the intended target, of course, but those witnessing the event cannot explain the cause of the explosion because the speed of the projectile is such that it arrives before the sound of its passage is heard. Press statements are minimal and the public remains in the dark for two months. The Allies will find it difficult to fly raids against the mobile launch vehicles even though they quickly trace the area in which they are operating. The V-2 programme will have a minimal effect on the war as a whole, the daily bombardment barely equalling the effect of a single Allied bomber over Germany.

In Belgium, Liège, Nieuport and Ostend fall to the Allies, and in southern France Besançon is taken by US VI Corps.

212

9 September In Belgium the Canadians walk into Bruges, and more advances are made in southern France. De Gaulle forms a new cabinet with Georges Bidault as Foreign Minister.

In the Pacific aircraft from twelve of Task Force 38's carriers bomb airfields on Mindanao.

Mindanao bombed

10 September A protracted debate about the wisdom of a major airborne mission against strategic bridges over canals and rivers in Holland is won by Montgomery when Operation 'Market Garden' is given the go-ahead. The action is scheduled for 17 September. For the present, the Allies prepare for a raid on Le Havre with a bombardment by HMS *Warspite*, the Canadians attack Zeebrugge and the Americans enter Luxembourg.

In Italy US II Corps advances towards the Futa and Il Giogo Passes north of Florence.

11 September In Europe British I Corps attacks Le Havre, British Second Army crosses into Holland and US troops reach the German border. A scouting patrol by US 5th Armored Division sees the first entry into German territory near the Luxembourg border.

Allies enter Holland

Allied forces moving up from the Mediterranean reach Dijon and link up with French 2nd Armoured Division in US Third Army.

At a meeting in Quebec the existing policies for prosecuting the conduct of the war are confirmed. It is agreed that British naval forces should join with the US Navy in the final push against the Japanese.

Second Quebec conference

12 September The German garrison at Le Havre surrenders. Further advanced units of US First Army reach the German border close to Aachen and Trier.

13 September The Russians begin air drops to the Polish Home Army which is still embroiled in the harsh battles for Warsaw.

In the Pacific US forces begin a bombardment of Peleliu and Angaur in the Palau group of islands.

14 September In Italy Eighth Army pushes forward towards the river Marano, having cleared the Germans from their stronghold on the Gemmano and Coriano Ridges.

The Soviet forces surrounding Warsaw take the suburb of Praga but choose not to drive into the city. The Soviet air force continues to drop supplies to support the local uprising.

In the Pacific Mindanao is hammered by more than 2,000 US carrier aircraft sorties; more than 200 Japanese aircraft are destroyed.

Mindanao bombed

15 September The French government issues warrants for the arrest of Pétain and his Vichy Cabinet.

US forces take Maastricht and Nancy. The US and French forces which have advanced from the Mediterranean now come under Eisenhower's control.

German frogmen mount a daring raid on the floodgates at Antwerp and make the port unusable to large vessels for six weeks.

German special forces raid Antwerp docks

British bombers again attack *Tirpitz*, this time from Russian bases. Once again smoke-screens save the ship from major hits.

In the Pacific the US forces who have landed on Peleliu encounter Japanese resistance after they have left the beachhead. The defenders have turned the island's network of caves into formidable strongholds. The Americans also land on the Moluccan island of Morotai, nearly 20,000 men getting ashore on this first day.

16 September The Soviets mount fresh attacks against Riga and Tallinn, and in the south Sofia is captured. The advance of Soviet forces this far south has begun to prejudice a German retreat from Greece.

'Market Garden' (Arnhem) operation

17 September Operation 'Market Garden' is launched. The Allied command believe that the retreating German forces are so disorganised and dispirited that a surprise airborne landing could speedily capture intact the many bridges across rivers and canals in Holland. The plan, most avidly urged by Montgomery, is suspect; it ignores the stronger case for securing the Scheldt Estuary and putting the port of Antwerp to work; it also under-estimates German resilience. Three airborne divisions participate: US 82nd, whose mission to take canal bridges north of Eindhoven is accomplished on the first day; US 101st, whose requirement to take bridges at Grave and Nijmegen is only partially achieved; and British 1st Airborne, who are dropped a little way from Arnhem to take the bridge in the town that crosses the lower Rhine. The chosen dropping zone is too far from the objective and this allows the Germans time to respond. An SS Panzer Division is among the units available and, while some British troops reach the bridge, they have insufficient numbers or firepower to take it and a long, bitter struggle for this strategic feature begins. More than 35,000 airborne troops are committed – twice as many as for the Normandy landings; the Allies deploy more than 4,600 aircraft and gliders. One early effect of the landing is the removal of the V-2 rocket launch area in The Hague to a safer area near Haarlem.

Elsewhere, the Canadians launch an attack on Boulogne following a heavy raid by RAF bomber aircraft.

In the Pacific US 8th Infantry Division lands on Angaur in the Palau Islands and meets immediate Japanese resistance.

18 September German reinforcements are hurried to Arnhem. US 101st Division links up with British XXX Corps at Eindhoven, but these and the other airborne units are struggling to hold their positions let alone advance.

US B-17s drop supplies to the Polish Home Army in Warsaw, but only 10 per cent fall in Polish-held areas.

19 September The British battalion which has reached one end of the bridge at Arnhem remains isolated from the main body of paratroops but continues to hold its position. XXX Corps has now linked up with 82nd Airborne at Grave and the united teams move on Nijmegen.

214

In Brittany the German garrison at Brest is finally defeated.

In the Palau Islands there is heavy fighting on Angaur and Peleliu.

20 September Nijmegen is taken by a swift attack by British Guards Armoured Division and 82nd Airborne which also captures the important bridge over the Waal before the Germans can destroy it. At Arnhem the paratroop unit loses its hold on one end of the bridge.

In Italy Eighth Army's V Corps enters San Marino.

21 September British paratroops have retreated from the centre of Arnhem to its western boundaries, still north of the river; a Polish parachute brigade is dropped south of this position, on the opposite bank. Progress from Nijmegen of British XXX Corps' vehicles is slowed by low-lying marshy land.

In Italy Eighth Army takes Rimini. *Rimini liberated*

In the Pacific Task Force 38 attacks Luzon in the Philippines; Manila is the prime target. *Luzon attacked*

22 September Boulogne is taken by the Canadians. The struggle around Arnhem continues as the scattered British units desperately try to link up.

Tallin, the capital of Estonia, falls to the Soviets. *Soviets take Tallin*

23 September An RAF bombing raid destroys an aqueduct on the Dortmund–Ems canal and brings to a halt the shipment of prefabricated U-boat parts by this route.

The Russian advance reaches the Baltic at Parnu and the Hungarian border.

In the Pacific US forces land on Ulithi Atoll, north of the Palaus, to build a naval base there.

24 September British XXX Corps is at the south bank of the Rhine west of Arnhem while paratroops north of the river are still holding out despite shortage of food and ammunition and constant German attacks.

25 September Many of the paratroopers in Arnhem are evacuated across the Rhine in small boats. More than 1,000 have been killed and 6,400 taken prisoner, but 2,400 escape. It proves to be the last German victory of the war. Operation 'Market Garden' has suffered from bad weather but the main reasons for the German success has been the under-estimation of their strength by the Allies and the availability of 2nd SS Panzer Division.

Calais is attacked by Canadian forces operating on the north coast of France.

26 September The Arnhem bridge is still in German hands.

In Italy Eighth Army crosses the Rubicon.

At a meeting the exiled Greek government and various guerrilla groups agree to certain future practices and to delegate military authority to the British General Scobie, whose first task will be to eject the Germans from Greece.

27 September In France US Third Army begins an attack on Metz, south *Allies attack Metz* of Luxembourg.

In Estonia German resistance is at an end, but counter-attacks take place against the Soviets moving into Hungary.

29 September In France the Canadians are still trying to wrest Calais from the stubborn German garrison.

Calais liberated

30 September The Germans surrender Calais; Canadian units press north and west from Antwerp.

Constant Allied air attacks on the synthetic fuel sites supplying the German war effort begin to take effect. Needing a minimum of 150,000 tons per day, production falls to less than 7,000. Fuel of any type is in such short supply that aircraft have to be towed to their hangars by horses and oxen.

The Americans announce that they have occupied the Palau Islands, though pockets of resistance remain.

OCTOBER 1944

1 October In Italy US Fifth Army's II Corps starts a new drive north to Bologna.

In Greece Allied landings get under way with British Commandos on Poros and Greek forces on Mitilini, Lemnos and Levita.

2 October US First Army begins to attack the West Wall (Siegfried Line) north of Aachen.

End of the Warsaw uprising

The brave action of the Home Army in Warsaw comes to an end as the German forces finally smash the locals into submission despite the presence of huge Soviet forces on the outskirts of the city. More than 200,000 Poles have died and the few buildings left standing in the city centre will soon be demolished in accordance with Hitler's directive that the Polish people be punished for their bravado.

3 October British aircraft bomb the Scheldt estuary around Walcheren Island, damaging the dikes and hampering German defensive moves. US First Army breaks through the West Wall.

Me 262 jet deployed

General Galland gets his way; the Me 262 jet is finally deployed as a fighter – Hitler had pressed for a bomber version. Forty of the aircraft are based near Osnabruck.

4 October North of Aachen German counter-attacks delay US forces but do not push them back.

The Me 262 fighters see their first action but are ineffective. They will eventually shoot down 25 Allied bombers, but their cumbersome take-off and landing, and the routing restrictions necessitated by their high fuel consumption, sees 35 of them lost.

In Greece more Allied landings are made on the Peloponese and Aegean islands.

5 October In Riga more pressure is exerted on German Army Group North units holding out.

6 October In the Scheldt Estuary, Canadian units begin to move against German forces there, but the terrain is very marshy and movement is difficult.

The Soviet Information Bureau reports the encirclement of Belgrade by Soviet and Yugoslav units. Elsewhere, Soviet 38th Army secures the strategically important Dukla Pass in the Carpathians.

7 October In France US Third Army gains some ground around Luxembourg and Metz but German resistance is strong. The Canadians make modest advances in the Scheldt estuary.

8 October On the Western Front fighting is at its fiercest as the Germans, after their lengthy retreat, turn and fight at their own border.

Finnish forces capture Kemi, the last of their ports to have been in German hands.

In Greece the British take Corinth and Samos as more Commando landings are made at Nauplion.

Allies take Corinth and Samos

9 October Canadian troops land on the south bank of the Scheldt, across the river from the Germans holding the town of Flushing.

In Moscow a conference begins between the Soviets and a British delegation led by Churchill and Anthony Eden. The topic is the future of Eastern Europe and Stalin cleverly reminds his visitors of his readiness to help defeat the Japanese as a means of wringing concessions from them. While Greece is to remain under British influence and the power somewhat divided in Hungary and Yugoslavia, the Russians insist that Bulgaria and Roumania remain under their umbrella, and refuse to yield to demands for autonomy from the exiled Polish government.

Moscow conference

10 October The Soviet forces reach the Baltic Sea when armoured spearheads encircle the port of Klaipeda in Lithuania.

In the Pacific the war moves inexorably against the Japanese as the carrier fleets of US Task Force 38 are deployed against the Ryukyu Islands. Two groups concentrate on Okinawa, the others on Sakashima and Onami-O-shima. Again many Japanese aircraft are shot down and merchant ships sunk as the American ships complete their missions with minimal opposition from air or sea.

11 October In the Scheldt Estuary Canadian forces cut the causeway between the mainland and Walcheren Island.

The German garrison at Aachen is under great pressure and has been invited to surrender; they decline and severe street fighting will be seen in the city during the next few days.

A Hungarian delegation signs an armistice in Moscow.

Hungarian armistice

In the Pacific Task Force 38 attacks airfields north of Luzon in the Philippines

12 October In Greece the Germans evacuate Piraeus as Allied paratroops land at Athens airfield and the British land on Corfu.

In the Pacific B-29 Superfortresses land in the Marianas to begin a strategic aerial war against Japan.

Task Force 38 begins an attack on Formosa. The Allies fly more than 2,300 sorties, the Japanese a mere handful, most of which are intercepted and shot down. The Australian cruiser *Canberra* is badly hit and the US carrier *Franklin* slightly damaged.

13 October The Germans launch V-1 and V-2 flying bombs against Antwerp in an attempt to stop the port being used by the Allies. The close-quarter fighting in Aachen continues and elements of British VIII Corps attack south from Nijmegen in the direction of Venlo.

In Greece the first troops of what will be a substantial British and Greek force land at Piraeus.

Outside Riga the German defence is broken and the Soviets reach the outskirts of the town.

14 October The death of Field Marshal Rommel from wounds suffered in battle is announced to the German nation. The broadcast does not disclose that the great commander has been forced to commit suicide by poison rather than face a humiliating public trial to answer the charge of being part of the July Bomb Plot. The Desert Fox is given a state funeral.

In Greece, Athens and Piraeus are liberated and more forces land.

In the Pacific the US cruiser *Houston* is put out of action by a torpedo attack during action off Formosa, but the assault there continues and B-29 Superfortresses join the mission from their Chinese bases.

More raids on Luzon strike north of Manila and on Aparri airfield. In these actions US aircraft losses continue to be less than a quarter of those suffered by the Japanese.

15 October In Latvia Riga falls, and in the north of Finland Petsamo is occupied.

Miklos Horthy, prime minister and regent of Hungary, is kidnapped by the German Otto Skorzeny and taken to a concentration camp. The armistice is declared null and void and the puppet Ferenc Szalasy is appointed to replace Horthy.

In Norway an SOE agent notifies London that *Tirpitz* has moved from Altafiord to a shallow anchorage in Tromsofiord.

16 October Aachen is now isolated but the German garrison fights on. Similar staunch defence is met by US VI Corps near Bruyères on the Moselle.

In the Pacific US forces begin to bombard Leyte, and their aircraft from Biak, Sansapor and Morotai, and ships from Task Group 77.4 attack Mindanao.

17 October More US sorties against Leyte and Mindanao, and aircraft from Task Group 38.4 join the bombardment of Luzon. Minesweeping begins in Leyte Gulf to clear the way for the landing-craft.

18 October The German *Volkssturm* (home defence force) announces the likely call-up of all males aged 16 to 60.

In Greece the exiled government returns and British forces occupy more towns and islands.

The Germans are speeding-up their retreat from Greece and southern Yugoslavia as the risk of isolation increases; Soviet forces are now in Czechoslovakia.

Aircraft from the carrier HMS *Implacable* locate *Tirpitz*. She is now 100 miles nearer RAF bases.

19 October On the Franco-German border Bruyères falls to US 36th Division and German resistance at Aachen weakens.

20 October The Allies begin a drive north-east from Antwerp whilst Patton's Third Army has the Germans trapped by flooding caused by the bombing of the dam at Dieuze.

Belgrade is liberated in a joint action by Tito's Partisans and Soviet units. The ancient coastal town of Dubrovnik is also captured.

In the Pacific Admiral Kinkaid's US Seventh Fleet escorts the first landing-parties from General Krueger's Sixth Army to Leyte. The ground forces have fire support from battleships offshore and, although the cruiser *Honolulu* is severely damaged by an aerial torpedo, there is little early resistance from Japanese 16th Division. The first day sees more than 130,000 US troops ashore, including General MacArthur who reminds the Filipino people, in a radio broadcast, that he had promised to return, and has.

The Japanese are sending a carrier force from Japan and other vessels from Brunei.

21 October In Europe Aachen is finally in Allied hands; the centre of the city has been ravaged by the long battle for control.

In the Pacific US forces from the various beachheads on Leyte have failed to link up, but some units have gained ground including the capture of Dulag airfield. Neighbouring islands are attacked by groups from Task Force 38.

In the Palau Islands resistance ends on Angaur, and other islands are by-passed as being unimportant now that their Japanese garrisons are cut off.

22 October On the Eastern Front Soviet Fourteenth Army has reached the Norwegian border, and at the other end of the front the Soviets take Baja on the Danube, south of Budapest.

The US push on Leyte gathers momentum and the Battle of Leyte Gulf is about to start. The Japanese strike forces from Brunei are split between Admiral Kurita's Force A and Admiral Nishimura's Force C, plus two more from the north, under Shima and Ozawa. It is intended that the latters' ships draw the main US forces away from their own invasion forces so leaving the other Japanese ships an easier route in from the west. These

219

massed Japanese fleets face Admiral Halsey's remaining twelve carriers and six battleships, and Kinkaid's eighteen escort carriers and six ageing battleships. The Americans also have three times as many destroyers as the Japanese.

23 October The German news bureau reports vast numbers of volunteers flocking to join the *Volkssturm* territorial army, including boys and men younger and older than the specified age groups.

US submarines sight Kurita's ships west of Palawan and, though they lose a vessel in the resulting engagement, the Americans sink two heavy cruisers and force another to retire damaged.

Admiral Onishi, CinC Japanese Naval Air Fleet, forms the *Kamikaze* corps from 210 Air Wing stationed at Clark Field, south of Manila.

24 October US 1st Cavalry Division units cross from Leyte to Samar.

The US carrier *Princeton* is crippled by Japanese aircraft from Luzon. Kurita's weakened fleet is attacked throughout the day by US carrier aircraft; the battleship *Musashi* is sunk and another cruiser is forced to retire causing Kurita to turn away from his course. Nishimura's ships are located and an ambush is set in Surigao Strait. Ozawa loses most of his aircraft, having sent them off on a fruitless mission from which they have to divert to land bases on Luzon; he is left with just 25 aircraft. At the end of the day Halsey believes Kurita has withdrawn completely, that Admiral Oldendorf's Support Force is positioned across the Surigao Strait and will ensnare Nishimura, and that he can safely send his carriers to do battle with Ozawa.

25 October At about midnight Nishimura's ships, and later those commanded by Admiral Shima, attempt to pass through the Surigao Strait. Oldendorf sends fast attack craft and then destroyers against the Japanese, keeping his larger ships in reserve. The battleship *Fuso*, a cruiser and three destroyers are sunk. The battleship *Yamashiro* runs straight into the fire of the entire US battle line and is sunk with all hands including Admiral Nishimura, in the last action fought between battleships. The Japanese cruiser *Mogami* limps away badly damaged. Kurita's ships are now through the San Bernardino Strait where they encounter Admiral Sprague's Task Force 77.4.3. This has been supporting landings and lacks the anti-ship weapons needed now. Sprague's ships have to turn away and are pursued by the Japanese until US TF 77.4.2 ships arrive. The Japanese cruiser *Chikuma* is sunk but the Americans also take hits and lose an escort carrier and three destroyers. Kurita becomes nervous about the increasing US aircraft attacks, believing they may be coming from Halsey's fleet. He withdraws, thereby forgoing his chance of reaching the Leyte invasion fleet, unaware that the first planned Kamikaze missions have sunk four US escort carriers. Halsey meanwhile has been steaming towards Ozawa's approaching decoy force and his first strike takes out two Japanese carriers before news of events farther south prompts him to return there with one carrier group and his battleships, leaving two carrier groups to engage Ozawa. The remaining two Japanese carriers, *Zuiho* and *Zuikaku*, are sunk together with a cruiser and two destroyers; now Ozawa's only capital ships are two carrier-battleships.

26 October The Americans continue to take their toll of Japanese warships around the Philippines; three more cruisers are sunk. This epic battle was decisive; from now on the US Navy had no serious opposition in the Pacific.

27 October In Europe the Germans mount a strong counter-attack against British forces near Venlo as winter conditions begin to play a part here and in Italy.

In the Pacific two Japanese destroyers are sunk off Luzon, but the US battleship *California* is damaged. During the next few days about 100 Japanese aircraft are destroyed at bases in Luzon.

28 October Allied reinforcements are brought up to Venlo.

In the Pacific the B-29 bombers based in the Marianas raid Japanese submarines' base on Truk Island in the Carolines.

US forces take heavy losses on Leyte but they have virtually cleared the strategic Catmon Hill and have secured Buri airfield.

30 October RAF Bomber Command raids Cologne for two nights running; more than 6,300 tons of bombs are dropped.

Cologne bombed

On Leyte US 7th Infantry Division take Dagami.

31 October RAF Bomber Command make a successful precision attack on the Gestapo HQ in Aarhus, Denmark, destroying many of the records held there.

Aarhus Gestapo HQ air raid

In Greece many of the island garrisons are isolated when the Germans evacuate Salonika.

Germans evacuate Salonika

NOVEMBER 1944

1 November The Battle of Walcheren. Three Commando groups land alongside British 52nd Division. Inclement weather reduces air support but the battleship *Warspite* and other ships provide gunfire. Several landing-ships are lost on their approach to the garrisoned island.

Battle of Walcheren

In the Far East the Japanese land 2,000 reinforcements on Leyte as the US advance continues.

A US aircraft flies a reconnaissance mission over Tokyo, the first flight over the capital since the Doolittle raid of April 1942.

2 November On the island of Walcheren the port of Flushing falls to 52nd Division but the Germans are defending stoutly.

Flushing falls

4 November As British minesweepers clear the approaches to Antwerp, the fighting continues on Walcheren. Access to the front through Antwerp is essential if the Allied push into Germany is to be adequately supplied.

221

In Burma 5th Indian Division's advance gathers pace and Kennedy Peak is taken.

5 November In the Pacific three groups from Task Force 38, now under Admiral McCain, attack Luzon and the surrounding area as the battle for the Philippines continues. The Japanese lose 400 aircraft and a cruiser; the Americans lose 25 aircraft and the carrier *Lexington* is damaged by a *Kamikaze*.

6 November On Walcheren British troops take Middleburg.

In Yugoslavia Tito's forces enter Monastir and now control most of the border with Greece.

Roosevelt re-elected

President Roosevelt is re-elected for a fourth term despite failing health.

7 November In the Pacific the last Japanese pockets on Bloody Ridge on Leyte are destroyed by a US 96th Division raid. The US advance northwards is held by strong resistance.

8 November Goebbels having finally announced the V-2 rocket campaign on the UK, Churchill follows suit. At last the residents of south-east England have an explanation for the mysterious explosions of recent weeks.

On Walcheren the German garrison surrenders.

In Burma the Allied advance takes Fort White.

9 November In France US Third Army units cross the Moselle near Metz and troops from British XII Corps quicken the advance which has crossed the Seille.

In the Pacific 2,000 more Japanese reinforcements reach Leyte, but the troop transports are forced to withdraw before they can off-load all the supplies.

10 November An Associated Press News Agency report states that the new V-2 rockets 'fall like stars' across London.

11 November In the Pacific as fierce fighting continues on Leyte, a Japanese convoy off Ormoc is attacked by TF38 carrier aircraft. Four destroyers and a minesweeper are sunk, as are four transports carrying 10,000 troops.

End of Tirpitz

12 November The German battleship *Tirpitz* is capsized at anchor off Haakoy Island in Tromsofiord by a raid by 29 RAF Lancasters which deliver a dozen Tallboy bombs, three of which hit the vessel. Few of the crew manage to abandon ship as the vessel turns over within thirteen minutes of the explosion; more than 1,000 are lost. The success will be triumphantly announced by the British Air Ministry on the 14th. Dönitz writes: 'With the loss of *Tirpitz*, naval activities with surface units came to an end.' Certainly it ended a most remarkable commitment of Allied resources to bringing about the demise of the great ship whose potential menace had occupied Allied planners for months.

13 November In the Pacific more US carrier attacks against Japanese shipping off Luzon sink a cruiser and four destroyers.

14 November In Europe Free French forces begin an action at the southern end of the Allied front to take Belfort. British XII Corps are still clearing German pockets around Venlo.

15 November On the Eastern Front the Soviets are 30 miles from Budapest.

16 November In Germany Hodges' US First Army advances east of Aachen as the defenders are pushed back. Allied air attacks soften up German lines west of the Roer ahead of attacks by US First and Ninth Armies aimed at reaching this important river.

17 November The Allied push into Germany gathers strength as First and Ninth Armies advance north-east of Aachen, Third and Seventh Armies hurry forward from the Moselle and the French offensive does well in the Belfort area.

The Japanese lose the aircraft carrier *Junyo* to an American submarine in the China Sea. *Junyo sunk*

18 November In France Metz is taken by the Allies. Farther north, the Roer towns of Julich and Duren also fall. *Metz liberated*

19 November The Germans mount a futile counter-attack at Geilen-kirchen which is beaten off and does not prevent the town being occupied. To the south, the French are at the perimeter of Belfort.

More Japanese vessels are sunk off Luzon.

20 November Advance units of the French forces fighting near Belfort by-pass the town and move on to the Rhine.

The Japanese deploy *Kaiten* manned torpedoes for the first time. *Kaiten manned torpedoes*

21 November The Allies have almost cleared the Germans out of southern Holland as they push on towards Venlo, but farther south the defenders are resisting to the west of the Roer.

Albanian resistance fighters take control of Tirana after the Germans evacuate the city. *Tirana liberated*

In the Pacific Japanese resistance in the Ormoc valley in Leyte is proving troublesome and US 7th Division moves in that direction to assist US 32nd Division there.

The US submarine *Sealion* torpedoes and sinks the Japanese battleship *Kongo* and a destroyer north of Formosa. *Kongo sunk*

22 November The whole of the Metz area is now in Allied hands and farther south Mulhouse is taken after a brief German counter-attack.

23 November German Seventh Army begins a series of sharp counters against US Ninth Army which stops the Allied advance east of the Ardennes. Hitler has been planning a major counter-attack in the west, convinced that the British and US forces are operating with different aims and ambitions and have scant belief in each other's ability. The Führer has convinced his own advisers that a drive at the centre of the Allied lines entering Germany, on a route similar to that taken in 1940, can recapture Antwerp, cut off many Allied units to the north, and blunt the Americans' enthusiasm for the fight. Von Rundstedt and Model argue that the scheme is ludicrously ambitious and that its defeat would mean the end of Germany.

The British government is told of the failure of their scientists to disrupt the remote-control system of the V-2 rockets. The launching vehicles are proving so mobile that the only way to stop them would be to destroy transport routes in the launch zones.

24 November Troops from US Third Army cross the Saar to north of Saarbrucken. To the south French 2nd Division has captured Strasbourg.

The last German forces are evacuated from Saaremo Island off Riga by the German Navy. The exodus has been protected by *Lützow*, *Admiral Scheer* and *Prinz Eugen*.

The Japanese achieve their last victory of the war when they occupy the US air base at Nanking in China.

25 November A single V-2 rocket kills 160 people when it lands on a Woolworth's store at Deptford in south London.

In the Philippines *Kamikazes* damage four US carriers off Luzon although these ships sink two cruisers; the land battle on Leyte is proving so equally balanced that US progress is negligible.

Munich bombed with 'Tallboy'

27 November RAF Bomber Command uses the 12,000lb Tallboy bomb for the first time against a German city when it raids Munich. More than 600 buildings are destroyed or rendered useless.

28 November The Germans mount rocket attacks on the port of Antwerp as it receives its first supply convoy since the floodgates were damaged by German frogmen.

In the Pacific fighting on Leyte continues to be fierce and the Japanese are on the verge of recapturing Burauen airfield.

29 November More *Kamikazes* damage US ships off Leyte.

The US submarine *Archerfish* sinks the Japanese carrier *Shinano* off Honshu.

Tokyo bombed

Thirty-five B-29 bombers raid Tokyo by night.

DECEMBER 1944

2 December In Europe progress remains slow, but US Third Army seizes bridges across the Saar and US Ninth Army takes Linnich north-east of Aachen.

3 December US Ninth Army's XIII Corps reaches the Roer.

In Italy British Eighth Army begins a new drive up the Adriatic coast.

Civil strife breaks out in Greece which will take the British some weeks to quell.

In the UK the Home Guard is stood down.

4 December Air raids against V-2 launch sites destroy only two rockets, but prompt the Germans to limit launches to the night hours.

6 December This day, the anniversary of Pearl Harbor, sees the last significant Japanese airborne operation when 400 sabotage troops are landed on Leyte. They are joined by other troops who emerge from the mountainous interior where earlier US attacks had driven them, and fighting is severe before the more numerous US forces wipe them out.

7 December The new Roumanian government sets out to purge the country of pro-Nazi factions and assist the Allies. This former Axis power is now committed to the Allied cause.

In the Pacific US 77th Division lands on Leyte, south of Ormoc.

8 December The Soviets continue to secure towns close to Budapest as they occupy more and more of Hungary.

In the Pacific the Americans renew naval bombardment of Iwo Jima.

9 December In Europe the winter weather is reducing operations, but German preparations for their imminent counter-attack continue.

The Soviet 2nd Ukraine Front reaches the Danube north of Budapest.

Some Japanese reinforcements reach Leyte as US forces gain more ground south of Ormoc.

10 December In Europe US First Army's VII Corps advances towards Duren.

In Leyte US 77th Division takes the main Japanese base at Ormoc.

12 December In Burma three British divisions advance towards Akyab in the Arakan.

13 December In the Pacific US naval command receives a setback when the flagship of a force on its way to the landings on Mindanao, the heavy cruiser *Nashville*, is badly damaged by a *Kamikaze* attack; several officers are among the casualties. *Nashville damaged*

14 December Carrier aircraft from Task Force 38 sortie against Luzon airfields in preparation for the landings on Mindanao. The landing force is escorted by thirteen carriers, eight battleships plus cruisers and destroyers. The troops will go ashore at San Augustin on the 15th with little resistance and ground will be quickly gained.

16 December In the Ardennes the Germans receive the order from von Rundstedt: 'The time has now come when the German Army must rise again and strike,' and the offensive is launched by 24 divisions on a front between Trier and Monschau. Tactical and strategic surprise is achieved and US V and VIII Corps are quickly forced to give ground. The assembling of German forces for the assault has been concealed from the Allies by an almost complete radio blackout; communications have been made by land line or messenger. *Battle of the Bulge*

The strike is intended to split the British and US units and recapture Antwerp. The forces used come from Model's Army Group B with von Rundstedt in overall command. The early pushes are completed in bad weather which removes the threat of Allied air supremacy and includes diverse sabotage missions by German units, some of whom wear American uniforms and speak English. The six US divisions facing the offensive include many untried troops and a large number of battle-weary men who have been fighting for many months. The first day of the Battle of the Bulge goes to the Germans.

17 December Although physically exhausted by their efforts around Arnhem, US 82nd and 101st Airborne Divisions are sent to the Ardennes. Elsewhere, Patton sends some of his units and stalls his advance in the south.

In Italy 10th Indian Division crosses the river Senio near Faenza.

In the USA Colonel Paul Tibbetts is leading a series of training flights with B-29 Superfortresses in the Utah desert, to determine whether atomic bombs can be safely dropped from these aircraft.

18 December In the Pacific Task Force 38, regrouping after recent attacks on Luzon, is struck by a fierce typhoon which inflicts worse damage than the Japanese. Three destroyers sink in the heavy seas and carriers and other destroyers are severely damaged.

19 December In the Ardennes the Germans have gained ten miles in places and the important road junction at Bastogne is under threat. In a change of command structure by Eisenhower Montgomery is given command of the forces to the north of the bulge created by the German push and Bradley command of the forces to the south. This means more US forces come under British control – a logical move – but it is not made known to the public at large.

20 December On the northern edge of the sector the German troops are halted near Stavelot and they have to withdraw. More centrally, the strategic towns of St-Vith and Bastogne are under increasing pressure from the Germans who realise they must progress in the centre of the 'Bulge' before the Allies can get their air forces effective.

21 December The 82nd Airborne Division is pushed out of Houffalize, and Bastogne is almost isolated by the pace of the German advance on each side of it. The front from Monschau to Trier is in five segments with the Allied strongholds around St-Vith and at Bastogne, and German strikes between these towns and to the north of St-Vith and south of Bastogne. US troops have held the German thrust in the north and retaken Stavelot.

22 December St-Vith falls to the Germans but not before the commanders, von Rundstedt, Model and Guderian have decided that the offensive is serving little purpose and will be unable to achieve its objective of Antwerp because of the worsening weather as well as the likely strengthening of Allied resolve. This determination is shown by General McAuliffe's rejection of the German demand that he surrender his forces at Bastogne; his reported response to the suggestion is 'Nuts!'

In the Philippines US forces advance towards Palompon on Leyte where the main Japanese forces are now positioned.

23 December Despite the German generals' reluctance to continue their counter-attacks, their troops are 25 miles west of Bastogne, where the Americans still refuse to yield. Allied air strikes against these forward units and their supply lines are beginning to have an effect with the advent of clearer weather; ammunition is dropped to the troops holding Bastogne.

24 December The Swedish newspaper *Svenska Dagbladet* quotes Portuguese travellers from London telling of the huge damage caused by the V-2 rockets. It reports (quite falsely) three Thames bridges destroyed and no building left standing within a 500-yard radius of Leicester Square.

In the Ardennes the spearhead of the German wedge is almost at Dinant, some sixty miles forward from their starting-point, but the drive has run out of steam. The campaign has secured an area of approximately 400 square miles but has been only a temporary embarrassment to the Allied drive for Berlin; the attempted separation of British and US forces has failed, and far from being able to recapture Antwerp, the Germans have been unable to get beyond the rugged terrain of the Ardennes. Hitler refuses a withdrawal; he is planning an offensive from Alsace in the New Year and is determined that both forward pushes succeed.

The Soviets are closing on Budapest which is almost cut off by units that have by-passed it. The German supply corridor to the west is barely 20 miles wide.

In the UK a group of Heinkel He-111s mount a V-1 raid on Manchester. One of the flying bombs hits the centre of the city, the others fall outside.

25 December US 4th Armored Division drives north from Martelange in an attempt to relieve the beleaguered troops at Bastogne.

In the Pacific the Americans at Leyte move some of their forces by sea from Ormoc to San Juan, north of Palompon, in a move to encircle the Japanese. The landing at San Juan is unopposed.

26 December Bastogne is reached by US relieving units, and the forward German troops are now vulnerable to Allied counter-attack.

Relief of Bastogne

A Japanese fleet from Indo-China arrives to bombard the US beachhead on Mindoro. This is the last offensive sortie by the Japanese Navy in this theatre.

29 December In the Ardennes the Allies are building up their forces close to the German front line. It will take another month to retake this territory.

There is fighting in Budapest as Soviet action beyond the city effectively cuts it off from resupply. Negotiations with the German garrison come to nothing when some of the Russians sent to discuss terms are killed in error.

30 December In the USA General Groves, head of the Manhattan Project, reports that the first two atomic bombs should be ready by 1 August 1945.

31 December In the Ardennes the Allies recapture Rochefort at the western point of the German salient, to begin the retaking of the area.

Hungary declares war
on Germany

Hungary declares war on Germany.

In the Pacific there is heavy fighting on Leyte. Severe losses are suffered by both sides and the bloody campaign will eventually cost the Japanese more than 60,000 dead and the Americans more than 15,000 dead or wounded.

1945

JANUARY 1945

I January Operation 'Bodenplatte'. In Europe Allied air forces operating from airfields in Holland, Belgium and northern France are surprised by a sudden attack by more than 800 diverse aircraft which the Luftwaffe has assembled from all possible locations, despite their loss of so many in recent weeks. The motley collection is flown by novices who are led to their targets by the few remaining skilled pilots. The Allies lose 300 aircraft but can replace these quickly; the Luftwaffe count is just over 200. These, and their pilots, are irreplaceable and the action has rendered the Luftwaffe almost powerless in the west.

2 January In the Ardennes the Allied counter-attacks gather pace, but Hitler rejects pleas from Model to withdraw around Houffalize.

In an attempt to relieve the siege of Budapest, German troops are brought from the crucial Warsaw area without the knowledge of Army Chief of Staff, Heinz Guderian.

In the Pacific the US landing force bound for the Philippines leaves Leyte: six battleships, sixteen escort carriers, ten cruisers and dozens of destroyers, landing-ships and support vessels, some from the Australian Navy. Japanese aircraft drop bombs on Saipan in the last such raid on the Marianas.

3 January In the Ardennes German troops continue to harass the Americans in Alsace and make sniping attacks against the Allied forces near Bastogne, the Allied advance is progressing.

In Burma the Japanese do little to prevent an Allied landing on Akyab Island in the Arakan. Inland British troops are advancing towards the Irrawaddy.

In the Pacific the Japanese launch frantic attacks against the US fleet heading for the Philippines, but only superficial damage by *Kamikazes* is caused.

4 January In the Ardennes units of Sixth SS Panzer Army are withdrawn to be sent to the Eastern Front.

In Burma Akyab falls to the Allies and British carriers raid oil refineries on Sumatra.

5 January In Greece General Alexander arrives in Athens; fighting between Greek Communists and British forces ends there.

The US fleet en route to the Philippines continues to suffer minor Japanese raids. Ships are damaged but the mission is not delayed.

6 January In the Ardennes Hitler refuses a request from von Rundstedt to withdraw.

Churchill and Stalin liaise about increased Soviet action in the east which might accelerate progress in the west.

The 4th SS Panzer Corps attempts a relief drive to Budapest from Komorn but fails.

The US fleet begins preliminary bombardment of targets in the Lingayen Gulf on the east coast of Luzon. It comes under heavy attack; a minesweeper is sunk and twelve other vessels are damaged. Carriers from Task Force 38 join the fray and send their aircraft against Japanese airfields operating the *Kamikazes*.

In Italy the Allied advance is slowed by bad weather and a shortage of supplies and reinforcements.

9 January American news agencies report US naval seniors as claiming that Germany has plans to launch rockets against the mainland from U-boats it is grouping in the Atlantic.

In the Pacific the landings on Luzon begin and make progress because the Japanese commander, General Yamashita, has decided not to fight his battle here. He has more than a quarter of a million men at various locations. Continued Japanese attacks from the air and at sea are an irritant but cause no substantial damage. The US beachheads are in Lingayen Gulf where the Japanese had landed three years before.

Units from TF38 link up with B-29 bombers to attack targets on Okinawa and Formosa.

10 January In Burma the Allies continue to advance along two lines: XXXIII Corps pushing towards the Irrawaddy and IV Corps, west of the Chindwin, taking Gangaw and moving on.

In the Pacific US forces have established strong beachheads on Luzon.

11 January In the Ardennes the German wedge is being reduced daily and their initiatives further south are also running out of steam.

More US forces land on Luzon as the first action is seen ashore.

12 January On the Eastern Front a new Soviet offensive begins with a push by nine armies north of Warsaw, by Zhukov nearer and to the south of the city, and by Konev's 1st Ukrainian Front north of the Vistula. These, and other pushes, find the Germans short of equipment and unable to hold the advance despite fierce fighting.

In Burma the British sweep southwards is just north of Mandalay but now faces tough Japanese defences.

13 January On the Eastern Front German resistance is swept aside.

14 January The last V-1 launched from Heinkel He-111s lands in Yorkshire. Barely one in ten of the weapons delivered like this have got close to a chosen target; most have been brought down by AA fire or have crashed prematurely.

In Greece a ceasefire is agreed to by British military authorities and the Greek Communists.

On the Eastern Front the Soviets cut several German rail and road supply routes. Further attempts to relieve Budapest are stopped by Soviet forces there.

15 January In the Pacific US forces move out from the beachheads, north, east and south; I Corps closes on Rosario but cannot take it.

Lingayen Gulf landings

Major Soviet offensive

Greece ceasefire

231

16 January In the Ardennes a German salient west of the Maas is put under extra pressure by British XIII Corps, and First and Third Armies are able to combine.

On the Eastern Front Warsaw is encircled by Soviet forces who begin to fight their way through the city from which most German troops have already escaped.

In Burma Chinese units which have moved along the Ledo Road from Myitkyina capture Namhkam.

Warsaw falls to Soviets

17 January Polish units fighting with the Red Army finally clear Warsaw of German resistance. The last four days have seen the Soviet White Russian Front break through the German defensive lines along a front of 160 miles with penetrative drives of up to 80 miles. The German defence along the Vistula has been destroyed.

18 January The German evacuate Krakow to avoid being encircled.

Soviets take Krakow

19 January Tarnow, Lodz and Krakow now fall to the Soviet advances beyond Warsaw.

In the Pacific US forces on Luzon begin to fight their way out of their bridgehead to the south, with Manila as their objective.

B-29 aircraft from their Marianas base damage Japanese engine and aircraft production in raids on Japan.

20 January In the Ardennes Brandenburg is taken in the Allied advance, as the French look to gain ground in the Vosges.

On the Eastern Front Tilsit falls to the Soviet pushes; German resistance remains determined but under strength. The Soviets are in control of much of Budapest.

21 January In Burma there is little resistance to British landings on Ramree Island which sees 4th British and 71st Indian Brigades brought to the theatre.

Formosa and Okinawa bombed

Aircraft from Task Force 38 begin two days of raids on Formosa and Okinawa. More than 100 Japanese aircraft are shot down, but three of the US carriers are hit.

22 January The Dutch factory which manufactures the liquid oxygen to fuel V-2 rockets is destroyed by Spitfires after its location has been traced by SOE agents.

23 January In the Ardennes the Germans' withdrawal accelerates, but they are constantly harried by Allied air attacks and their ability to turn and fight again is much reduced.

Allies cross Irrawaddy

In Burma as Allied units begin to cross the Irrawaddy they face enhanced Japanese counters. General Slim is forcing the Japanese to concentrate their attention on the perceived threat to Mandalay while he intends to send his main advance farther south.

Army Group Vistula established

24 January The mauled morale of the German Army commanders is further dented by Hitler's appointment of SS leader Heinrich Himmler to head a new Army Group Vistula to oppose the Soviet advance from the east. The man has no battlefield expertise and will soon be found wanting.

Allied troops clearing mines laid by the retreating Germans report that many of the mines are no longer encased in steel but often in glass, wood or cardboard.

Japanese resistance on Mindoro is all but eliminated as Calapan falls to US forces.

25 January In East Prussia the evacuation of isolated troops is rushed into action, using every available merchant and naval ship, including the cruisers *Emden* and *Hipper*. Many of the vessels are lost to Soviet submarines and British mines.

In the Pacific Iwo Jima is bombarded from the sea and air in preparation for forthcoming US landings.

Iwo Jima bombarded

27 January In the Ardennes German forces have now been forced to retreat from all territory taken by them, and the troops are now ill-prepared for defensive action.

On the Eastern Front although the German garrison still holds the Polish city of Poznan, Soviet forces have by-passed it and are continuing their advance to the Vistula. The Lithuanian port of Memel is finally occupied by the Soviets. The third and most determined attempt by German forces to relieve Budapest is held by the Soviets.

Ardennes 'bulge' eliminated

In Burma the Ledo Road to China is finally cleared and the advance to Lashio and Mandalay can be speeded up.

Ledo Road cleared

28 January Soviet forces are on German territory and Zhukov's troops are barely 100 miles from Berlin. Katowice has fallen to Konev's troops.

29 January In the Pacific US XI Corps lands at San Antonio in Luzon to attempt to clear Japanese defenders from the neck of the Bataan Peninsula.

30 January Churchill, Roosevelt and their advisers meet in Malta in preparation for the Yalta Conference with Stalin.

Malta meeting

31 January US First Army units cross into Germany east of St-Vith at the conclusion of their counter-attack in the Ardennes.

Zhukov's forces are at the river Oder, fifty miles from Berlin.

Soviets reach Oder

More US forces land unopposed on Luzon.

FEBRUARY 1945

1 February Soviet forces have paused at the Oder while pockets of German resistance are mopped up behind them. Soviet advances will be restricted to the flanks for the time being.

On Luzon the Americans now face tough resistance and are struggling to complete the breakthrough at the neck of the Bataan Peninsula

2 February In Europe British forces attack across the Maas north of Breda.

3 February Berlin suffers its worst air raid of the war when more than 1,500 US bombers and fighters hit the city with more than 2,000 tons of bombs.

Berlin bombed

In the Pacific US 11th Airborne Division is dropped on Luzon.

4 February The Yalta Conference begins. Roosevelt's ill health and subsequent reluctance to conduct overlong debate, US and British determination to get the Soviets strongly committed to defeating Japan, and Stalin's constant reminders of his country's part in defeating Hitler, will secure concessions over the Polish borders and the Soviet role in post-war European and world politics.

In the Pacific advance US forces reach the outskirts of Manila from the north; 11th Airborne approaches from the south. There are 20,000 Japanese defending the city.

5 February In Europe German forces are bisected near Colmar by a French/American move.

8 February South-east of Nijmegen, a British/Canadian thrust gains ground despite strong German resistance.

In the Pacific there is heavy fighting in and around Manila. The 11th Airborne Division strikes into the south-eastern suburbs; 1st Cavalry are in the east and 37th Division also engages.

9 February The Allied push near Nijmegen reaches the Rhine and captures Millingen.

While both vessels are submerged, the submarine HMS *Venturer* sinks *U864* to register the first successful underwater attack.

In Burma Ramree Island is captured by 26th Indian Division.

10 February The Soviet submarine *S13* sinks the passenger liner *General von Steuben* which has sailed from Pilau the previous day with more than 6,000 passengers. Only 300 are saved, and Soviet claims that among those lost were élite officers, SS men and Nazi Party officials cannot alter the fact that many refugees go down with the ship.

11 February In Europe Allied advances in the west take Cleve as the drive from Nijmegen continues, and Prum, east of St-Vith, also falls.

Konev's forces advance from their Oder bridgehead near Steinau and strike north and west.

12 February In Burma the Allies have crossed the Irrawaddy in several places, but heavy Japanese resistance is being encountered on the push for Lashio.

In the Pacific Japanese forces on the Bataan Peninsula have been cut off by US moves. US XI Corps advances into the peninsula.

13 February The Budapest garrison surrenders after an eight-weeks' battle; more than 100,000 prisoners have been taken.

US bombers hit Corregidor and landing sites around Manila Bay.

More than 750 RAF bombers attack the city of Dresden, and will follow this with USAAF and RAF daylight raids during the next two days. The resulting firestorm will claim upwards of 70,000 lives, many of whom are civilian refugees from the east.

14 February The British/Canadian push to the Rhine has reached the river at Emmerich.

In Burma so many Japanese troops are being diverted to defend Mandalay, that Allied drives can gather pace. The 7th Indian Division crosses the Irrawaddy near Myangu.

16 February In the Pacific US forces make seaborne and airborne landings on Corregidor Island. The heavy pre-landing bombardment has not neutralised the Japanese resistance from solid defensive positions. *Corregidor landings*

Carrier aircraft from Task Force 58 attack targets in and around Tokyo and will extend this to Yokohama before the carriers and supporting ships sail for Iwo Jima. More than 2,700 sorties are flown for only 88 losses. *Tokyo bombed*

17 February In Europe US Third Army units begin to advance from southern Luxembourg. Farther south Seventh Army advances towards Saarbrucken.

RAF bombers raid Trieste harbour and sink the Italian battleship *Conte di Cavour* and the incomplete *Impero* to prevent their use by the Germans. *Conte di Cavour and Impero sunk*

In the Pacific the preliminary bombardment of Iwo Jima reaches its height after bad weather reduces its early effectiveness.

18 February US Third Army units break through the West Wall (Siegfried Line). *West Wall breached*

19 February In the Pacific Iwo Jima is strategically and politically significant to both sides. The Americans need it as a fighter base for their Japanese raids and as a relief base for damaged bombers flying from farther afield. US Marine divisions land on the south-east of the island, some 30,000 getting ashore on this first day. The Japanese garrison of just over 20,000 has prepared elaborate defences but allows the landing to take place before opening fire. Despite heavy casualties, the Marines extend their beachhead and cross the island. *Iwo Jima landings*

US forces begin landings in the north of Samar Island in the Philippines. *Samar landings*

21 February In Burma Allied forces strike forward towards Meiktila from Myangu.

In the Pacific *Kamikazes* attack US ships supporting the Iwo Jima landing; the carrier *Bismarck Sea* is sunk and several others damaged. On the island, advances towards the heavily defended airfields and its high point, Mount Suribachi, are slow and small despite offshore bombardment support. *Bismarck Sea sunk*

22 February In Germany US Third Army's advance into the Eifel area bordered by the rivers Moselle and Rhine is proving dramatically successful, threatening to isolate many troops of German Seventh Army.

In a show of strength Operation 'Clarion' sees Allied air forces deploy more than 9,000 aircraft on relay raids against every German city.

In Burma 6,000 men from British 3rd Commando Brigade among others land near Kangaw. *Kangaw landings*

23 February A new advance from the Roer by the US First and Ninth Armies is opposed by units of German Army Group B.

On the Eastern Front Poznan falls after four weeks of fighting, but the other long-standing battle for Breslau continues, and will do so until the end of the war.

In the Pacific US forces on Iwo Jima have secured much of Mount Suribachi and their national flag flies at the summit, but elsewhere fierce fighting continues.

Manila is close to falling into US hands after heavy bombardment.

25 February In Germany Julich and Duren are taken as US First and Ninth Armies advance beyond the Roer. Farther south, the river Saar has been crossed at Saarburg.

Fierce fighting continues on Iwo Jima and heavy losses are suffered by both sides.

Tokyo bombed

It is estimated that more than 27,500 buildings are destroyed in Tokyo by the latest US air raid. These raids are being made by night and at lower altitudes, and are becoming more effective.

26 February In Burma the Allies capture valuable airfields on their advance south.

Corregidor secured

The fighting ends on Corregidor. More than 5,000 Japanese are dead including some trapped in the many collapsed tunnels all over the island.

27 February In Germany Allied forces are advancing on many fronts; Trier, Mönchengladbach and Cologne are under threat.

More US carriers are called to Iwo Jima where fighting is focused on the heavily defended second airfield.

28 February In Burma Meiktila is attacked by Allied forces that are more numerous than the Japanese defenders have been led to believe. This important Japanese communications centre has been left in the hands of local troops while more expert troops have been moved to Mandalay.

In the Pacific 8,000 men of US 41st Infantry Division land at Puerto Princesa on Palawan Island against minimal resistance.

MARCH 1945

1 March In Germany Mönchengladbach and Neuss fall to the Allies; US First and Third Armies are making good ground.

In one of their last offensive actions German armoured troops mount an attack in lower Silesia and temporarily retake the city of Lauban.

In the Pacific Manila is all but occupied by the American forces, the Japanese defenders holding just a few government buildings.

On Iwo Jima both airfields are now in US hands, but the strong Japanese defence launches spirited counter-attacks.

Okinawa bombarded

Okinawa, and shipping near its coasts, is bombarded by Task Force 58 aircraft.

2 March In Germany US Third Army occupies Trier; Ninth Army secures Roermond and Venlo and its right flank reaches the Rhine at Düsseldorf.

236

The first sign of Stalin's readiness to abuse the agreements reached at Yalta is seen when Soviet pressure is brought to bear on King Michael of Roumania to dismiss his government. It will be replaced with one dominated by the Communists.

3 March In Burma units of British IV Corps occupy Meiktila, cutting the supply route to Japanese forces farther north.

Allies take Meiktila

In the Pacific US forces on Iwo Jima take the third airfield and occupy more of the island after vicious close-quarter fighting.

The shattered city of Manila falls to the Americans as the last of the 20,000 Japanese defenders are wiped out.

Manila secured

5 March In Germany US VII Corps enters the city of Cologne. Boys as young as 15 are called up for the German Army.

In Burma Japanese counter-attacks threaten the Allied forces in Meiktila, but air supply enables 17th Indian Division to hold its position.

6 March US Third Army advances towards the Rhine at Koblenz; all the other Allied fronts are also advancing. US 9th Armored Division is leading the push through Cologne and on to Remagen and, further north, the last units of German rearguards west of the Rhine are being mopped up.

In Hungary the arrival of Sixth SS Panzer Army, withdrawn from the Ardennes, enables a counter-offensive with other units to be launched against Soviet 27th Army, with the aim of retaking ground between the Danube and Lake Balaton. Reinforced by 3rd Ukraine Front, 27th Army puts a stop to the initiative.

In Burma Chinese First Army finally reaches and captures Lashio on their push southwards.

Chinese take Lashio

7 March In Germany a swift advance by US III Corps units reaches the damaged Ludendorff Bridge at Remagen and forces are across before it can be completely destroyed by the retreating Germans. This considerable setback to German hopes of holding this point causes Hitler to sack von Rundstedt as CinC West. Eisenhower's reaction to the bridge's capture: 'That bridge is worth its weight in gold.'

Rhine crossing at Remagen

In Yugoslavia Tito and his supporters emerge as the dominant partners in a government shared with the Royalists.

In the Pacific with the fall of Manila US advances continue to the south of Luzon while elsewhere minor pockets of resistance are dealt with.

8 March In Germany, having failed to hold the Remagen bridge, the Germans bring in aircraft to disrupt Allied attempts to move more units across the Rhine at this point. The air strikes do not destroy the bridge but a congestion of Allied troops is inevitable.

In Burma an advance by 2nd British and 20th Indian Divisions from the Irrawaddy heralds an Allied break forward west of Mandalay.

Japanese defenders on Iwo Jima have now been pushed back to a small pocket on the northern coast.

9 March In Germany Bonn and Erpel are taken.

In Burma 19th Indian Division is at the outskirts of Mandalay and other Allied forces are approaching from the west. The Japanese have brought troops from the Mandalay area in an attempt to retake Meiktila.

In a massive air raid on Tokyo by US B-29 Superfortresses 10,000 lose their lives in the firestorm created among the wood and paper-built houses. It signals the start of a bombing campaign against other Japanese cities.

10 March As Kesselring arrives from Italy to replace von Rundstedt as CinC West, the last German forces west of the Rhine withdraw, leaving the Allies holding the west bank north of Koblenz.

In Hungary the German counter-offensive grinds to a halt for lack of equipment and supply problems. Rain has reduced the terrain to a morass, preventing vehicular movement.

On Iwo Jima the Japanese launch a series of dramatic suicide attacks which are wholly futile.

More US forces land on Mindanao as fighting continues on Luzon and ends on Palawan.

11 March On the Eastern Front Hitler makes his last visit to the front at Castle Freienwalde on the Oder. He urges his commanders to delay the Soviet push on Berlin until he can release a new weapon: 'Each day and each hour is precious,' he claims, though he does not disclose what the new weapon is.

More than 1,000 RAF bombers make a daylight raid on Essen, effectively destroying the city and rail junction with 4,700 tons of bombs. A similar attack on Dortmund will follow.

12 March German Seventh Army units attempt a counter-attack around the Remagen bridge.

14 March The Allied advance across the Rhine slowly expands despite fierce German counter-attacks; XII and XX Corps press on from the Moselle near Koblenz and from Trier and Saarburg. The rail viaduct at Bielefeld is destroyed by a 22,000lb Grand Slam bomb dropped from a specially converted Lancaster bomber.

In Burma the last rail link to Mandalay is cut when Maymo follows Mongmit into Allied hands. Much of Mandalay has been captured in vicious close-quarter battles.

15 March The 17th Indian Division, supplied from the air and supported by air strikes, are holding Meiktila.

Despite every effort by US forces to end the battle, the last Japanese survivors are still fighting on Iwo Jima.

16 March The salient created by the German counter-attack in Hungary is now put under pressure by Soviet forces. Third Hungarian Army suffers heavy losses.

In the Pacific fighting continues south-east of Manila and on the many offshore islands where Japanese garrisons are being engaged by US forces.

17 March US Third Army takes Koblenz and the temporary bridges built by Allied engineers around Remagen come into use when the Ludendorff Bridge finally succumbs to bombing and heavy traffic. Allies take Koblenz

18 March In an awesome raid on Berlin more than 4,000 tons of bombs hit the city centre and cause much structural damage. Berlin bombed

Soviet forces are close to the cities of Gdynia and Danzig.

In Burma heavy fighting continues in Mandalay and around Meiktila.

In the Pacific Task Force 58 begins a campaign against the Japanese Home Islands, particularly the airfields. The defence is restricted to a few *Kamikaze* attacks which are accurate but do not cause excessive damage.

19 March Hitler orders all manufacturing units and food preparation and storage points to be destroyed on all fronts. This is strongly resisted by Albert Speer and the Army chiefs who conspire to delay the implementation of the policy.

In Germany the Allied advance is nearing Mainz and Kaiserslautern

In East Prussia a final Soviet push will see the defenders eliminated or withdrawn within the next few days.

20 March The Allies secure Saarbrucken and Kaiserslautern. The Remagen bridgehead is nearly 600 square miles in extent, but the fighting here is as fierce as anything the Allies have experienced.

General Heinrici replaces Himmler as Commander of Army Group Vistula, but finds the troops depleted by the battles in Pomerania and ill-prepared to build defences along the Oder ahead of the Soviet push for Berlin.

In Burma Mandalay falls to 19th Indian Division. The tough Japanese defence could have been stronger had not Allied tactics confused the Japanese leaders. Allies take Mandalay

21 March The Japanese 5th Air Force deploys the first *Ohka* piloted bombs slung under Mitsubishi bombers. The flight of eighteen is intercepted by US carrier aircraft and all but one are shot down.

22 March Variable tactics used in the Allied advance into Germany are seen as Patton's Third Army hurries ahead of other sectors, especially those under the command of Montgomery farther north. This will not prove strategically damaging because the German defence has little or no ability to disrupt either pattern of progress, but it does raise some tricky issues of personality for Eisenhower to deal with. Montgomery's caution is, in part, brought about by the terrain in which his armies are operating, but he is a meticulous planner whereas Patton is more of a 'get the job done' practitioner.

On the Eastern Front Soviet forces are breaking across the Oder in Silesia.

23 March British Second and Canadian First Armies cross the Rhine south of Wesel. US 8th Air Force HQ announces that more than 8,000 British and US aircraft have been active in daylight raids on Germany the previous day.

In Burma Wundwin is taken by the Allies.

In the Pacific San Fernando on Luzon is taken by a combined force of US troops and Filipino guerrillas.

Action begins in preparation for the landing on Okinawa with attacks from TF58's carriers. Also involved is the British Pacific Fleet, coded as TF57. The Japanese defence on the first days consists of weak submarine and *Kamikaze* attacks, and some explosive boats are deployed.

24 March In Germany British troops occupy Wesel and extend their advance as German resistance weakens further; they are deploying token armoured groups against large Allied formations.

In Hungary German and Hungarian forces are retreating in disarray as more towns are taken by Soviet forces. In Poland the cities of Gdynia and Danzig are separated by the capture of Spolot between them.

25 March In Germany Allied advances continue at three principal points. In the north they press east from Wesel down the river Lippe and into the Ruhr; from Remagen and Koblenz they strike towards Limburg and Giessen and, taking Darmstadt, move south of Frankfurt to push on to the river Main at Hanau. Moves south by units of V Corps and north by XX Corps will isolate many German troops west of Wiesbaden.

In the Pacific TF52 enters the fray off Okinawa to allow other units to refuel. The battleship *Nevada* is hit by a *Kamikaze*.

26 March A further 14,000 US troops land in the Philippines, south of Cebu City.

Iwo Jima secured

The last suicide attack by the remaining Japanese on Iwo Jima is annihilated by US forces. Barely two hundred of the 20,000 Japanese garrison have survived to be taken prisoner; the Americans have lost nearly 6,000 dead and more than 17,000 wounded. From now on more than 2,000 aircraft will make emergency landings at the base after missions over Japan.

In the Okinawa campaign US 77th Infantry Division lands on Kerama Retto Island and quickly overcomes the small Japanese resistance there. This occupation is to protect the channel through which the major landing-ships will pass.

27 March The last V-2 rocket to land in the UK hits Orpington in Kent. The V-2s have killed 2,754 civilians and 6,523 have been seriously injured. The last V-1 launched at the UK lands in Kent on the 29th; V-1s have killed 6,184 civilians and seriously injured 17,981. But Hitler's 'terror weapon' has not succeeded in breaking the British spirit. A fact usually ignored in histories of the war is that German long-range coastal batteries opposite Dover killed 148 and seriously injured 255 people.

In Germany US Third Army reaches Wiesbaden.

On the Eastern Front Sixth SS Panzer Army suffers heavy losses in its defensive action along the river Raba as 2nd and 3rd Ukraine Fronts continue their attacks.

240

In the Pacific Cebu City falls to the US forces and resistance in the Philippines weakens as garrisons on the smaller islands withdraw to mainland defensive positions. The American forces will only be required to clear Luzon, Mindanao and Negros; elsewhere the groups of Filipino guerrillas will suffice to wear down the remaining Japanese forces.

The main bombardment of Okinawa has begun and the Japanese unsuccessfully deploy explosive boats against the US ships.

28 March Eisenhower discloses his plan to Stalin that the Allied advance will proceed through southern Germany and Austria. The British are infuriated because the agreed plan was to advance to Berlin. Churchill's appeal to Washington is not dealt with by the infirm President Roosevelt but by General Marshall and the Joint Chiefs of Staff, who ratify Eisenhower's plan. With hindsight it can be suggested that the direct run to Berlin would have given the Western Allies a better stance in European post-war politics.

Hitler dismisses Guderian, his sole remaining battlefield commander from the early years. Guderian has been the cohesive factor in keeping the Army chiefs unified despite the Führer's increasingly manic directives. Guderian is replaced by the inferior General Krebs.

Guderian dismissed

Gdynia falls to the Soviets.

Soviets take Gdynia

In Burma the effort made by the Japanese to recapture the communications centre of Meiktila has not only failed but has taken troops away from other areas where the Allies have now pushed forward at greater pace. The Japanese commander, Kimura, decides that his weakened position calls for a retreat and directs many of his men east to Thazi.

29 March Troops of US 185th Regiment land on the Philippine island of Negros. They will face long and determined resistance.

30 March US Army Air Force attacks on ports in northern Germany destroy the cruiser *Köln* and fourteen U-boats.

Danzig finally falls to the Soviets and 3rd Ukraine Front has entered Austria from Hungary.

The Burma campaign is proving a *tour de force* on the part of General Slim. Japanese forces in the centre of the country have been beaten by the methods he laid down. In unfavourable terrain Slim has masterminded tactics which have drawn the Japanese out of position and dispersed their considerable resources.

Off Okinawa the US cruiser *Indianapolis* is badly damaged by a *Kamikaze*.

APRIL 1945

1 April In Germany US First and Ninth Armies link up to cut off more than 300,000 troops of Fifth and Fifteenth Panzer Armies in the Ruhr.

Ruhr pocket closed

Soviet forces capture the Hungarian town of Sopron to the south of the Austrian border and Vienna. Another break across the German defences on the Oder is made at Glogau.

In Italy the British attack across the river Reno.

In the Pacific a US landing at Legaspi in the south-east of Luzon quickly gains ground including an airfield. More resistance is encountered in other areas.

Okinawa landings

The invasion of Okinawa begins; it is the largest naval operation in the Pacific theatre. Nearly 500,000 men in 1,200 transports head for beaches in the south-west of the island. The 130,000 Japanese on the island are settled in caves and defensive positions away from the landing area. A beachhead is quickly established which the Allied naval ships support with continuous heavy bombardment; they themselves come under attack from *Kamikaze* and conventional aircraft. On this first day the US battleship *West Virginia* and the British carrier HMS *Indomitable* are among those hit.

2 April In Germany Münster is taken as British Second Army advances through the Ruhr; French First Army occupies Karlsruhe.

Troops of 3rd Ukranian Front reach the suburbs of Vienna.

Off Okinawa, *Kamikazes* target troop transports and inflict many casualties.

3 April While most of Hungary is cleared of Axis forces, Soviet troops occupy Wiener Neustadt in Austria.

4 April Osnabruck falls to the Allies and Minden is threatened. US Ninth Army units have reached the Weser opposite Hameln, and US Third Army has captured Kassel and Gotha.

Soviet troops under Malinovsky take Bratislava.

In the Pacific the first Japanese ground resistance is encountered as bad weather sets in to hamper further troop landings.

5 April Ahead of the planned invasion of Japan, General MacArthur is given command of all army forces in the Pacific, Admiral Nimitz taking

Suzuki replaces Koiso

the equivalent naval role. In Japan, General Koiso and his cabinet resign and Admiral Suzuki takes over with Togo as Foreign Minister. The new men believe that any offers of peace should be considered if this will prevent an invasion.

6 April Vienna is effectively besieged by Soviet troops; the Germans are forced out of Sarajevo by local Yugoslav soldiers.

In the Pacific most of the invasion forces on Okinawa are held by the Japanese at the Shuri defensive line, but General Geiger's US Corps is not so delayed en route northwards. *Kamikaze* attacks continue and five destroyers are lost and others damaged.

The 72,800-ton battleship *Yamato*, with a cruiser and eight destroyers, has left the Inland Sea bound for Okinawa on a one-way mission to smash the invasion; it has sufficient fuel for the outward passage only. She is spotted by Allied reconnaissance aircraft and the US submarine fleet is notified.

7 April German troops trapped in the Ruhr pocket try to fight their way out by engaging elements of US First and Ninth Armies.

Yamato is located and attacked by 380 Allied aircraft. Five heavy bombs and ten torpedoes hit their target and, remarkably, are sufficient to sink the giant vessel. Only 269 men are rescued; almost 2,500 are lost.

Yamato sunk

8 April In Vienna close-quarter fighting is taking place. In East Prussia the German defence of Königsberg is being worn down at last.

In Burma the British forces that have driven the Japanese from the centre of the country can begin a motorised advance south through the Sittang and Irrawaddy valleys.

In the Philippines more US troops are landed on Negros where resistance is proving very tough.

On Okinawa, US III Corps has crossed the Motobu Peninsula and 6th Marine Division moves in to clear the area.

9 April In the Ruhr the Allied advance has reached Essen and the Krupp industrial plants. In Kiel harbour, the German pocket battleship *Admiral Scheer* ends its war in an RAF air raid. The cruiser *Emden* and other vessels are critically damaged.

In Italy US Fifth and British Eighth Armies prepare their spring offensive.

The Königsberg garrison surrenders to the Soviets.

Soviets take Königsberg

10 April Hanover falls to the Allies who are pressuring the remaining German positions in Holland and moving on Bremen, Erfurt and Nuremberg.

In Italy Eighth Army makes early progress, the Germans having been led to expect the push to come further west; US Fifth Army also advances and takes Massa.

On Luzon the US advance south of Manila has reached Lamon Bay and the town of Mauban, which is captured.

11 April The Soviets have penetrated Vienna as far as the Danube Canal.

In the Indian Ocean, Sabang is bombarded from the battleships HMS *Queen Elizabeth* and the French *Richelieu*.

12 April The death is announced of President Roosevelt. Admired by the other Allied leaders, he has given consistent support to the war effort from long before the USA was formally involved, and his ability to fill important political and military posts with ideal candidates has proved a feature of his time in office. Many tributes are paid including one by Stalin who tells Churchill that the President was 'an unswerving champion of close co-operation between our three countries'. He is succeeded by the inexperienced Vice-President Truman who has to be quickly updated on the progress of the atomic weapons programme.

Death of Roosevelt

Truman president

In Germany Erfurt and Baden Baden are taken in Allied advances.

13 April In Germany Jena and Bamberg fall to the Allies.

When Allied troops enter the Belsen and Buchenwald concentration camps, the full horror of the Nazis' attempt to exterminate the Jewish race is brought to light.

Belsen and Buchenwald liberated

Vienna falls to the 3rd Ukraine Front after fierce street-fighting.

In the Pacific the Americans complete the clearance of Japanese defenders on the islands in Manila Bay with the destruction of garrisons on Fort Drum and, on the 16th, Fort Frank.

14 April Heavy attacks against the isolated German forces in the Ruhr pocket split the German forces.

In Italy US Fifth and British Eighth Armies link to mount a substantial offensive. Vergato is captured.

In the Pacific US forces on Luzon are engaged in the north near Baguio and in the Bicol Peninsula where Calaung is occupied. The Japanese are defending stoutly.

The 'Seewolf' U-boat pack is formed with the sole purpose of launching V-2 rockets against the US eastern seaboard.

15 April In Holland eight months after the Operation 'Market Garden' débâcle, Arnhem falls to Canadian units who move on towards Groningen; US First Army captures Leuna. A surprise move by German Twelfth Army prompts US Ninth Army to cross the Elbe, but it is forced to retreat.

16 April The Colditz prison camp is liberated and US Seventh Army is poised to attack Nuremberg.

Stalin has ordered a major, fast-paced offensive on Berlin. He doubts the validity of Eisenhower's message of 28 March and believes the Western Allies may still head for Berlin. His instructions to his commanders are not entirely complete, neither Zhukov nor Konev being awarded the honour of making the final assault, but these two fine Marshals have more than two million men, 6,000 tanks, more than 5,500 aircraft and 16,000 guns available for the task. The German defensive lines at the Oder have already been weakened by earlier attacks and they are hopelessly short of guns, tanks and air support.

The German pocket battleship *Lützow* is sunk in Kaiserfahrt Canal by an RAF raid. It is refloated but scuttled on 4 May.

In the Pacific the Americans land on the islet of Ie Shima, close to Okinawa, but will take five days to capture the island and its airfield after fierce battles which see nearly 5,000 Japanese killed.

The Soviet submarine *L3* fires on the German motor vessel *Goya* which is carrying refugees from the Hela Peninsula. The ship sinks quickly and only 165 of the 6,385 passengers are saved.

17 April Allied forces in the Ruhr are now finding that some German units are surrendering rather than fighting on or retreating. Elsewhere resistance is still strong.

In Italy the Allied drive is gaining impetus with Argenta falling to V Corps and, with the Argenta Gap now free, Bologna is under threat.

German troops in defensive lines east of Berlin begin a spirited battle to stop the Soviet advance but are forced to give ground slowly. In Austria and Czechoslovakia the German scene is even more bleak, losses of ground and men even greater.

18 April On a dark day for Germany the German pocket in the Ruhr surrenders and Model commits suicide; more than 300,000 prisoners are taken. US Ninth Army takes Magdeburg, and Patton's forces accelerate their advance to reach and cross the Czech border.

Ruhr pocket surrenders

19 April In Burma the Allied push south is proceeding well with ground gained in both the Sittang and Irrawaddy valleys.

On Luzon, US troops moving north have reached and occupied the coastal town of Vigan.

On Okinawa US XXIV Corps attacks with three divisions after air and ground bombardment.

20 April Nuremberg and Stuttgart are taken by the Allies.

Allies take Nuremberg and Stuttgart

The Soviet push to Berlin and northern Germany gathers pace as 2nd Belorussian Front joins the forces of Zhukov and Konev. The first German defensive lines on the Oder and Neisse are now in tatters; south-east of Berlin, Konev's troops are across the Spree and just 20 miles from the outskirts of the capital. On Hitler's 56th birthday Soviet artillery fire reaches the centre of Berlin. Zhukov has taken Protzel.

The northern sector of Okinawa is secured by the Americans when they capture the Motobu Peninsula. The Japanese continue to defend the Shuri Line stoutly.

21 April Advance units from Zhukov's forces enter Berlin. At a meeting in the Führer's bunker Dönitz is ordered to leave Lobetal and retire to Schleswig-Holstein; the Luftwaffe HQ near Potsdam is ordered to be vacated.

In Italy Bologna is taken by Polish II Corps and US Fifth Army has fought its way on to the Lombardy Plain which will hasten its forward pace.

Allies take Bologna

In Burma the Allied advance accelerates in the Sittang valley with the capture of Yedashe and the return to Allied control of several airfields. On the Irrawaddy, Yenangyaung falls to British XXXIII Corps.

On Luzon US forces are meeting heavy Japanese resistance near Baguio inland from Lingayen Gulf.

22 April Himmler betrays his true colours when he has a private meeting with Count Bernadotte of the Swedish Red Cross, seeking to use him as an intermediary and courier for a message of German surrender to the Western Allies. The message takes 48 hours to reach Allied hands and is not treated seriously. Himmler, a cruel and callous man at the height of his powers, has attempted this because he fears the retribution the Red Army will exact from him.

US Seventh Army crosses the Danube in two places as the Allied push matches that of the Soviets.

23 April Hitler orders the arrest of Hermann Göring after the Luftwaffe leader, whose efforts during Germany's retreat have not been impressive and whose influence has accordingly diminished, sends the Führer a

Hitler orders Göring's arrest

message offering to assume control of the Reich if Hitler is unable to continue operating from the Berlin bunker. Had he assumed power, Göring was planning to fly to Paris to negotiate with Eisenhower.

The Allied advance in the west is now unopposed in places. Dessau is taken by US First Army and Ulm is occupied.

Allies cross Po

24 April In Italy US Fifth and British Eighth Armies are crossing the Po, and La Spezia is taken. Now out of the mountainous terrain the Allied forces in this theatre are advancing at a great pace.

Advance Soviet units are now well within the suburbs of Berlin and begin encircling the city. The moves have isolated large elements of Ninth Panzer and Fourth Armies.

RAF Bomber Command flies its last significant mission over Germany with a raid against Hitler's mountain retreat at Berchtesgaden.

In the Pacific the increasing strength of the US assault on the Shuri Line on Okinawa causes the Japanese to move back to their secondary positions.

US-Soviet meeting on Elbe

25 April US First Army links up with Soviet forces at Torgau on the Elbe.

Parma and Verona liberated

In Italy Parma and Verona are liberated by the rampaging Allied forces who now find resistance non-existent and many German units ready to surrender.

Berlin is now surrounded on all sides and the noose is tightening as forward units edge in to the city centre. Hanna Reitsch, a leading German test pilot and a fanatical Nazi who literally adores Hitler, flies from Austria to collect General Ritter von Greim from Munich and fly him to a meeting with Hitler. On reaching Gatow air base they find their next machine, a Storch light aircraft, has been destroyed by shellfire and have to use the sole surviving Storch to make a dangerous flight to the capital. Reitsch lands the plane with von Greim badly injured from a tank missile which has struck the cockpit. At the planned meeting the General is promoted to Field Marshal and given command of the Luftwaffe, and is flown out of the capital by Reitsch piloting an Arado Ar 96, the last airworthy aircraft in the city.

In Burma the Allied advance southwards is causing many of the Japanese forces in Rangoon and further south to withdraw eastwards so as to escape into Thailand.

San Francisco conference

A Conference begins in San Francisco to draw up the constitution of a United Nations Organisation which will include a Security Council of which the permanent members will be the United States, the Soviet Union, Great Britain, France and China.

Pétain arrested

26 April Marshal Pétain is arrested while trying to escape from France into Switzerland. His subsequent death sentence will be commuted to life imprisonment by de Gaulle.

In Italy Allied forces are converging on Milan, Venice and Trieste.

In the Pacific more US forces have to be landed on Negros because of fierce resistance.

27 April In Berlin Templehof airfield is captured by the Soviets as the city's suburbs are systematically cleared of the German military.

On Luzon the Allies finally take Baguio.

In Borneo the Tarakan region in the north-east is bombarded prior to planned US landings.

Off Okinawa *Kamikaze* attacks increase.

28 April In Berlin there is bitter street fighting and a relief attempt by German Twelfth Army is aborted because of shortage of men.

Mussolini, his mistress and some Fascist colleagues are captured by partisans near Lake Como as they flee for Switzerland. They are quickly shot, their bodies are mutilated and hung by the heels from meat hooks on a petrol station forecourt. The Allied drive through Italy continues and Brescia and Bergamo are liberated.

Mussolini executed

In Berlin Soviet units are but a mile away from Hitler's bunker.

On Okinawa the Americans deploy flame-throwers and heavy armour in their endeavour to break through Japanese defences.

29 April In Hitler's bunker Admiral Dönitz, much to his surprise, is appointed successor to Hitler. The Führer marries his companion Eva Braun. In his last message Hitler accuses the German people of failing him in his drive to rid the world of Bolshevism. For his part, Dönitz sees his task as saving as many German lives as he can with unconditional surrender so close.

Dachau concentration camp is liberated by US Third Army, saving 30,000 inmates.

Dachau liberated

The surrender of German troops in Italy is signed in the southern town of Caserta after secret negotiations set up by Allan Dulles, head of the Office of Strategic Services in Switzerland with SS General Wolff.

Surrender of German troops in Italy

In Berlin the Red Army is clearing the capital street by street; areas of central Germany are being occupied.

30 April Hitler and Eva Braun commit suicide at 3.30 p.m. Although the nature of their deaths and disposal of their bodies is disputed to this day, the likelihood is that the bodies were taken out to the courtyard and burned. Just three hours before, Soviet troops have occupied the Reichstag and other government buildings. The once mighty German military force now holds only a portion of Moravia and much of Bohemia.

Hitler suicide

On Okinawa the Japanese attempt counter-attacks but are beaten off. More US troops are landed.

MAY 1945

I May German radio announces Hitler's death and the appointment of Dönitz as Führer. Goebbels has his children murdered and at his order an SS man kills him and his wife with a shot to the head. Other Nazi leaders flee Berlin.

Dönitz Führer
Death of Goebbels

The Allied forces are well into Austria and, in the north, are closing on Lübeck and Hamburg. US First and Ninth Armies have reached the agreed demarcation line of the Soviet occupation zone and go no further.

General Krebs attempts to negotiate a surrender with Zhukov as only small sectors of Berlin remain in German hands. He is firmly told that unconditional surrender is his only option.

Yugoslavs take Trieste As the surrender terms for the Italian theatre are confirmed, Tito and his men capture Trieste which, though it is eventually returned to Italy, will remain a disputed region.

In Burma as the monsoon breaks the Allies make an amphibious landing to take Rangoon. Paratroops drop on the east bank of the Irrawaddy.

In Borneo there is minimal opposition to the landing of 18,000 men, mostly Australians, at Tarakan.

Fall of Berlin **2 May** The report of Hitler's death by German High Command speaks of him having 'died at the head of the heroic defenders of Germany's capital city'. At 3 p.m. the German garrison stops fighting and is taken prisoner.

Lübeck is taken by British Second Army and US units ride on through Austria and Bavaria.

In Italy Allied forces reach Milan and Turin, and move on to the Brenner Pass and contact with US Seventh Army.

In Burma the attack on Rangoon continues and further north Pegu falls to IV Corps.

Allies take Hamburg **3 May** Hamburg falls to the British and Innsbruck to the Americans as the Allied forces in the west advance almost unmolested.

More contact points are made between Soviet and British and US forces as the former reach the Elbe west of Berlin.

The German cruiser *Admiral Hipper* is scuttled in Kiel Bay, having been previously damaged by an air raid.

Allies take Rangoon Rangoon is taken unopposed and Prome, further north, also falls. The British/Indian force in Burma can now look to attack Singapore.

On Okinawa the Japanese begin a vigorous counter-offensive but fail to break through US lines. The attack serves to identify the Japanese positions which have proved difficult to locate. More *Kamikaze* attacks are flown against Allied ships offshore.

Luneburg Heath surrender **4 May** German envoys meet Montgomery at Luneburg Heath and surrender unconditionally. But fighting continues as Salzburg is captured and other US troops continue their advance in Czechoslovakia. Flossenburg concentration camp, which houses the Hitler conspirators Canaris and Oster and where more than 14,000 inmates have perished, is liberated.

Allies enter Copenhagen **5 May** German Army Group H surrenders to the Americans in Bavaria and British troops land in Copenhagen to replace local militias which have taken to fighting the Germans there. Resistance fighters are also active in Prague where they take on local SS units.

In the USA six civilians are killed in Oregon, in the only success for a Japanese balloon bomb and the only deaths to the air war on the US continent. More than 9,000 of these primitive explosive devices have been launched to drift over America, but even this number, in comparison to the land-mass targeted, makes it a futile exercise and shows the desperate state of the Japanese to make some offensive impact.

In southern Burma British carrier aircraft and battleships begin attacks on Japanese bases.

6 May In Germany General Patton's troops take Pilsen but are prevented, much to the General's disgust, from advancing further because of the occupation agreement with the Soviets.

In Burma mopping-up operations are under way as organised Japanese resistance ceases.

On Okinawa the Japanese counter ceases, having cost the lives of more than 5,000 troops, and US forces make more gains.

7 May Representatives from the USA, Great Britain, France and Russia are present at Eisenhower's headquarters at 2.41 p.m. as General Jodl and Admiral Freideburg sign the unconditional German surrender documents.

Unconditional German surrender to Eisenhower

Still active off the eastern Scottish coast, *U2336* records the final U-boat success of the war when she sinks two merchant ships.

8 May VE Day. Victory in Europe is celebrated as Churchill, President Truman and King George VI broadcast speeches; the remaining German pockets of resistance in Prague and eastern Germany surrender.

VE Day

9 May Some fleeing Nazis are captured, including Göring and Kesselring, as the surrender documents are ratified in Berlin.

Göring and Kesselring captured

10 May Resistance fighters in Norway capture Vidkun Quisling and others of his party.

In the Pacific the war against Japan continues. There is still heavy fighting in the Philippines as more US troops land at Macalajar Bay.

11 May The remnant of German Army Group Centre surrenders to the Soviets. Apart from a few days of skirmishing in Yugoslavia, fighting in Europe is at an end.

Final German surrenders

On Okinawa US forces begin a concerted attack on Japanese positions without early success.

13 May On Mindanao the Americans secure Del Monte airfield.

14 May One of Germany's most successful U-boat commanders, Wolfgang Luth, is shot dead at the Flensburg Naval Academy when he fails to hear a sentry's challenge. The fate of the sentry is not known.

15 May On Okinawa fierce battles continue as Japanese units resist US attempts to break through their defences.

The Japanese cruiser *Haguro* is sunk by torpedoes from five British destroyers in the Malacca Straits in the last action between major warships.

Haguro sunk

17 May The US carrier *Ticonderoga* encounters no resistance as she attacks the Japanese-held islands of Taroa and Maleolap in the Marshalls.

18 May On Okinawa the strategic Sugar Loaf Hill is captured by American units.

21 May The Japanese begin to withdraw from their Shuri Line as American gains on Okinawa increase.

23 May Heinrich Himmler escapes interrogation by committing suicide after capture by British forces.

The heaviest bombardment of Japanese home territory to date sees 750,000 phosphorus bombs dropped by more than 500 US bombers. A similar number will raid Tokyo in the next 24 hours; almost half of the residential area of the capital will be laid waste by this bombing.

27 May On Okinawa fierce fighting continues. US forces have taken Yonabaru and Naha but are delayed by stout defence elsewhere.

JUNE 1945

1 June Off Okinawa the carrier groups continue to support the US forces on the island despite *Kamikaze* attacks during the coming days.

4 June The Americans land two regiments of 6th Marine Division on the Oruku Peninsula which is heavily occupied by retreating Japanese who will put up strong resistance.

10 June In Borneo a large contingent from 9th Australian Division land in Brunei Bay after a bombardment by cruisers and destroyers.

12 June Mass suicides among the Japanese force in the Oruku region of Okinawa indicate the hopelessness of their situation.

18 June In London William 'Lord Haw Haw' Joyce goes on trial. He will be found guilty of broadcasting war propaganda from Germany and will be executed.

The American General Buckner is killed by Japanese fire on a visit to Okinawa; he is succeeded by General 'Vinegar Joe' Stilwell. On the island US forces have secured the Oruku, Mount Yagu and much of the Kunishi Ridge.

21 June General Ushijima's body is found when the Americans capture the Japanese HQ on Hill 69. The Japanese have suffered the loss of 160,000 dead, more than 7,500 aircraft and many ships; and more than 10,700 men have been taken prisoner. In this crucial battle for a very small piece of land the Americans have lost 12,500 men and 35,000 wounded, 36 ships and more than 750 aircraft. But the Japanese air force and its remaining naval fleet have been all but destroyed in the struggle.

25 June On Luzon the constant landings of US reinforcements has seen the remaining 50,000 Japanese hopelessly outnumbered and mostly holed up in the Sierra Madre.

28 June It has taken almost six months to recapture the Philippines, but General MacArthur is able to broadcast the end of the campaign. Pockets of Japanese resistance will be encountered for a few months yet, but organised fighting is beyond them now.

29 June President Truman approves plans for the invasion of Japan. The start-date is set for 1 November, with further landings in the spring of 1946.

JULY 1945

1 July In Borneo more than 30,000 men from 7th Australian Division land at Balikpapan after a naval bombardment during the previous week. They will make rapid gains including an airfield and oilfields.

Balikpapan landings

2 July Yet another B-29 raid on Japanese cities sees thousands more incendiary bombs delivered. There is a mass exodus of terrified people from the cities and a collapse of public morale. Tokyo is evacuated; only 200,000 essential workers remain.

10 July US and British carrier forces begin a campaign against the Japanese Home Islands; more than 1,000 bombers are again sent against Tokyo.

14 July In the Tsugaru Strait much Japanese shipping is sunk by Allied carrier forces.

16 July The first ever test of an atomic weapon takes place at Los Alamos, New Mexico, USA. The explosion can be seen from 180 miles away and vaporises the steel structure which holds the device. The military authorities report the event as 'an ammunition depot' blowing up and that 'light phenomena and pressure waves were observed'.

Los Alamos atomic test

17 July The Potsdam Conference opens at which, Churchill, Truman, Stalin and their advisers refine their plans for the post-war world and focus on the defeat of Japan.

Potsdam Conference

20 July A US test flight from the Marianas simulates delivery of the atomic bomb. This aircraft carries conventional weapons which weigh 10,000lb.

24 July Truman takes the decision to use his atomic weapon against the Japanese if they fail to agree to an unconditional surrender. Stalin is given some details about the bomb but is not told of its planned deployment.

26 July The British learn that they have elected a Labour government and will have Clement Attlee as their Prime Minister in place of their war leader, Winston Churchill.

Attlee replaces Churchill

A broadcast, which will become known as the Potsdam Declaration, is made to the Japanese demanding unconditional surrender, but offering the assurance that the Allies do not wish to destroy the Japanese economy. No mention is made of the future status of the Emperor, a vital factor in the Japanese view of any surrender.

Potsdam Declaration demands Japanese surrender

The Royal Navy minesweeper HMS *Vestal* is damaged by a *Kamikaze* and later scuttled by fire from a British destroyer to become the final British warship casualty of the war.

28 July At a press conference the Japanese Premier Suzuki gives a confusing response to the Declaration. The Allies' translation seems to indicate his unwillingness to take any notice of the demand, but could also be interpreted as meaning that he wished to make no comment at this time.

Indianapolis sunk

29 July The Japanese submarine *I.58* sinks the US cruiser *Indianapolis* en route for Leyte from the Marianas, having delivered requisite components for the atomic weapon. It is the greatest but last success for a Japanese submarine.

30 July In Singapore harbour the British midget submarine *XE-1* attaches mines to the hull of the Japanese heavy cruiser *Takao*. The mines explode next day to make the last operation of this type in the war a success.

31 July Pierre Laval's attempt to evade capture via an escape route through Germany and Spain comes to nought when he is found in Austria and returned to the French authorities. He will be tried and executed.

AUGUST 1945

2 August In the heaviest air raid of the war, 800 US B-29s drop more than 6,000 tons of incendiary bombs on Japanese cities and manufacturing plants; 80,000 people are killed.

3 August The blockade of Japan is completed by the mining of all Japanese and Korean harbours.

Hiroshima atomic
bombing

6 August To Colonel Paul Tibbetts falls the task of delivering the first atomic bomb. He takes off at 2.45 a.m., the bomb is dropped at 8.15 a.m.; the flight, in a heavily overladen aircraft, is difficult and the Colonel is led to the target by three B-29s acting as weather observers. The uranium 235 fission weapon is dropped from his aircraft, 'Enola Gay' (named after his mother!), on the city of Hiroshima, producing an explosion equivalent to 20,000 tons of TNT. From the resultant blast and the firestorm which quickly follows, more than half the city is laid waste. More than 80,000 people are killed outright and thousands more maimed and burned, and yet more unfortunates destined to suffer wretched illness in subsequent decades. The total effect is awesome, but does not match the devastation already visited upon Tokyo. It is the demonstration of the havoc and damage caused in an instant by a single bomb dropped by a single aircraft which is to have the telling impact.

7 August Radio Tokyo reports unspecifically about an attack on Hiroshima. The Americans are unable to assess the results because impenetrable cloud over the site precludes reconnaissance flights. Late in the day Imperial Japanese HQ refers to a 'new type of bomb' having been used on Hiroshima, admitting that 'only a small number of the new bombs were released, yet they caused substantial damage'.

8 August In its first full report on the Hiroshima bombing, Radio Tokyo ends its assessment with the claim that the US have used methods which 'have surpassed in their hideous cruelty those of Genghis Khan'.

The Soviets declare war on Japan after what they see as that country's rejection of the Potsdam terms.

9 August A second atomic bomb is dropped, this time on Nagasaki. This one is more sophisticated but has a slightly less damaging impact. Even so, 40,000 people are killed and the same immediacy of carnage is evident. President Truman announces that more bombs will follow if the Potsdam Declaration is not accepted though, in fact, he hasn't any more to use. The Japanese Supreme Council convenes to agree to the Allies' demands provided the monarchy can be allowed to survive. Hesitancy, from some of the military, is personally dispelled by the Emperor.

By now the Soviets have followed up their declaration of war by massing 1,500,000 troops to move against the Japanese forces in Manchuria.

More air and sea bombardment of Japanese islands and the mainland takes place.

10 August The Japanese broadcast their readiness to accept the Potsdam terms provided that the future status of the Emperor is safeguarded. The Allies will reply that the continuity of monarchy would be a decision taken by the Supreme Commander of their forces in the region. The Japanese will not be satisfied by this, but all parties sense that the wrangling will end with surrender.

14 August The Japanese Emperor records a speech to his people repeating the message he has given to his politicians, that they should 'bear the unbearable' and unconditionally surrender. There is an attempt to steal the taped message before it can be delivered but it fails and his words will be heard by Japan and the world. The fear of more atomic weapon attacks and the certainty of land defeat by the Soviets have combined to secure the complete surrender.

15 August VJ Day. The Emperor's broadcast is made. For many Japanese people these are the first negative words they have heard from leaders who have kept the parlous state of the war from them. There remain many soldiers, sailors and airmen who would fight on if allowed. Overall there is a feeling of great humiliation which only the retention of the Emperor's powers and standing can allay. The Emperor will issue a formal ceasefire to his forces within hours and Prince Higashi-Kuni heads the new government.

18 August Most of Manchuria has been occupied by the Soviet Army. The Kwantung Army will surrender within the week.

SEPTEMBER 1945

2 September The US battleship *Missouri* is the venue for the signing of the Japanese surrender. The leading Allied officers present are General MacArthur, who accepts the surrender, and Admirals Nimitz and Fraser who sign for America and Great Britain. MacArthur ends the ceremony with the words, 'Let us pray that peace be now restored to the world and that God will preserve it always. These proceedings are closed.' The defeat of Japan has been accomplished without any of its home territory being occupied by ground forces; a unique circumstance. The conflict which has become known as The Second World War has lasted six years and one day.

OCTOBER 1945

United Nations
Charter

24 October The United Nations Charter comes into force, initially with 29 members.

NOVEMBER 1945

In Yugoslavia Tito's National Front Party wins power. In Austria the Communists secure only three seats and fare little better in Hungary.

Nuremberg Trials

The Nuremberg Trials begin with 21 leading Nazi officials in the dock including Göring, Dönitz, Raeder, Jodl and Keitel. The event discloses to the world the horror of the Nazi regime; Rudolf Hess, who had been an SS Brigadier-General, gives appalling details of the systematic mass murder at Auschwitz. The trials continue until October 1946.

DECEMBER 1945

The Japanese General Yamashita who commanded the infamous Death March of Allied prisoners in 1942, is sentenced to death by an American Military Commission.

POSTSCRIPT

The conflict of 1939–1945, which affected more than 200 nations and brought misery and death to millions, could have been avoided. Many politicians were slow, reluctant or unable to foresee the warning signs; most civilians could not believe that the world would fail to avoid a war so soon after 'the War that will end War' had been suffered. Some historians believe that the growth of Nazism came only from the insecurity felt by the German nation and that political wisdom could have accommodated and calmed those fears; others claim, perhaps with the beloved benefit of hindsight, that the war was fought against the wrong foe. What is sure is that there were still deep structural faults in the political basis of the geographical area called Europe and perhaps it was always going to need a war to enable redefinition and rebuilding to take place.

Once Hitler had stimulated conflict, his undoubted drive, the years of clandestine planning and construction, and the able administrators and military leaders he had around him ensured that he could get very close to achieving the dominant position he sought in order, he would argue, to secure his nation from threats from East and West. That he did not succeed can be put down to many factors that include his inexperience, and impatience of battlefield reversals. He had too few international allies and those he chose were weak performers. Had he secured the support of Franco, the European war would have surely taken a longer course and, perhaps, a different one.

When the Japanese entered the war for, they would claim, the same defensive reasons quoted by Hitler, they did so with traditional national commitment but with inadequate forces to secure the vast area they sought to control. Once the USA committed itself to both the European and Pacific theatres – Roosevelt had long believed that US troops would become involved and had given Great Britain much support from the early months of the war – a far greater German–Japanese integration than was the case would be required if defeat were to be avoided.

As ever in large-scale warfare, personalities emerged who would be hugely instrumental in the outcome. While in both peace and war it is the anonymous background planners and desk-bound strategists who influence the actions of the men who state the policy, conflict requires that there be a leader to follow, and World War Two certainly had its fair share of these.

Inevitably Winston Churchill heads many lists for, despite his many previous failings and his dogmatic, intransigent approach which riled so many, he achieved his absolute objective; he kept his nation at war and fuelled its determination to win. Because he did this, and accepted no compromise, he has a unique standing.

Adolf Hitler could boast military and political geniuses among his hierarchy, just as we can quote his failure to maximise this benefit as a major cause for his defeat. It is intriguing to consider how the merits of Guderian, Rommel, von Manstein and von Rundstedt might have been used by a different commander-in-chief, what Kesselring, Raeder and Dönitz could have achieved with more consistent supplies and support, and what the many fine administrators in the Reich could have built had their abilities not been stultified by manic dictates and the relentless brutality and cruelty which was the hallmark of the enormous number of thugs and psychopaths who were given a free hand by the Nazis. .

At the outbreak of hostilities the USA was fortunate to find that it had elected a masterful statesman and a brilliant judge of personality as its President. Franklin Roosevelt had already shown skill in bringing his country out of recession with the help of carefully chosen appointees to lead each programme; during the war years he demonstrated the same art, disclosing an uncanny knack of finding the right man for the job on so many occasions. In Dwight Eisenhower was found the right mix of military skill and diplomatic awareness to lead the Allied effort in taking the fight back to Germany, but many of Roosevelt's other placements also proved inspired.

Josef Stalin was perhaps more fortunate. This complex man caused his forces to be ill-prepared for the war, but his ruthless devotion to the protection of his country and the successful infusion of this creed into his commanders and their men brought victory in the end, even if the Russian climate again proved a most valuable 'weapon' in defeating an aggressor. In battlefield masters such as Zhukov and Konev he found men who, having tasted reversal, were capable of leading one of the greatest counter-offensives in history.

But it was not the leaders, political or military, who were closest to World War Two. The ordinary soldier, sailor and airman, the resistance fighter and the espionage agent, were at the front line and all too many stayed there, never to return. Because fewer of those who did return remain to give us their personal accounts, we should not neglect to study the events of World War Two for only by studying the past can we learn from the errors and omissions of those times and determine not to repeat them.

THEATRES
OF WAR

**Theatre of Operations
for the German Western
Offensive, 1940**

**Theatre of Operations for
the German Invasion of the
Soviet Union, 1941–1942**

BALTIC SEA

Helsinki

Leningrad

Tikhvin

Tallin

ESTONIA

Demyansk

Pskov

LATVIA

Riga

USSR

LITHUANIA

Moscow

Königsberg

Vitebsk

Vyazma

Vilnius

Smolensk

Tula

EAST
PRUSSIA

Grodno

Minsk

Mogilev

Roslavl

Bialystok

Rogachev

Bryansk

Beresina

Orel

BELORUSSIA

Warsaw

Bug

PRIPET MARSHES

POLAND

Kursk

Korosten

Novigrad Volynsk

SLOV-
AKIA

Lvov

Zhitomir

Kiev

Kharkov

UKRAINE

Dnieper

Dniester

Bug

HUNGARY

Uman

Kirovgrad

Dnepropetrovsk

Krivoy Rog

Prut

Jassy

Nikolayev

Kishinev

Korsun

ROUMANIA

Odessa

CRIMEA

Bucharest

Danube

Sophia

BULGARIA

BLACK SEA

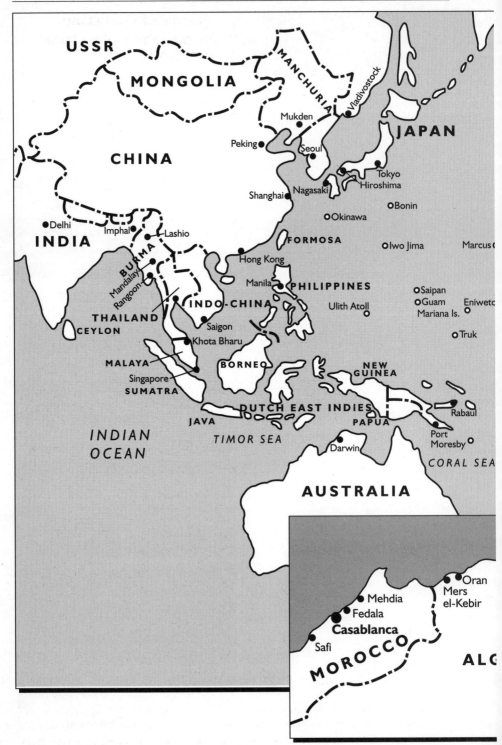

**Theatre of Operations
for the War against Japan,
1941–1945**

Attu
Kiska Aleutian Is.

PACIFIC OCEAN

O Midway

Hawaiian Is.
Pearl Harbor

O Wake

O Kwajalein

Marshall Is.

O Tarawa
Gilbert Is. O

Soloman Is.
Guadalcanal

**Theatre of Operations
for the North African
Campaign, 1941–1943**

Algiers
Bône   Bizerte
Bougie   Bija   **Tunis**
Tebessa Thala Souke el Arba
Biskra   Mahdia
         Kasserine
         Djerba   Tripoli
                                    Benghazi
         Mareth
         Medenine
RIA   TRIPOLITANIA
                    El Agheila
              LIBYA   CYRENAICA

Gazala
Tobruk
Bardia   Sidi Barrani   Mersa Matruh   Alexandria

Beda
Fomm   Bir Hacheim   El Alamain   **Cairo**

EGYPT

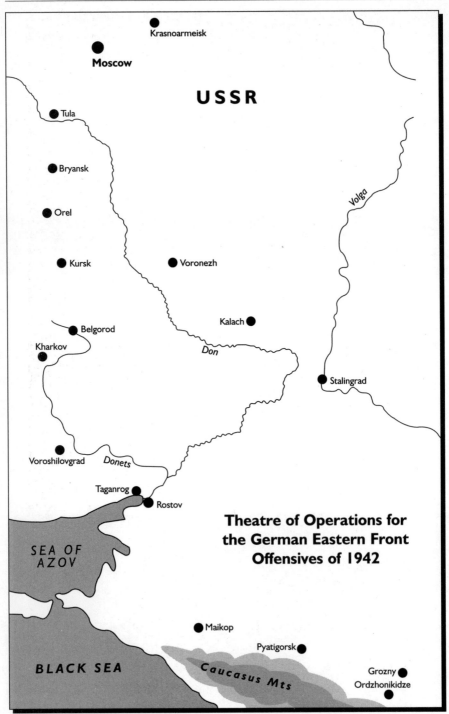

USSR

Krasnoarmeisk

Moscow

Tula

Bryansk

Orel

Volga

Kursk

Voronezh

Kalach

Belgorod

Don

Kharkov

Stalingrad

Voroshilovgrad

Donets

Taganrog

Rostov

**Theatre of Operations for
the German Eastern Front
Offensives of 1942**

**SEA OF
AZOV**

Maikop

Pyatigorsk

Caucasus Mts

Grozny

Ordzhonikidze

BLACK SEA

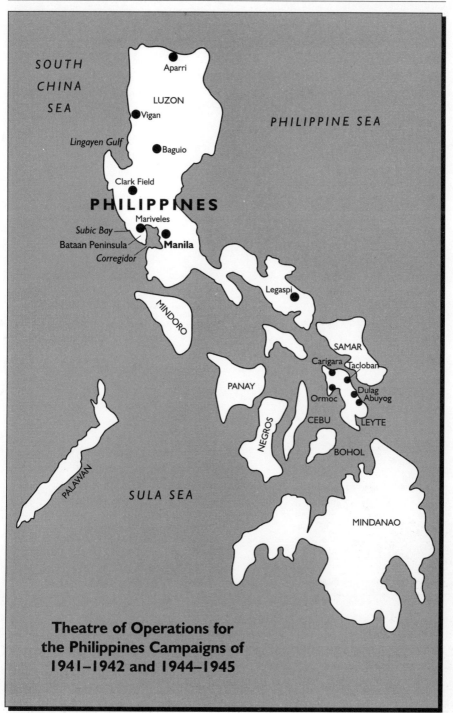

**Theatre of Operations for
the Philippines Campaigns of
1941–1942 and 1944–1945**

Theatre of Operations for the
Soviet Counter-Offensives of 1943–1944

Theatre of Operations for the
Soviet Offensives of 1944–1945

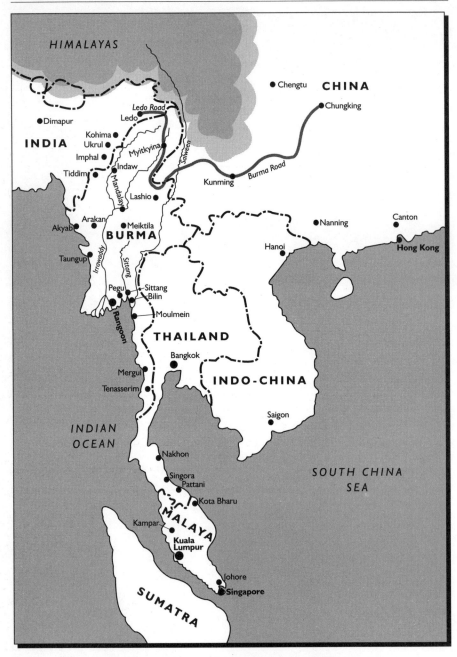

Theatre of Operations for the
Malaya and Burma Campaigns, 1941–1945

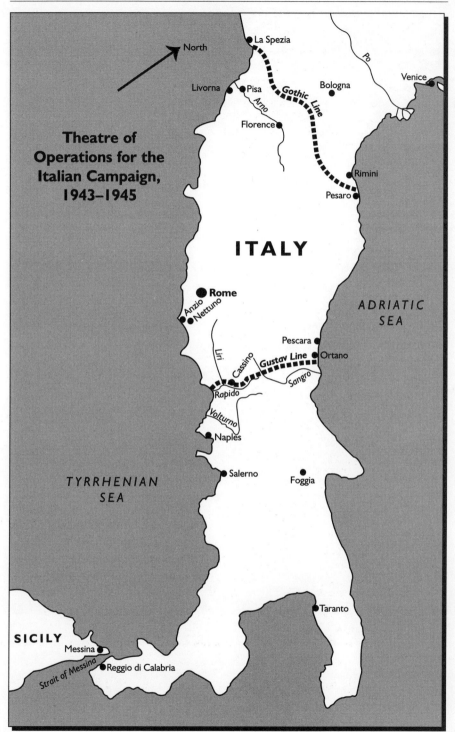

Theatre of
Operations for the
Italian Campaign,
1943–1945

North

La Spezia

Po

Venice

Livorna

Pisa

Gothic Line

Bologna

Arno

Florence

Rimini

Pesaro

ITALY

*ADRIATIC
SEA*

Rome

Anzio
Nettuno

Pescara

Liri

Cassino

Gustav Line

Ortano

Rapido

Sangro

Volturno

Naples

Salerno

Foggia

*TYRRHENIAN
SEA*

Taranto

SICILY

Messina

Strait of Messina

Reggio di Calabria

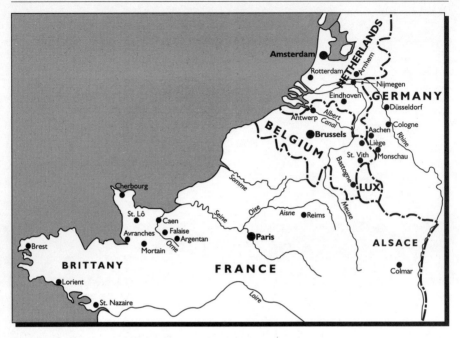

Theatre of Operations for the
Western Front Campaigns, 1944–1945

INDEX